Handling Special Materials

Handling Special Materials in Libraries

A Project of the South Atlantic Chapter, SLA

Edited by
FRANCES E. KAISER
Georgia Institute of Technology Library

SPECIAL LIBRARIES ASSOCIATION
New York
1974

© 1974 by Special Libraries Association
235 Park Avenue South, New York 10003

Printed in the United States of America

Library of Congress Cataloging in Publication Data
Main entry under title:

Handling special materials in libraries.

  Includes bibliographical references.
  1. Libraries—Special collections. 2. Libraries—Special collections—
Bibliography. I. Kaiser, Frances E., ed. II. Special Libraries Associa-
tion. South Atlantic Chapter. III. Title.
Z688.A2H35   025.17   73-21956
ISBN 0-87111-211-6

Contents

Preface

Libraries must acquire, handle and make available all kinds of special materials for their users. Special materials here include government publications, technical reports, maps, proprietary publications, company and trade literature, patents and trademarks, standards, symposia and conference records, and related miscellaneous materials. Information knows no boundary of format or medium. Thus, if a library collects in depth in a particular subject area, important items will be acquired regardless of their physical format or specialized nature.

Because of the importance of these kinds of materials to the researcher-user, the librarian must know where to go to obtain quickly a patent issued in one of the less industrialized nations or recently published standards or specifications. Methods of handling these materials in the collection for efficient retrieval must also be determined.

Libraries of all kinds—special, academic, public—need and collect special materials for use by their clientele. It is often difficult to find moderately up-to-date information collected in one place on the availability of diverse special materials. This volume should be of value to the fledgling librarian as well as to the experienced professional, particularly if a library may not have previously collected a particular type or format. It should also prove to be a useful instructional tool.

For the reader in need of more detailed information, a lengthy bibliography with subject index is included.

This collection of papers is an outgrowth of a Short Course on *Handling Special Materials in Libraries*, held at the Georgia Institute of Technology, Feb 2-4, 1972, under the joint sponsorship of the South Atlantic Chapter of Special Libraries Association, the Price Gilbert Memorial Library and the School of Information and Computer Science at Georgia Tech. Experienced librarians presented papers in their fields of expertise. Most of the lectures presented during the Short Course are included in this volume.

The volume is a project of the South Atlantic Chapter; Safford Harris (special collections librarian, Georgia Institute of Technology) and Eugenia Abbey (librarian, VA Hospital, Atlanta, Georgia) helped to edit the manuscript.

Frances E. Kaiser, Head
Department of Library Instruction
Price Gilbert Memorial Library
Georgia Institute of Technology
Atlanta, Georgia

Organization of a Government Documents and Technical Reports Collection

RICHARD LEACY

This paper concentrates on the organization of federally sponsored materials, particularly publications distributed by the U.S. Government Printing Office and technical reports emanating from the Atomic Energy Commission, the National Aeronautics and Space Administration, and the National Technical Information Service. Maps and patents are excluded. Publications by state governments are included; but they are not given the same close examination as their federal counterparts receive. Significant titles useful to both librarian and patron are cited. The description of each title relies on introductory information appearing in the respective publication. This paper suggests some of the questions and problems that a librarian confronts in handling government publications, suggests the courses of action he may follow, and explains some of the relevant procedures adopted by the library at the Georgia Institute of Technology.

The first matter the librarian must resolve is perhaps also the crucial one. Shall government publications be integrated into the library's regular collection, or shall they be organized into a special collection? There are three questions that need to be answered to determine the most advisable disposition of the material.

1. How large a part of the library's collection will be composed of government publications?
2. Is the acquisition of material to be on a frequent or infrequent basis?
3. Is the library to be a depository, and, if so, what percentage of available item categories are to be selected?

If only a few government publications are to be acquired, or, if acquisition is to be concentrated in only a few subject areas, it would seem advisable to integrate the material into the regular collection. If

Richard Leacy is government documents librarian, Price Gilbert Memorial Library, Georgia Institute of Technology, Atlanta, Ga.

the library is used primarily by grade school students, the most efficient procedure may be a vertical file arrangement of material by subject areas relating to the school curriculum. On the other hand, if the library is to become a depository for either federal or state government publications, the question becomes more complicated. One school of thought adheres to the concept of one collection, supported by one card catalog, and one classification schedule. This school asks, "Is it fair to give one publication of the same merit less cataloging, and supposedly less availability, than another? Is it fair to deny the library user one complete subject–author card catalog to the library's holdings?"

The fundamental problem is not one of equity, but, rather, one of utility. There is a more relevant question. What provides a reasonably efficient organizational and retrieval process for a given information form? It is this question that needs to be addressed to the problem of handling government publications.

As a matter of fact, the card catalog has never been a complete retrieval tool to the library's holdings (7, p. 61). For periodicals it does little more than identify titles; for monographic serials it does little more than list numbers received in the series. Librarian and user alike are almost wholly dependent on subject–author book indexes such as the *Readers' Guide to Periodical Literature, Engineering Index, Chemical Abstracts,* and *Index Medicus* as retrieval tools. It is doubtful that even the most zealous of the profession would undertake indepth indexing of periodicals so that the user would have the advantage of a more complete card catalog.

There is another question, frequently asked, in determining how to handle this material. Are government publications different from those issued by a commercial publisher? This author tends to think they are and would like to suggest what may be some of their unique aspects. First, governmental reports and Congressional hearings are an analysis of national problems; they are the record of popular response to national political questions. The volumes compiling laws, administrative policies, and federal programs tell how the government finally responded to those problems and to the prevailing political climate. Statistical compendiums are the nation's linear measurement. Therefore, government publications through the years provide in print the most reliable, comprehensive, documented textual and statistical record of the life of the nation. Second, the United States Government, reportedly, produces more titles than any other publisher in the world. Third, the government constantly creates new authors in the form of new bureaus, agencies, and departments. Each of these units creates new series and alters old ones. Fourth, the government is its own publisher, printer, and distributor dispensing its materials at minimal cost and often without charge. Fifth, it catalogs, classifies, and indexes its own works. These factors make government publications unique and, combined, form the basis for the argument to organize this material into a collection housed, maintained, and staffed separately from the general collection.

FEDERAL GOVERNMENT PUBLICATIONS

Having noted some of the reasons for having a special collection, it is necessary to examine specific aspects of maintaining that collection—classification, cataloging, acquisition of material, and utilization of retrieval tools. The Government Documents Collection of the Georgia Tech Library serves as the working model for the following analysis.

Classification

The Superintendent of Documents classification system is what is called a vertical schedule which relates to the administrative structure of the government, rather than a horizontal schedule which relates to subject of material such as the Dewey or Library of Congress classification systems. The vertical arrangement is based on what is known as the principle of provenance. At the 1936 Conference of the American Library Association, Dorsey Hyde described the system as follows:

The adoption of this basic principle of archival classification occurred after the unfortunate experiences of the French and Belgian national archives in attempting to devise a rearrangement by subject . . . of their public records.

Under this plan (which was first promulgated in France by the Ministerial circular of 1841) the aim of the archives classifier is to devise a system which takes the government agency concerned, rather than the subject, as its starting point and unit, and which "breaks down" this unit into its logical subdivisions of offices, bureaus, sections and the like, and finally reaches and assigns numbers to the various archival series of each such final administrative subdivision (15, p. 182).

The actual scheme used by the Superintendent of Documents was devised by Adelaide R. Hasse about 1895 (6, p. 472). Hasse had a particularly noteworthy and productive life as a librarian. Her career began in 1889 when she became assistant librarian in the Los Angeles Public Library. She served as a librarian at the Office of the Superintendent of Documents from 1895 to 1897. She then went on to become the Chief of the Document Department at the New York Public Library from 1897 to 1918. In 1919 she organized the records of the War Industries Board and the Council of National Defense. She served as bibliographer of the Brookings Institution from 1923 until 1932. During the depression she worked as a consultant to the Temporary National Economic Committee. She served as editorial analyst and bibliographer for the Institute of Economics and the Securities and Exchange Commission. She also held the title of lecturer at George Washington University and the Catholic University of America. In July 1953, at the age of 84, she died at a hospital just outside Washington, D.C. (8, 23, 24, 26)

Miss Hasse began working on the classification scheme while she was an assistant librarian at the Los Angeles Public Library and completed it after she went to work at the newly created Office of the Superintendent of Documents. The scheme, which is still used today with modifications, carefully follows the archival principle. Departments or independent agencies come first, followed by subordinate bureaus, offices, and administrations. One or several initials from the main words of the parent department are used to separate the important units. Thus the 11 main executive departments are designated as follows:

A —Agriculture Department
C —Commerce Department
D —Defense Department
HE—Health, Education, and Welfare Department
HH—Housing and Urban Development Department
I —Interior Department
J —Justice Department
L —Labor Department
S —State Department
T —Treasury Department
TD—Transportation Department.

Some independent agencies and commissions that may report directly to the President are given two or more letters relating to the name of the specific organization, while other parts of government are assigned an "X" or "Y" designation.

CC —Federal Communications Commission
CS —Civil Service Commission
DC —District of Columbia
FHL—Federal Home Loan Bank Board
FR —Federal Reserve System Board of Governors
IC —Interstate Commerce Commission
X —Covers proceedings on the floors of the House and Senate
Y 3 —Covers publications of more than 50 independent commissions of government both temporary and permanent
Y 4 —Assigned to hearings and prints by Congressional committees.

Having used letters to designate parent departments, numbers are used next to code the major operating offices within a department. While these numbers are arranged consecutively, the next immediate number is seldom used for the next immediate agency. The Agriculture Department is an example:

1—Identifies the Secretary's office
13—Identifies the Forest Service
17—Identifies the National Agricultural Library
43—Identifies the Federal Extension Service
67—Identifies the Foreign Agricultural Service
68—Identifies the Rural Electrification Administration.

Following the letter designating the parent department and the number indicating the major subordinate office comes the series designation preceded by a period and followed by a colon. The series designation identifies the type of publication such as a periodical or a monographic serial. Years ago specific numbers quite uniformly were used for types of publications such as handbooks, manuals, or instructions, but that practice has to a certain extent been supplanted by using the numbers to identify a definite named series. Some series designations are still reserved for types of publications (*39*, p. 1-2)

.1: Annual reports

.2: General publications (unnumbered publications of a miscellaneous nature)

.3: Bulletins

.4: Circulars

.5: Laws (administered by the agency and published by it)

.6: Regulations, rules, and instructions

.7: Releases

.8: Handbooks, manuals, guides.

After the series designation, the numbers are followed by a colon. The colon is the dividing point between administrative classification, and, either a specific number to identify one particular publication or a Cuttering process. If only numbers follow the colon, they are used to place a periodical, or monographic serial, in either chronological or numerical order. In such case, the numbers may stand for a year, a volume, a volume and a particular issue number of a periodical, or the number of a specific title in a monographic series. If letters and numbers are used following the colon, the letters are usually taken from the primary word in the title of the publication and serve to provide some subject order. Either procedure assigns to each title a unique classification number, which is necessary for effective organization of the collection and for maintenance of a shelf list.

There are some inherent difficulties in this system. An agency or bureau brought into being after the classification schedule has been set up usually is added to the end of the schedule for the parent department and is assigned a higher number within that schedule than would otherwise have been assigned. As the government grows, the classification schedule takes on a chronological arrangement which cannot be avoided. While the fact of chronology does intrude, new divisions are kept within their administrative structure and the basic cohesion of the vertical system remains.

A few words need to be added about the classification of Congressional publications. All Congressional hearings are given a "Y 4" designation followed by letters and numbers to identify specific committees. The committee designation is followed by a colon, which, in turn, is followed either by a Cutter number for some committees, or a serial accession number for other committees. The serial accession numbers provide a single numerical sequence either for a session, or for an entire

Congress. In a serial accession number, the first two digits indicate the number of the Congress. Hearings are followed by committee reports, which are issued first separately and later in bound volumes. These bound volumes form what is called the Serial Set, each volume being assigned a unique serial number.

Finding a publication in the Serial Set requires a few special steps. Material is arranged in the volumes of the Serial Set by report or document number by House or by Senate. The volumes of the Serial Set do not have continuous pagination; the pages of each title in a volume are numbered separately. The first step in finding a report or document has three parts: 1) Find out if the publication was issued by a House committee or a Senate committee. 2) Determine the number and the session of Congress in which it was issued. 3) Determine the number of the report or document. This step may be accomplished in either of two ways through the *Monthly Catalog*. The person may look in the index under the name of the Congressional committee for a listing of reports issued. He may also look in the index under the appropriate subject term which will list both the hearings and the resultant committee report. The second step is to go to the *Numerical Lists and Schedule of Volumes of the Reports and Documents* issued for each session of Congress. Each numerical list is divided into four parts: Senate reports, House reports, Senate documents, and House documents. Each part is arranged numerically by report or document number. The number is followed by the title of the publication. After the title, the serial number is given in heavy print. The publication itself is placed in numerical order by its own number within the specified volume of the Serial Set.

There is, however, a more complicated problem which may arise concerning the classification schedule. This problem involves the creation of a new agency growing out of an older agency. The new agency may become a separate bureau or it may become a larger unit encompassing the earlier organization. When the Department of Health, Education, and Welfare was created by Reorganization Plan 1 of 1953, it was decided to keep the "FS" classification of the Federal Security Agency rather than establish a new schedule. In 1969, sixteen years later, that decision was changed, and in 1970 an entirely new "HE" classification schedule appeared.

Undoubtedly, the factor of bureaucratic growth was the reason for establishing the new schedule. The "FS" classification schedule did not allow for the degree of publication expansion by new agencies, especially the growth of the U.S. Public Health Service and the National Institutes of Health. Some bureaus kept a similar number. The Social Security Administration which had been "FS 3" became "HE 3"; and the Education Office changed from "FS 5" to "HE 5," giving birth in 1973 to the National Institute of Education, "HE 18." The Public Health Service was entirely rescheduled according to the specific operating units of the various National Institutes of Health; here there were no similarities in classification numbers. The basic question was, "What changes should be made in the library's government documents collection?" The library finally adopted the following rules of procedure:

1. The entire "FS" schedule would not be reclassified into the "HE" schedule;
2. Issues of monographic series classed in "FS" would be left in the "FS" classification—later issues classed in "HE" would establish a new series ("See" references would be made directing the user to the corresponding entry);
3. A serial with a single title such as an annual report would be transferred entirely to the "HE" number;
4. A periodical run would be transferred entirely to the new "HE" number;
5. If a periodical or a monographic serial more closely approximated a new series, no "See" reference would be established.

While these rules may not have been perfect, they did provide a practical course of operation within which an orderly transition could be made.

Cataloging

This section of the paper concerns cataloging and other forms of record keeping. If a library integrates government publications into its main collection, then the library will apply its regular cataloging procedures to government material. Either Dewey or Library of Congress rules will be used to determine corporate author and subject headings; specific serial records will be established according to the individual library's application of the appropriate rules. The Georgia Institute of Technology Library keeps federal government publications in a special collection and maintains a separate card catalog for them. Three rules have been used in developing the catalog: 1) Do not duplicate something that is already done and may be utilized as a working retrieval tool for the collection. 2) Have one card in the catalog for each publication—this does not mean that each publication, necessarily, has its own card. 3) Have one alphabetic arrangement for all records. Now, in practice what do these rules mean?

Rule 1: "Do not duplicate something that is already done and may be utilized as a working retrieval tool." The *Monthly Catalog of United States Government Publications* serves the function of a subject catalog. Its indexes are cumulated on an annual and decennial basis and provide an adequate subject approach to the material. It does not have a corporate author index; therefore, the library makes one corporate author card for each publication exclusive of periodicals and other title main entries which are listed in the annual appendix entitled "Directory of United States Government Periodicals and Subscription

Publications" appearing in each February issue.

Rule 2: "Have one card in the catalog for each publication." Upon receipt of a publication which is not part of a periodical or other title main entry serial, one corporate author card is typed and filed in the catalog. The corporate author is determined by the *Monthly Catalog* or the *List of Classes of United States Government Publications Available for Selection by Depository Libraries.* The card includes item number, classification number, corporate author, full title of material, and date of publication. Periodicals are given a title main entry. Each periodical title card is also a check-in record of issues received. When the library binds a title for the first time, it makes a "bound volume" card which serves as a cumulative record showing particular volumes and years bound together. Numbered monographic serials are given two records in the catalog both of which are filed by corporate author, which is determined by the Superintendent of Documents. The first is a check-in record by name of the series; the second is a card with the title of the specific issue and a series added entry.

This procedure allows the user two avenues of approach in locating the material. He will find the series title card filed alphabetically by corporate author. He will also find a title card for a specific number of a monographic series filed by corporate author. There is a third approach for locating a periodical or a monographic serial. The library produces, on microfiche, a *Serials Holdings List* of 15,890 current and inactive serials in its collections. This list has one alphabetic arrangement of material classified in the Dewey or Library of Congress schemes following current Anglo-American rules interfiled with material in the Government Documents Collection following Superintendent of Documents entry form. Location symbols are given for specific entries, e.g., "DOC" indicates Government Documents Collection.

Rule 3: "Have one alphabetic arrangement for all records in the card catalog." This rule means that corporate author cards and title main entry cards are interfiled in one alphabetic arrangement. When a periodical or a monographic series is to be bound, one slip with appropriate information about author and/or title, years, and date sent to the bindery is filed directly behind the series card. This practice provides one card catalog for corporate author cards, periodicals, annual series, other numbered monographic serials, and bindery records.

The card catalog and the *Monthly Catalog of United States Government Publications* serve as complementary bibliographic control tools. The *Monthly Catalog* and a few other related sources of information should be mentioned.

Retrieval Tools

Monthly Catalog of United States Government Publications. Washington, D.C., Government Printing Office.

This title, which began in 1895, is the primary listing of publications by the United States Government. Departments and agencies of the federal government are arranged alphabetically by the key word in the name. Thus, the Department of the Interior is listed as "Interior Department." The Bureau of Mines which is part of the Interior Department is listed as the "Mines Bureau." Keeping with the practice of having a single alphabetic listing of departments and their subordinate offices, the Mines Bureau appears somewhere between the Medicine and Surgery Bureau of the Department of the Navy and the Missouri Basin Inter-Agency Committee, an independent agency of the government. The publications of each office are listed under that office and are arranged alphabetically by the first word in the title of each excluding the articles "the" and "a."

Each entry gives all usual bibliographic information—full title, personal and corporate authors, year of publication, number of pages, and Superintendent of Documents classification number. The entry also gives availability which may be of help if the *Monthly Catalog* is being used as a source for ordering material. Usually, there are five categories of availability: 1) an asterisk indicates the title is for sale by the Superintendent of Documents; 2) a dagger indicates distribution is made by the issuing office; 3) a double dagger indicates official use, supposedly not available; 4) a circle with a vertical line through the center indicates for sale by the National Technical Information Service; and 5) a black dot indicates the title is sent to depository libraries.

Purchase of material sold by the Government Printing Office is relatively simple, since there are several order blanks in the back of each issue of the *Monthly Catalog*. The Government Printing Office requires prepayment for all material sold. A library may establish a Deposit Account against which it may draw for the acquisition of publications. This procedure is simpler than the purchase of coupons sold by the Superintendent of Documents. The library uses the coupons in lieu of money to purchase material. The library also may send a check to cover a purchase order. Acquisition of material sold by the National Technical Information Service is discussed in the section of this paper dealing with technical reports. Publications listed as "official use not available" may be acquirable if one uses the correct avenues of approach. Establishing personal contact with a bureau's administrator, or an administrator in the field, may prove helpful in obtaining such titles. A congressman or a senator is often a great aid in such circumstances. Good relations with congressional representatives have for many librarians been an effective acquisitions tool.

Along with the *Monthly Catalog* the Superintendent of Documents publishes a *Decennial Cumulative Index*. The citations under the subject headings are by year and entry number. Unlike the regular monthly and annual indexes, there are no entries for individual authors. While only titles of unique interest and importance are included, the 1951–1960 edition has 2,639 pages.

Edward Przebienda, *United States Government Publications Monthly Catalog: Decennial Cumulative Personal Author Index 1941–1970.* Ann Arbor, Pierian Press, 1971–1972. (4 v.)

These four volumes contain a total of 238,000 bibliographic citations to the *Monthly Catalog.* Each volume has a single alphabetic arrangement by surname of personal author. Three classes of authorship are noted, single authorship, co-authorship, and authorships with more than one other person. No titles or other bibliographic information are included. Each reference is to a specific entry in the *Monthly Catalog;* it is assumed that the user will go to that entry for a complete citation.

Cumulative Subject Index to the Monthly Catalog of United States Government Publications, 1900–1971. Washington, D.C., Carrollton Press, Inc., 1972. (14 v.)

These fourteen volumes have one alphabetic arrangement by common word subject. No titles or other bibliographic information are included. Each reference is to a specific entry in the *Monthly Catalog;* it is assumed that the user will go to that entry for a complete citation.

CIS Index. Washington, D.C.: Congressional Information Service, 1970–

This monthly publication is divided into two sections, a summary or abstract section and an index section. The summary section covers committee hearings, committee prints, House and Senate reports, House and Senate documents, House and Senate miscellaneous publications, Senate executive reports, and Senate executive documents. This section is arranged first by House, then Joint, and, finally, Senate committees. Within each of these divisions the respective committees are arranged alphabetically, and the materials of each committee are grouped together by common type such as hearings, prints, and reports. The Service attempts to include publications within a month after issuance.

The index section has a single alphabetic arrangement covering subject of publication, specific subjects discussed by witnesses, personal and corporate names, affiliations of witnesses such as businesses or organizations being represented, names of subcommittees, popular names of laws, reports and bills. There are additional indexes by bill number, report number, document number, and names of committee and subcommittee chairmen.

The indexes are cumulated quarterly. The entire publication is cumulated annually in two bound volumes one of which is a detailed index, the other contains the abstracts. A list of new Superintendent of Documents classification numbers is included with each quarterly index and is cumulated in the annual edition.

Federal Register Office, *United States Government Organization Man-*

ual. Washington, D.C., Government Printing Office.

This is the official organization handbook of the federal government. It contains sections describing the agencies of the legislature, judicial, and executive branches including the names and titles of department heads as well as departmental addresses. It includes brief descriptions of quasi-official agencies and of selected international organizations. There are charts of some of the more complex agencies, brief histories of agencies abolished or transferred since 1933, lists of government publications, and references showing where agency rules are published in the *Code of Federal Regulations*.

Congress. Senate. Government Operations Committee. *Organization of Federal Executive Departments and Agencies*. Washington, D.C., Government Printing Office. (Chart).

This chart lists the departments, independent agencies, and commissions with the main subordinate offices of each. The number of employees is included for each organizational unit. There are also comparison summary statistics going back 10 years of total paid employees.

Congress and the Nation, 1945-1964, a Review of Government and Politics in the Postwar Years. Washington, D.C., Congressional Quarterly Service, 1965.

This title concerns legislation, politics, and personnel. It covers such subjects as foreign policy, economic policy, natural resources and power, health, education and welfare, federal-state relations, lobbies, special investigations, and includes a biographic index to Congress 1945-1965, key votes in the House and Senate, controversial nominations, major Supreme Court cases, a chronology of major events from 1945 to 1964, and a section called "How a Bill is Passed."

Each chapter usually contains a summary, a program discussion when appropriate, background leading up to postwar years, and a chronology of legislative action from 1945 to 1964. Related programs or legislative action are sometimes included.

The first chapter, "Politics," is a brief history of the kind of Congress each was and the resultant election issues that developed, Congress by Congress and election by election, from 1945 through 1964. There is a detailed alphabetic index to the whole volume. There are, also, four related titles issued by the same publisher:

1. *Congress and the Nation: v. 2—1965-1968, a Review of Government and Politics;*
2. *Congressional Quarterly Weekly Report;*
3. *Congressional Quarterly Almanac, Annual* which cumulates the *Congressional Quarterly Weekly Report;* and
4. *CQ Guide to Current American Government*. 1969.

Biographical Directory of the American Congress, 1774-1971. Washington, D.C., Government Printing Office, 1971 (92d Congress, 1st Session, Senate Document No. 92-8).

This title is issued on an irregular basis in updated cumulated form as part of the Serial Set. It includes the Continental Congresses, Sep 5, 1774, to Oct 21, 1788, and the Congresses of the United States from the 1st to the 92d, Mar 4, 1789, to Jan 3, 1971, inclusive. It covers specifically the following subjects: executive officers, 1789-1971; places and times of meetings with officers of the Continental Congresses and the names of the delegates arranged by states; apportionment of representatives by decennial census; times and places of meetings with officers of the Congresses of the United States and the names of the delegates arranged by states; biographies of presidents who were not members of Congress; and, finally, biographies of members of Congress arranged alphabetically by surname.

Official Congressional Directory for the Use of the United States Congress. Washington, D.C., Government Printing Office.

This title is issued for each session of Congress. It includes information on such subjects as: alphabetical list and addresses of members; administrative assistants and secretaries; biographical section on members; committee assignments; department of the executive branch with names of individuals and offices held; District of Columbia government with names of individuals and offices held; foreign diplomats assigned to Washington; United States diplomats assigned abroad arranged alphabetically by name of country to which assigned; index of individual names; judiciary; maps of congressional districts; press representatives and services; and some statistical information.

Charles B. Brownson, ed., *Congressional Staff Directory.* Washington, D.C., The Congressional Staff Directory.

This title has been published annually since 1959. It covers state delegations; staffs of the officers and members of the Senate; staffs of Senate committees and subcommittees; staffs of joint committees; staffs of miscellaneous officers; staffs of House members; as well as the staffs of the various committees, subcommittees, and officers. It also includes brief biographies of each staff member.

Public Affairs Information Service Bulletin. New York, Public Affairs Information Service, Inc.

This title, which began in 1915, is published weekly and cumulated annually. It is a selective subject list of the latest books; pamphlets; government publications; reports of public and private agencies; and periodical articles relating to economic and social conditions, public administration, and international relations. Each entry gives full title, personal and corporate authors, source and availability, cost, number of pages, and date of issue. The bulletin includes a list of periodical references, directory of those publishers and organizations whose material is included, and a list of subject headings used. In 1970 the service somewhat reduced its coverage, but all substantive material remains.

STATE PUBLICATIONS

This section of the paper deals with state publications. Their acquisition and organization in the library's collection present more difficulties than do federal publications. There is no single printer for the publications of all states; rarely is there a single printer for the publications of any state. There is no established classification schedule, such as the Superintendent of Documents system, for state publications. Publishing, usually, is done by individual state agencies, and, often, is contracted out to a commercial printer. Since there is seldom centralized printing, there is seldom centralized distribution.

Many states do have designated depositories even though they do not have a single state printer; however, the practical result of decentralized distribution is nondistribution of a majority of agency publications. Decentralized distribution depends upon the maintenance of mailing lists by each state unit. As personnel changes occur and new agencies are created, sometimes small, and sometimes far away from the state capitol, distribution lags and gaps appear in library holdings. While acquiring and organizing state publications are difficult, the problems are not unsolvable.

Acquisition

The primary general bibliographic source is the *Monthly Checklist of State Publications*, which began in 1910, and is prepared by the Gifts and Exchange Division of the Library of Congress. Monographs are listed each month as they are received and are arranged by state and issuing agency. Included are annual publications and monographs in series. The monographs in series are listed as contents under the series title, except for publications in college and university bulletin series, and similar materials, which are listed under their monographic titles. Periodicals are listed semiannually in the June and December issues, the December list being cumulative for the year. Publications of associations of state officials and of regional organizations and library surveys, studies, manuals, and statistical reports appear in two sections at the end of the listing of monographs by state.

For each publication the price and pertinent bibliographic information, such as changes in titles and in names of issuing bodies, are given

when known. The Library of Congress card number is also shown at the
end of each entry when available. A few categories of publications, such
as college and university catalogs, loose-leaf additions, slip laws, and
certain ephemeral material such as blank forms and publishers announcements, are not included. Listings of state university press publications are limited to those which by reason of their content or series
title appear to be official publications of the university. The publications listed are not distributed by the Library of Congress but may be
obtained from the agencies issuing them. The Library of Congress also
produces a separate annual index.

The real solution to the problem of collecting and organizing state
documents may be within the operation of the federal government. The
National Technical Information Service could establish a liaison with the
Library of Congress and issue a microfiche edition of those state documents which are listed in *The Monthly Checklist of State Publications*.
Libraries could then subscribe to the publications of one or more states
in much the same fashion they subscribe to other microfiche services of
NTIS. A library could arrange the microfiche by year and by serial number assigned to each publication included in the *Monthly Checklist*.
Active support by national library organizations and individual librarians for such a program would solve what is at present a difficult problem.

Classification

The next problem is classification of material. Some states have
developed a vertical classification schedule similar to that used by the
Superintendent of Documents. Perhaps the most effective system is the
one devised by the state of California for its own publications.

The California State Library at Sacramento publishes a version of
the *Monthly Catalog* called *California State Publications*. It is issued
monthly and cumulated annually. The State Library has devised a classification schedule based on the organizational structure of the state
government—in principle it closely resembles the Superintendent of
Documents classification scheme. California also has an official state
printer and a system of depository libraries within the state. California
is a model of what other individual states need to do to make available
their public papers to schools, universities, and libraries. The entries in
California State Publications are arranged by classification number,
which roughly provides an alphabetic arrangement by issuing agency.
The full address of each issuing agency is given if that address is different from that of the state capitol. Each entry includes classification
number; corporate author, if different from that of the issuing agency;
and subject descriptors. There is a single alphabetic index which includes
corporate authors and subjects. The classification schedule, with sugges-

tions for similar state schedules, is obtainable from the California State
Library in a publication called *California State Publications, Manual for
Acquisition, Processing, Use.*

The *California Blue Book,* which also gives the names of specific
officeholders, is an aid to understanding the California classification
system. The table of contents lists the major departments with the subordinate offices of each. There is a detailed alphabetic index in the back
of the volume. For those planning to have an extensive collection of
state publications, the acquisition of the state blue books would be
helpful. A listing of available titles by state appears in the *State Manuals,
Blue Books, And Election Results* by Charles Press and Oliver Williams
published by the Institute of Governmental Studies, University of
California, Berkeley.

FEDERALLY SPONSORED TECHNICAL REPORTS

The last part of this paper concentrates on federally sponsored technical reports. Technical reports have long been a problem for librarians.
The reports do not easily fit into the regular collection and their volume defies the resources of the cataloging departments of most libraries.
Because these reports now are, usually, in some form of microtext, they
tend to be kept in a special collection. Three particular aspects of this
material and its handling merit further attention, the characteristics of
technical reports, the background of Georgia Tech's technical reports
collection, and the classification of the reports, as well as the tools for
acquisition and retrieval.

There are ten characteristics which may help in defining the unique
nature of the technical report (*8,* pp. 1–2).

1. Report literature is voluminous in the number of titles issued and
in the number of agencies involved in their publication. The number of
distributing agencies is somewhat more limited, but, still, complex and
varied enough to cause considerable confusion. The actual number of
copies of each report is relatively small.

2. The reports are heterogeneous, differing widely in form and content, some of ephemeral nature, others, well-organized and comprehensive, are of permanent value.

3. The distribution of certain reports is limited by security classification; others may be limited because they are politically sensitive. Not
everyone may have access to all reports.

4. They are not available from book trade sources, but only through
specified government agencies, and, often, through military channels.
Much of the material is free if distribution is made to qualified persons.
Those reports which are available to the general public tend to be for
sale.

5. Usually, they are not referenced in conventional bibliographical

tools for either books or periodicals. The librarian must become familiar with a different set of retrieval tools.

6. There is no union list to the holdings of reports in specific libraries. The Library of Congress and the National Technical Information Service have the largest known collections of this material. Early in 1957 it was announced that the Technology Department of the Carnegie Library of Pittsburgh, Pa., had become the first depository for reports of the Office of Technical Services of the Department of Commerce.

7. These reports are difficult to handle, once acquired, because of size and multiple authorships both personal and corporate. They are rarely hard bound, thus, requiring special reinforcement if they are kept in paper copy. Today they are generally available in microtext—usually on fiche, less often in film, and, occasionally, an aberant microcard appears. Microforms require special reading equipment. With the advent of negative microtext came the reader/printer from which regular-sized paper copy could be produced.

8. The reports are serials and, usually, have multiple serial numbers coming from the various agencies with which they have some connection.

9. If the reports have a security classification they must be stored and handled according to elaborate controls enforced by the Department of Defense.

10. At this time the vast majority of reports are sponsored by the Department of Defense and the Atomic Energy Commission. Other departments and agencies combined account for a small percentage of the total material. All the report literature produced contains a great deal of basic and applied scientific data of use to industrial and academic researchers. In many cases these reports are the only source of advanced or specialized information, and, therefore, they are a significant part of the collection of a scientific and technological library.

History and Organization

The Georgia Tech Library's Technical Reports Collection dates from World War II when general use of the technical report came into being. Up to that time scholarly technical journals were the primary means of making known the results of scientific research. Formal printing, with its requirements of textual refinement and adherence to editorial rules, caused considerable delay in the publication of new scientific information. The war brought federal government funding both for technical research as well as publishing its results in a form more quickly available than the traditional journal article. The war ended but government financing of defense research and report publication continued. By the early sixties the form of the technical report had changed from an 8" x 11" mimeographed page to a 4" x 5" microform because of the factors of volume, storage, cost, and distribution. Initially, microreproduction consisted of microfilm and later microcard. Each was a positive print whose enlarged image was poor and neither could easily be reproduced. The positive microcard gave way to the negative microfiche and engineering work on lense and screen improved a once faulty image.

In 1962 as part of a program financed by the National Science Foundation, the Office of Technical Services in the Department of Commerce designated the Georgia Institute of Technology Library a Regional Technical Reports Center—one of 12 such centers in the United States. At this time the library's technical reports collection consisted mainly of reports sponsored by the Atomic Energy Commission and the National Aeronautics and Space Administration. The Atomic Energy Commission microtext reports date from 1953; the National Aeronautics and Space Administration microtext reports date from 1962.

With the establishment of the Technical Reports Center, the library began receiving two new categories of reports, "AD" and "PB", which were indexed in U.S. Government Research Reports. These acronyms were derived from two separate organizations no longer in existence— the Armed Services Technical Information Agency (Documents) whose functions are now performed by the Defense Documentation Center, and the Publication Board, a part of the Department of Commerce, whose functions are now performed by the National Technical Information Service. For the next decade, these reports had a spotty career as far as their lives at the Georgia Institute of Technology were concerned. For two years the library received both series on microfilm. Microfiche superseded microfilm and budget difficulties superseded film and fiche, interrupting, for the moment, the development of this area of the collection. It was not until the 1970s that the Library purchased subscriptions to "AD" and "PB" reports, and it would appear that both series are now a permanent part of its operation.

The library's technical reports holdings are essentially microtext, i.e., mostly microfiche with some microcards and some microfilm. The microtext collection is divided into four separate parts according to the sponsoring organization and classification system: 1) National Aeronautics and Space Administration reports arranged numerically by "N" number; 2) Atomic Energy Commission reports arranged by a vertical classification schedule using letters to identify immediate issuing offices, which, frequently, are laboratories, and numbers which serve as accession numbers; 3) Department of Defense reports arranged numerically by "AD" numbers; and 4) Reports from the civilian departments arranged by "PB" numbers. NASA microfiche comes to the Georgia Tech Library on deposit from NASA because of research it is sponsoring at the Institute. Atomic Energy Commission microfiche is purchased by the library on a subscription basis from Microsurance, Inc., Oak Ridge, Tenn. The library has a subscription to "AD" and "PB" reports distributed by the National Technical Information Service at Springfield, Va.

Cataloging and Classifying

The Atomic Energy Commission and the National Aeronautics and Space Administration pioneered not only in the form of the technical report, but also in its cataloging, classifying, and indexing. Their technical reports indexes have gone through many changes from general chronological listings, descriptor indexes, KWIC indexes, and, currently, to a book form of index with annual cumulations by author, title, subject, and accession/report number.

The means of bibliographic control established by these two agencies have been applied to technical reports in the civil field via *Government Reports Announcements* and *Government Reports Index*. Now, literally all federally sponsored material has the unique advantage of a publisher who provides cataloging, classifying, and indexing of his own publications. Thus a microform arrives in the library preclassified and precataloged by the publisher who will also issue an index which is the main retrieval tool for the library user.

To supplement these titles and to aid in handling reports, the Library produces a card catalog which is, essentially, a monographic series check-in record arranged alphabetically by primary corporate author. The catalog is divided into two parts: the first part is for reports sponsored by the Atomic Energy Commission; the second part is for all other reports. The microfiche edition of the Library's *Serials Holdings List* does not include any series which are a part of the Technical Reports Collection

Retrieval Tools

There are several titles which serve as the main retrieval tools and which merit a brief description. Several of these titles were mentioned previously in this paper.

Scientific and Technical Aerospace Reports. Washington, D.C., National Aeronautics and Space Administration.

This title, which began in 1963, appears on the 8th and 23d of each month. It is a comprehensive abstracting and indexing journal covering current worldwide report literature on the science and technology of space and aeronautics. Publications abstracted include scientific and technical reports issued by NASA and its contractors, other U.S. Government agencies, corporations, universities, and research organizations throughout the world. Pertinent theses, NASA-owned patents and patent applications, translations, and other separate documents are also abstracted. In addition to an abstract, each entry gives the NASA serial number, corporate source and location, full title, all personal authors, place of publication if different from location of corporate source, date of issue, number of pages, and availability. Citations and abstracts in *STAR* are grouped in 34 subject categories which are listed in the following abstract. The index section has six parts: 1) subject, 2) personal author, 3) corporate source, 4) contract number, 5) report accession number, and 6) accession report number. The accession/report number index ceased at the end of v. 9 (1971). Starting with v. 10 (1972), abstracts are arranged numerically by this number. Cumulative volumes of each index are published annually. Prior to v. 10, each entry in an index indicates a page number directing the user to the correct page on which the abstract appears.

By arrangement between the National Aeronautics and Space Administration and the American Institute of Aeronautics and Astronautics, the AIAA publication, *International Aerospace Abstracts,* provides parallel coverage of scientific and trade journals, books, and conference papers in the same subject areas using a common NASA thesaurus to determine subject headings.

International Aerospace Abstracts. New York, American Institute of Aeronautics and Astronautics under contract with the National Aeronautics and Space Administration.

IAA, which began in 1961, is issued twice monthly on the 1st and the 15th for the purpose of alternating with the issuing dates of *STAR*. In June and December three issues are published. This title is divided into two major sections, an abstract section and an index section. The abstract section contains complete bibliographic citations for each entry giving full title of article, all personal authors and their places of employment, the title of the publication in which the article appears, date of publication, volume, and page numbers of the article, and the *IAA* accession number. All documents abstracted are available from the Technical Information Service, American Institute of Aeronautics and Astronautics, 750 Third Ave., New York, N.Y. 10017. The abstracts are arranged by appropriate subject categories to facilitate scanning. The subject categories are numbered from 01 to 34; the scope of each is outlined in the "Table of Contents" of each issue and again at the beginning of each category in the "Abstracts Section." The "Index Section" has five parts: 1) subject, 2) personal author, 3) contract number, 4) meeting paper and report number, and 5) accession number. Each index is prefaced by explanatory notes to guide the user to the desired abstract. Cumulations of each index are published quarterly and annually.

By special arrangement between the National Aeronautics and

Space Administration and the American Institute of Aeronautics and
Astronautics, *STAR* and *IAA* provide comprehensive access to the
national and international unclassified report and other published literature of current significance to aerospace science and technology. *IAA*
and *STAR* both utilize identical subject categories and indexes; the 34
subject categories are listed below.

01 Aerodynamics	18 Materials, nonmetallic
02 Aircraft	19 Mathematics
03 Auxiliary systems	20 Meteorology
04 Biosciences	21 Navigation
05 Biotechnology	22 Nuclear engineering
06 Chemistry	23 Physics, general
07 Communications	24 Physics—atomic, molecular, and
08 Computers	nuclear
09 Electronic equipment	25 Physics, plasma
10 Electronics	26 Physics, solid state
11 Facilities, research and suport	27 Propellants
12 Fluid mechanics	28 Propulsion systems
13 Geophysics	29 Space radiation
14 Instrumentation and	30 Space sciences
photography	31 Space vehicles
15 Machine elements and processes	32 Structural mechanics
16 Masers	33 Thermodynamics and combustion
17 Materials, metallic	34 General

Nuclear Science Abstracts. Washington, D.C., Government Printing
Office.

This title, which began in 1948, is published biweekly covering scientific and technical reports by the U.S. Atomic Energy Commission
and its contractors, other U.S. Government agencies, foreign governments, universities, and industrial and research organizations. Particular
attention is given to the literature published in the United Kingdom,
Japan, Canada, Sweden, Denmark, Norway, Finland, West Germany,
Australia, and France. In addition, books, conference proceedings, individual conference papers, patents, and journal literature on a worldwide basis are abstracted and indexed. Each abstract includes full title,
personal authors and their places of employment, title and date of publication, volume and page numbers of article, and AEC classification
number when appropriate. The abstracts are arranged by 22 main subject categories, each category being divided into several subgroups. The
main categories are as follows.

Chemistry	Materials
Engineering	Nuclear materials and waste management
Environmental and earth sciences	Particle accelerators
Instrumentation	Physics, astrophysics and cosmology
Isotope and radiation sources	Physics, atmospheric
technology	Physics, atomic and molecular
Life sciences	Physics, electrofluid and magnetofluid

Physics, high-energy	Physics, radiation and shielding
Physics, low-temperature	Physics, solid-state
Physics, nuclear	Physics, theoretical
Physics, plasma and	Reactor technology
thermonuclear	General

There are four indexes: 1) subject, 2) personal author, 3) corporate author, and 4) report number. Prior to v. 27 the indexes were cumulated annually with one volume produced per year. Starting with 1973 there will be two volumes per year with the indexes being cumulated for each volume. A list of journals scanned regularly appears in the Jan 15 issue and is supplemented in the July issue.

Each entry in the indexes gives a number which is the abstract number; abstracts are arranged in a single numerical sequence. Listings in index cumulations of more than one volume include the volume number in heavy type followed by the particular abstract number in lighter type. The library's collection of AEC sponsored reports is in microtext, which is arranged by the Atomic Energy Commission classification number given in each abstract. Book and periodical literature cited are generally in the library's main collection and may be located through the card catalog, or its microfiche edition, copies of which are distributed throughout the Georgia Institute of Technology.

Government Reports Announcements, and *Government Reports Index.* Washington, D.C., Government Printing Office.

These titles, which began in 1946, are issued on the 10th and 25th of each month by the National Technical Information Service located at Springfield, Virginia. These titles cover research and development reports funded by the federal government, but, usually, produced by nongovernmental organizations. The reports listed are sold to the public by the National Technical Information Service. Individual titles may be purchased by citing the serial number and full title on an order form which appears in the back of each issue of *Government Reports Announcements*. NTIS accepts subscriptions by subject category to certain series. The subscriptions are called "Selective Dissemination of Microfiche." For more detailed information those interested should write to the Customer Services Division, National Technical Information Service, U.S. Department of Commerce, 5285 Port Royal Road, Springfield, Va. 22151.

Some of the reports included are also distributed by the Atomic Energy Commission, the Department of Defense, the National Aeronautics and Space Administration, the Government Printing Office, and other departments and agencies of the federal government. Some technical translations of reports from foreign governments are included. Reports in the NTIS collection are available indefinitely. Each abstract appearing in *GRA* gives full title, corporate source, federal sponsor, all personal authors, date of issue, number of pages, and contract number. Citations include both patent information and references to other abstracts when pertinent. Each issue of *GRA* has a classified subject arrangement by 22 main fields listed below. Each field is divided into appropriate subgroups. For example:

01 Aeronautics	12 Mathematical sciences
02 Agriculture	13 Mechanical, industrial, civil, and
03 Astronomy and astrophysics	marine engineering
04 Atmospheric sciences	14 Methods and equipment
05 Behavioral and social sciences	15 Military sciences
06 Biological and medical sciences	16 Missile technology
07 Chemistry	17 Navigation, communications,
08 Earth sciences and oceanography	detection and countermeasures
09 Electronics and electrical	18 Nuclear science and technology
engineering	19 Ordnance
10 Energy conversion (non-	20 Physics
propulsive)	21 Propulsion and fuels
11 Materials	22 Space technology

GRI, which is the index for *GRA,* is divided into five parts: 1) subject, 2) personal author, 3) corporate source, 4) contract/grant number, and 5) accession/report number. Each index is cumulated annually.

The library's holdings are in microtext arranged by the serial numbers assigned by NTIS.

Selected Rand Abstracts. Santa Monica, Calif., The Rand Corporation.

This title, which began in 1963, is issued quarterly. Rand is an independent, nonprofit organization engaged in scientific research and analysis. It conducts studies in the public interest supported by the United States Government, by state and local governments, and by its own funds derived from earned fees, and by private sources, including foundations. The work involves most of the major disciplines in the physical, social, and biological sciences, with emphasis on their application to problems of policy and planning in domestic and foreign affairs.

Selected Rand Abstracts is a complete guide to the current unclassified publications of the Rand Corporation. The volume is cumulative through the year. Each issue is divided into an index section and an abstract section. The index section contains subject and author indexes covering all the material abstracted in the current volume. The abstract section is divided into four parts—books, reports, Rand memoranda, and papers. Books are arranged alphabetically according to the surname of the first author. Each of the other three sections is arranged numerically according to the serial number of the publication.

Index of Selected Publications of the Rand Corporation, Volume I: 1946–1962. Santa Monica, Calif., The Rand Corporation, 1962.

Reta C. Moser, *Space-Age Acronyms, Abbreviations and Designations.*
New York, IFI/Plenum, 1969.

In the "Foreword," Woods states, "Acronym agglomeration is an
affliction of the age, and there are acronym addicts who, in their weak-
ness, find it impossible to resist them." The technical reports librarian
will find it impossible to avoid them. This title includes some 15,000
acronyms and 25,000 definitions arranged alphabetically.

SUMMARY AND CONCLUSIONS

This paper has examined the three main categories of government
printed material—federal government publications, state government
publications, and technical reports. Peculiarities of each have been
noted and particular titles of help to the librarian have been cited. The
practices of the Georgia Institute of Technology Library have been used
as working examples of the procedures one library has adopted to
handle this type of material.

State publications remain, largely, unorganized, unrecorded, and
undistributed. The problem is a lack of centralized procedures. Federal
distribution of a microfiche edition of titles listed in the *Monthly
Checklist of State Publications* would solve some of the difficulty. Such
a program could be accomplished through a cooperative arrangement
between the Library of Congress and the National Technical Information Service. State library organizations should petition their legislatures
for the passage of laws establishing state printers charged with the responsibility of gathering, publishing, and distributing the public papers
of their respective states.

The literature from the federal government, grouped separately by
classification schedules but physically housed together, combines to
form a cohesive collection. Administrative policy, national politics, and
technical research are inextricably interwoven. Federal publications are
the exposition of each. Organization of these publications into a single
collection allows librarian and researcher alike efficient access to the
information they contain. The librarian may utilize the cataloging, classifying, and indexing done by the federal government for its own publications. It is not within the capacity of the normal library staff to perform these functions adequately for this material. Utilizing all the federally produced resources both of published literature and bibliographic
control tools, a library would have the advantage of a quality collection
whose acquisition, maintenance, and retrieval would make a minimal
demand on its operating budget.

Bibliography

1. Andriot, J. L. / *Guide to Popular U.S. Government Publications.* Arlington, Va., Documents Index, 1960.

2. Andriot, J. L. / *Guide to U.S. Government Serials and Periodicals.* McLean, Va., Documents Index, 1959-.

3. Andriot, J. L. / *Guide to U.S. Government Statistics.* Arlington, Va., Documents Index, 1956-.

4. Caldwell, G. / University Libraries and Government Publications, a Survey. *College and Research Libraries* 22:30-34 (Jan 1961).

5. California. State Library, Sacramento. / *California State Publications; Manual for Acquisition, Processing, Use.* 2d rev. ed. Sacramento, Calif. Department of Finances, Organization and Cost Control Division, 1961.

6. Childs, J. B. / Bibliographic Control of Federal, State and Local Documents. *Library Trends* 15:6-26 (Jul 1966).

7. Clarke, N. F. / Cataloging, Classification and Storage of Government Publications when Incorporated into the General Library Collection. *Library Trends* 15:58-71 (Jul 1966).

8. Dale, D. C. / The Development of Classification Systems for Government Publications. *Library Resources and Technical Services* 13:471-483 (Fall 1969).

9. Darling, R. E. / The Government Bookstore. *Special Libraries* 62:8 (Jan 1971).

10. Deaths—Adelaide Hasse. *Library Journal* 78:1497 (Sep 15, 1953).

11. Federal System of 12 Centers to Collect Technical Reports. *Library Journal* 87:1870 (May 15, 1962).

12. Hasse, A. R. / *United States Government Publications, a Handbook for the Cataloger: Part I, the Government at Large—the Constitution, Statutes, Treaties.* Boston, Library Bureau, 1902.

13. Hasse, A. R. / *United States Government Publications, a Handbook for the Cataloger: Part II, the Legislative Body.* Boston, Library Bureau, 1903.

14. Holzbauer, H. / Bibliographic Organization in the Federal Government. *Wilson Library Bulletin* 40:719-720 (Apr 1966).

15. Hyde, D. W., Jr. / Public Archives and Public Documents as Aids to Scholarship. *Public Documents.* Paper presented by the Committee on Public Documents at the 1936 Conference of the American Library Association. Chicago, American Library Association, 1936.

16. Jackson, E. P. / Cataloging, Classification and Storage in a Separate Documents Collection. *Library Trends* 15:50-57 (Jul 1966).

17. Jackson, E. P. / *A Manual for the Administration of the Federal Documents Collection in Libraries.* Chicago, American Library Association, 1955.

18. Kane, R. / The Future Lies Ahead; the Documents Depository Library of Tomorrow. *Library Journal* 92:3971-3973 (Nov 1, 1967).

19. Keefer, M. / Simplified Cataloging of Federal and State Documents. *Library Resources and Technical Services* 6:262-264 (Summer 1962).

20. Kiraldi, L. / Government Abstracting Services. *Library Journal* 93:4634-4635 (Dec 15, 1958).

21. Kirkland, J. / *Guide to the Use of Technical Report Literature in the Georgia Tech Library.* Atlanta, 1967. (Unpublished).

22. Leavitt, E. P. / Government Publications in the University Library. *Library Journal* 86:1741-1743 (May 1, 1961).

23. Levy, G. M. / Cuttering the Corporate Entry. *Special Libraries* 60:657-658 (Dec 1969).

24. Lweinson, P. / Preservation of Government Publications. *American Archivist* 22:181-188 (Apr 1959).

25. Miscellaneous—Miss Adelaide R. Hasse In U.S. Library of Congress. *Information Bulletin* 12:13 (Aug. 3, 1953).

26. Miss Adelaide Hasse, A Bibliographer, 84. *New York Times* (Jul 30, 1953) p. 230.

27. Norden, M. / KWIC Index to Government Publications. *Journal of Library Automation* 2:139-147 (Sep 1969).

28. Obituaries—Adelaide R. Hasse . . . . *Special Libraries* 44:344 (Oct 1953).

29. Obituaries—July 28, Adelaide R. Hasse . . . . *Wilson Library Bulletin* 28:30 (Sep 1953).

30. Paulson, P. J. / Government Documents and Other Non-Trade Publications. *Library Trends* 18:363-372 (Jan 1970).

31. Schmeckebier, L. F. / *Government Publications and Their Use.* 2d ed. Washington, D.C., The Brookings Institution, 1969.

32. Scott, P. / The Present and Future of Government Documents in Microform. *Library Trends* 15:72-86 (Jul 1966).

33. Shaw, T. S. / Library Associations and Public Documents. *Library Trends* 15:167-177 (Jul 1966).

34. Shore, P. / An Evaluation of U.S. Document Bibliography. *Library Resources and Technical Services* 4:34-43 (Winter 1960).

35. Simmons, R. M. / Handling Changes in Superintendent of Documents Classification. *Library Resources and Technical Services* 15:241-244 (Spring 1971).

36. Smith, R. S. / Information Hang-Ups: Some Suggestions for DDC and the Clearinghouse. *Special Libraries* 60:672-676 (Dec 1969).

37. Spalding, C.S. / LC Practice with Regard to U.S. Documents. *Library Resources and Technical Services* 14:609-610 (Fall 1970).

38. Stevenson, C. G. / Control and Inventory of Classified Documents. *Special Libraries* 51:499-500 (Nov 1960).

39. U.S. Government Printing Office. Public Documents Department. Library. *An Explanation of the Superintendent of Documents Classification System,* 1970.

40. Van de Voorde, P. / Official Use Trend in the Monthly Catalog of United States Government Publications. *Library Resources and Technical Services* 14:455-457 (Summer 1970).

Patent and Trademark Literature

SAFFORD HARRIS

Although authorities on patents and trademarks differ on the chronological history of patents, they do agree that some form of protection for creativity has been in existence since 500 B.C. (I,A,17,p.10). When America was colonized, the British patent system became the basis for protection by the colonial governments (I,A,17,p.11). After Independence, the United States Constitution included a statement about patents (I,A,5,p.617,col.2); many U.S. patent laws have been passed since that date. However, the basic principle has been the same since the Act of 1836 (I,B,52,p.6).

Patent Definitions

A *patent* indicates the official or legal grant issued by a government giving the inventor the right to exclude all others from making, using, or selling the invention for a specific period of time. The statute states that anyone who "invents or discovers any new and useful process, machine, manufacture, or composition of matter, or any new and useful improvement thereof, may obtain a patent" (I,B,27,p.3). Also, the idea must not be obvious to one skilled in the art.

There are about 200 countries which grant some form of the *complete patent* (II,A,9), a term used to mean any patent which a government has granted in whatever form chosen. When an idea is patented in the U.S., the Patent Office issues the document as a patent or letters patent. The complete patent includes text—with background information, objectives, how it works—and drawings. Near the end of every patent, there are one or more claims, or ways, in which one patent differs from another. The text does not include size of item, or standards.

A *brief patent* covers either a claim, or claims, or an abstract. The *Annual Report/Report of the Commissioner of Patents,* 1836-1871, included claims, or an abstract, and for that period the use of *brief patent*

Safford Harris is patent librarian, Price Gilbert Memorial Library, Georgia Institute of Technology, Atlanta, Ga.

covered both terms. From 1872, when the Patent Office began publishing the *Official Gazette,* through 1967, only claims were included in that publication.

In 1966, a Patent Office ruling created the *abstract of the disclosure,* or *abstract,* which is requried for each new patent application filed after a certain date. It must be "a non-legal technical statement of the contents," and should serve "to indicate whether there is a need for consulting the full specification for details" [I,B,21,v.906(no.1): item 165,p.48 (Jan 2, 1973)]. This abstract, if prepared for the application, has been required in the *Official Gazette* and the *Official Gazette: Patents* since January 1968.

Other basic information is included for each *patent* number, *design* patent number, *reissue* patent number, *plant* patent number, and *defensive publication*. This information is the *heading*. The heading includes the patent number, title, patentee and address, assignee and address, if one, serial number (Ser.No.) assigned to the application, date application filed, International Classification class and subclass (Int.Cl.), and U.S. Classification class and subclass (U.S.Cl., or Cl.).

In addition to the information formerly included in the heading, the new cover sheet, which became effective Jan 18, 1972, gives several additional machine readable elements. They include: 1) cross-references for the particular class and subclass, i.e., other subject areas where the same patent number has been classed; and 2) the field of search—other classes and subclasses where information on similar structures in the classification scheme can be found.

Class and subclass should be described together. The U.S. Patent Office has assigned every idea for an invention to a subject, *class*, and a more specific subject subdivision, *subclass*. These numbers are for identification purposes only and are established and abolished by the Patent Office as needed. Subclass numbers may or may not appear in numerical order in the outline for the schedule of that class in the Manual of Classification. In the explanations in the *Classification Definitions* for a particular class, however, the subclasses are consecutive.

Over the years the patent examiners created unofficial subclasses and digests (collections of patents related to many classes), to aid their searches. *Unofficial subclasses* are composed of a group of patents selected from an official subclass and identified with a term descriptive of the new specific subject. Detailed information on these terms is included in Section I,B, Item 53 in the selected bibliography.

Kinds of Patents

The U.S. Patent Office issues five kinds of patents: 1) *complete patent*, identified in bibliographic references as U.S. Patent; 2) *design patent*; 3) *reissue* patent; 4) *plant* patent; and 5) *defensive publication*.

The *complete patent* refers to patents granted weekly, issued in ascending numerical order from number one, dated Jul 13, 1836. The patents are granted for a 17 year period and can be extended only by an Act of Congress. Since 1872, the Patent Office, however, has provided the public with a brief form of the complete patent in the *Official Gazette*.

Since Jul 1952, complete patents have been issued in the following categories: General and Mechanical, Chemical, and Electrical. Brief forms of the patents are identified with a running title only in the *Official Gazette* and *Official Gazette: Patents*. The arrangement for each subject is in numerical order by class and subclass number for a particular group, and in consecutive order by patent number for a particular issue.

In the United States a patentee, or the assignee, may dedicate, or give to the public for use in any way, the whole patent for the entire term or any part of any term "of the patent granted or to be granted." In addition, the patentee, or the assignee, may disclaim "any complete claim," for the whole term or any part of the term upon payment of the required fee. Such a disclaimer must be in writing (I, B, 38, Chapter 1403, rev. 29, Jul 1971).

Design patents cover new, original, and ornamental designs for articles of manufacture. Only the "outward look" of the article is protected. Design patents are granted for a period of 3 ½, 7, or 14 years. The *Official Gazette* and the *Official Gazette: Patents* include brief forms of the design patents. The Disclosure Document Program, explained later, does not apply to design patents.

The *reissue patent*, is granted only for a complete patent and a design patent. It is cited as *Re, reissue patent*, or *Des.Re.*, *design reissue patent*. The patentee and/or the assignee apply for a reissue patent when corrections or changes in a patent must be made. Nothing new is allowed. All reissue patents expire on the original date of the patent.

The *plant patent* is issued to anyone "who has invented or discovered and asexually reproduced any distinct and new variety of plant, including cultivated sports, mutants, hybrids, and newly found seedlings, other than a tuber-propagated plant or a plant found in an uncultivated state. Asexually propagated plants are those that are reproduced by means other than from seeds, such as by the rooting of cuttings, by layering, budding, grafting, . . . etc." Plant patents have been issued since Aug 18, 1931, and are granted for 17 years. Since Dec 24, 1970, the Plant Variety Protection Act has protected sexually reproduced varieties (I,B,27,p.29-30).

The *defensive publication* became effective May 1, 1968, as a program open to applicants under certain conditions. The application abstract, upon receipt and approval, is published in the *Official Gazette* and the *Official Gazette: Patents*. The program provides better service to the public since the application abstract and suitable drawings became a part of the official search files. Defensive publications have been assigned a six digit number preceded by the letter "T," meaning technical disclosure. The first three figures indicate the volume number of the *Official Gazette* and the *Official Gazette: Patents* for a particular month; the last three figures indicate the item number for the month in consecutive order beginning with 001. [I,B,40,v.869(no.3):687-688(Dec 16, 1969)]. The earliest defensive publication is in the Nov 5, 1968, issue.

Significant Resources

There are two categories of basic resources for information on patent and trademark literature: nongovernmental and governmental. They may be used as a standard guide in building a collection in these fields.

Nongovernmental Sources. The most important nongovernmental source is the latest edition of *Ulrich's International Periodicals Directory*, in which there is a section called "Patents, Trademarks, and Copyrights." These listings include title, beginning date, frequency, cost, address, coverage, (abstr., bk.rev., pat., tr.mk., index), number circulated, where indexed, and specialized coverage, if unique.

Two sources also provide lists of countries and/or abstracts of patents: *Chemical Abstracts* and *Derwent Patents Manual.* Usually the first issue in January of *Chemical Abstracts* lists the countries covered, addresses, and cost of patents from 26 countries. It includes a wide range of patents in chemistry and related fields. *Derwent Patents Manual* discusses serials from more than ten countries, including the U.S. These descriptions are based on the complete patents. Each issue includes abstracts in English, a numerical location index, a patentee index, and the International Patent Classification. All patents are covered for Germany, Great Britain, and the Soviet Union. Only chemical and related patents are published for Belgium, France, India, Japan, Netherlands, South Africa, and U.S.

A useful tool is the "Patent Concordance" in *Chemical Abstracts*, published since 1963. Limited in subject matter, it is invaluable in locating a U.S. patent number when the patent was first granted in a foreign country. It is cumulated semiannually and at five year intervals. One drawback is the delay of probably two years between the time a patent is listed in the first foreign country and when it is granted in the U.S.

References to recently patented inventions may also be found in current periodicals, serials, monographs, and even newspapers, especially the Saturday issue of the *New York Times*.

Governmental Sources. One of the most important governmental sources covering information on patents and trademarks is the *Monthly Catalog of the United States Government Publications*, sold by the Superintendent of Documents. The *Monthly Catalog* is a valuable source of inexpensive patent and trademark publications. Other specialized titles are published by the Department of Commerce and the Patent Office. The September issue of the *Monthly Catalog* includes a list of depository libraries, many of which include patent and trademark materials.

Additional government sources of information are the *Official Gazette,* the *Official Gazette: Patents*, and the *Official Gazette: Trade-*

marks. They should be considered as first purchases for most collections. Another significant source is *Index of Patents,* especially *Part II. Subjects of Inventions.* This includes a list of depository libraries subscribing to the complete U.S. patents by state, town, and library name and a list, arranged by state and territory, city, and name of library, indicating where copies of the *Official Gazette* and/or *Official Gazette: Patents* or *Official Gazette: Trademarks* may be found. The U.S. Patent Office also issues at irregular intervals two invaluable and fairly inexpensive government publications: *General Information Concerning Patents* and *Patent Laws.*

Sources for Acquisition

There are several sources for locating information on the purchase of complete patents. These patents, both U.S. and foreign, may be ordered directly from the publisher. The U.S. Patent Office includes information on ordering of complete U.S. patents in the publications: *General Information Concerning Patents*; *Rules of Practice in Patent Cases*; and *Patent Laws.*

Two other sources for buying U.S. and foreign patent materials are available. *Ulrich's International Periodicals Directory* gives necessary information for placing an order directly to the publisher, whether in the U.S. or abroad. A source of information for ordering foreign patents is *Derwent Patents Manual* described earlier. Any complete foreign patent listed may be ordered directly from Derwent Publications Ltd., but by subscribers only.

Trademarks

The Trademark Act of 1946 defined a *trademark* as ". . .any word, name, symbol, or device, or any combination thereof adopted and used by a manufacturer or merchant to identify his goods and distinguish them from those manufactured or sold by others." The Act states further that trademarks indicate origin and "guarantee the quality of the goods bearing the marks and, through advertising, serve to create and maintain a demand for the product" (III,B,3,p.1).

U.S. trademarks are registered in the U.S. Patent Office to mean that the government recognizes the right of the owner of the mark "to distinguish his goods from those of others" (III,B,3,p.1). "Rights in a trademark are established. . .by the use of the mark on goods" . . . which "have been sold or shipped in interstate, foreign, or Territorial commerce" (III,B,7,p.3).

Trade names and *commercial names* cannot be registered in the U.S. Patent Office "unless actually used as trademarks." These "names are business names used by manufacturers, merchants, and others to identify their businesses or occupations, such as names of partnerships, companies, and other organizations" (III,B,7,p.4). A trade name identifies a producer, a trademark identifies a product.

The Trademark Act of 1946 also provided for the registration of *service marks, certification marks*, and *collective marks.* The term *serv-*

ice mark "means a mark used in the sale of advertising of services of others" (III,B,3,p.10). Service marks have been separated into eight classes numbered 100-107: miscellaneous; advertising and business; insurance and financial; construction and repair; communication; transportation; material treatment; and education and entertainment.

The term *collective mark* (Class 200) "means a trademark or service mark used by the members of a cooperative, an association, or other collective group or organization. Marks used to indicate membership in a union, an association, or other organization may be registered as Collective Membership Marks" (III,B,3,p.11).

The term *certification mark* (Class A and Class B) "means a mark used upon or in connection with the products or services of one or more persons other than the owner of the mark to certify regional or other origin, material, mode of manufacture, quality, accuracy or other characteristics of such goods or services or that the work or labor on the goods or services was performed by members of a union or other organization" (III,B,3,p.10). Certification marks identify "goods" (Class A), and "services" (Class B).

The Lanham Trademark Act of 1946 established two registers, Principal and Supplemental. The Patent Office accepts for registration on the Principal Register any mark the applicant has used "in commerce for the five years next preceding the date of filing of the application for registration." These categories include "Coined, arbitrary, fanciful, or suggestive marks, generally referred to as 'technical marks'." Not qualified for registration on the Principal Register are marks which "are capable of distinguishing applicant's goods and have been in lawful use in commerce for the year preceding the date of filing of the application for registration". These are registered on the Supplemental Register. They include "any trademark, symbol, label, package, configuration of goods, name, word, slogan, phase, surname, geographical name, numeral, or device, or any combination of any of the foregoing" (III,B,3,p. 2,3).

Generally, it is more difficult to locate information about trademarks than it is to find information about patents. There are, however, several sources in the literature for identifying trademarks. Again, *Ulrich's International Periodicals Directory* is most important. The *Monthly Catalog of the United States Government Publications* is also useful. Titles on or about trademarks are listed under Patent Office. The U.S. Patent Office publishes an annual index entitled *Index of Trademarks*, an alphabetical listing of the registrants of trademarks, Through 1926, the *Index of Patents* also included the indexes of trademarks. Beginning with 1927, a separate volume began publication.

The *Trademark Register of the United States,* published by the Patent Searching Service, is the only listing of trademark names by class. It is the most useful publication for identifying trademarks when a date is unknown and only the trademark name is available. This title is a cumulative listing from 1881 through June 1 of the most recent year publish-

ed. It is necessary first to identify the trademark by subject or class to
find the name under its class. The classes are arranged in numerical order,
then in alphabetical order under each. The information given includes
these items only: trademark name in capital letters, followed by Class
number (Cl. and number), date published in the *Official Gazette* or *Official Gazette: Trademarks*; and the assigned trademark number. For the
name of the registrant (individual, corporation, or a firm), consult the
brief form in the *Official Gazette* or in the *Official Gazette: Trademarks*
for the date published. Again, the trademark name will be given in capital letters, followed by the registrant, the SN number (serial number),
publication date (Pub. date), and Filed date.

In order to see the actual mark, the address of the registrant, or the
actual format of the trademark name, you must locate the trademark's
serial number under its class for the date published in the *Official Gazette* or in the *Official Gazette: Trademarks*. Additional information
given includes a detailed statement of the purpose of the trademark,
followed by its International Class (Int. Cl.), when it was filed, and its
date of first use.

The U.S. Patent Office issues, at irregular intervals, three helpful
publications giving detailed information about trademarks: *General
Information Concerning Trademarks, Trademark: Rules of Practice of
the Patent Office with Forms and Statutes,* and *Q[uestions] & A[nswers]
About Trademarks*. Since they are inexpensive, these titles should be a
part of every library's collection. Another title, *Manual of Patent Examining Procedure*, includes a section called "Trademarks and Names
Used in Trades." A "Partial List of Trademarks" gives the name of the
trademark and the "Particular goods on or in connection with which
the trademark is used." The list is used as a guideline for trademark
names when applying for a patent.

It should be stressed that patent and trademark literature is not
easily found. The librarian must know his collection, his tools, and his
sources. This knowledge will provide direction for developing whatever
collection is needed in these areas of specialization.

Selected Bibliography

I. U.S. Patents

A. *Guides, Aids, and Information Commercially Published*

1. American Association of Nurserymen / *Plant Patents with Common Names.*
   [Numbers] 1-2207: 1931-1962. Washington, D.C. [1963].
2. Arnold, Tom / *Invention Protection for Practicing Engineers.* New York,
   Barnes & Noble [1971].
3. *BNA's Patent, Trademark & Copyright Journal.* Washington, D.C., Bureau of
   National Affairs, Inc., Nov. 5, 1970-.
4. Bowker Associates, Inc., Washington, D.C. / *United States Patent Previews,*

1965-1970. Assignments of pending patents recorded in the U.S. Patent Office, Jan 1963-Jul 1965. Washington, D.C., Bowker Associates [1966].

5. Calvert, Robert, ed. / *The Encyclopedia of Patent Practice and Invention Management.* A comprehensive statement of the principles and procedures in solicitation, enforcement and licensing of patents and recognition and utilization of inventions, written by an eminent staff of contributing authors. New York, Reinhold Book Corporation [1964].

6. Fenner, Terrence W. / *Inventor's Handbook.* New York, Chemical Publishing Co., 1969.

7. Gilbert, O. Rundle / Illustrated Catalog. $2.00. Garrison, N.Y. [n.p.]
"The O. Rundle Gilberts' collection of 100,000 original United States Patent models inventions."
"The patent models are the original models that were submitted to the United States Patent Office by inventors between the years 1790 and 1890."
"Owners of the original United States patent models. Inventions dating from 1790-1890."

8. The Green Leaf Guide / *National Reference for the Patent Field.* 6th ed. Port Washington, N.Y., Paul Field, 1950.

9. Horwitz, Lester / *Patent Office Rules and Practice.* 3v. New York, Matthew Bender, 1972.

10. *Idea; the Patent, Trademark and Copyright Journal of Research and Education.* Washington, D.C., Patent, Trademark and Copyright Research Institute, George Washington University Institute. 1964-.

11. *The International Index of Patents: Chemical and Allied Arts, 1790/1960.* 6v. New York, Interdex Corp., 1964.

12. *The International Index of Patents: Electrical and Allied Arts, 1790/1960.* 5v. New York, Interdex Corp., 1965.

13. Jacobs, Albert L. / *Patent and Trademark Forms; for Applications, Prosecution, Appeals, Interferences, Arguments and Litigation:* v.1.—Patents; v.2—Trademarks. rev. ed. Brooklyn, N.Y., Central Book Co., 1967-1970.

14. Jones, Stacy V. / *The Inventor's Patent Handbook.* rev. ed. New York, Dial Press, 1969.

15. Jones, Stacy V. / *You Ought to Patent That.* New York, Dial Press, 1962.

16. Kessler, Kenneth O. / *The Successful Inventor's Guide; How to Develop, Protect and Sell Your Invention Profitably.* Englewood Cliffs, N.J., Prentice-Hall, 1965.

17. Kursh, Harry / *Inside the U.S. Patent Office: The Story of the Men, the Laws, and the Procedures of the American Patent System.* New York, W. W. Norton, 1959.

18. *The National Catalog of Patents: Chemical.* 1961-1962. New York, Rowman and Littlefield, Inc., 1963. 2v./year. (Patent numbers included from U.S. Patent Office. *Official Gazette* issues: 1961-1962).

19. *The National Catalog of Patents: Chemical Allied Patents.* 1961/62. New York, Rowman and Littlefield, Inc., 1963. (Patent numbers included from U.S. Patent Office. *Official Gazette* issues: 1961-1962).

20. *The National Catalog of Patents: Electrical Allied Patents.* 1961/62. New York, Rowman and Littlefield, Inc., 1963. (Patent numbers included from U.S. Patent Office. *Official Gazette* issues: 1961-1962).

21. *The National Catalog of Patents: Electrical, Including Communications and Radiant Energy.* 1961-1962. New York, Rowman and Littlefield, Inc., 1963. 2v./year. (Patent numbers included from U.S. Patent Office. *Official Gazette* issues: 1961-1962).

22. Noyes Data Corporation, Park Ridge, N.J. [For listings in the several series, with or without numbers, covering U.S. Patents granted during a specified time period on given subjects, see the May 1973 Catalog of Noyes Data Corporation]

23. *Patent and Trade Mark Review.* New York, Trade Activities, Inc. 1902-.

24. *Patent Licensing Gazette.* Willow Grove, Pa., Techni Research Associates, Inc. 1968-.

25. Patent Office Society, Washington, D.C. / *Journal.* Federalsburg, Md. 1918-.

26. *Patent, Trademark and Copyright Journal of Research and Education.* Washington D.C., Patent, Trademark and Copyright Research Institute, George Washington University Institute. June 1957-1963. (Superseded by: *Idea; the Patent, Trademark and Copyright Journal of Research and Education*).

27. Randall, Merle / *Finding List for United States Patent, Design, Trade-Mark, Reissue, Label, Print, and Plant Patent Numbers.* Berkeley, Calif., University of California Press, 1938.

28. *Shepard's United States Patents and Trademarks Citations.* A compilation of Citations to United States Patents, Trademarks and Copyrights and to Related Decisions by the Courts and Commissioner of Patents. (The citations which include letter-form abbreviations showing the status of patents, trademarks and copyrights and showing affirmances, reversals and subsequent decisions . . .) 1st ed. 2v. Colorado Springs, Colo., Shepard's Citations, Inc., 1968-. (Updated by cumulative supplements).

29. TTA Information Services Company / *Survey of Patent and Product Development Organizations.* San Mateo, Calif., 1971. (An affiliate of Technology Transfer Associates, Inc.).

30. *United States Patent Quarterly* / Washington, D.C., Bureau of National Affairs, Inc., 1929-.

31. Wade, Worth / *The Corporate Patent Department: Its Organization, Administration, Functions.* Ardmore, Pa., Advance House, 1963.

B. *Guides, Aids, and Information Published by the U.S. Patent Office and/or Other Government Agencies.*

1. Committee for International Cooperation in Information Retrieval Among Examining Patent Offices. [ICIREPAT] *Annual Meeting[s]* . . .; Proceedings. 1st-. Washington, D.C., U.S. Dept. of Commerce, Patent Office. 1961-.

2. Committee for International Cooperation in Information Retrieval Among Examining Patent Offices [ICIREPAT] / *Bulletin[s]* No. 1-. Washington, D.C., U.S. Dept. of Commerce, Patent Office. 1962-.

3. U.S. Agricultural Research Service. Eastern Regional Research Laboratory / *Publications and Patents.* Philadelphia, Pa., U.S. Dept. of Agriculture. 1939/60-. (Usually two issues a year. Author entries vary. Research covers: animal products: dairy, meat, fats, and leather; plant products: eastern fruits and vegetables, tobacco, honey, and maple).

4. U.S. Agricultural Research Service. Northern Regional Research Laboratory / *Publications and Patents.* Peoria, Ill., U.S. Dept. of Agriculture. 1948(?)-. (Usually two issues a year. Author entries vary. Research covers: cereal grains: corn, wheat, barley, grain sorghum, and oats; oil-seeds: soybean, flaxseed, and erucic acid-containing oilseeds; and new crops).

5. U.S. Agricultural Research Service. Southeastern Regional Research Laboratory / [As of 1973 no list has been published and no patent has been granted] Athens, Ga., U.S. Dept. of Agriculture. (Author entries vary. Research covers: southeastern poultry, fruits, vegetables; pecans, peanuts, forages and feeds; sunflower as an oilseed; pork; and tobacco).

6. U.S. Agricultural Research Service. Southern Regional Research Laboratory
/ *Publications and Patents*. New Orleans, La., U.S. Dept. of Agriculture. 1941-
(Usually two issues a year. Author entries vary. Research covers: cotton and
cottonseed; pine gum; Southern fruits and vegetables, including citrus and
sweet potatoes; rice; and peanuts).

7. U.S. Agricultural Research Service. Western Regional Research Laboratory /
List of Publications & Patents with Abstracts. Berkeley, Calif., U.S. Dept. of
Agriculture. 1948(?)-. (Usually two issues a year. Author entries vary. Series
vary. Research covers: western fruits, nuts, vegetables, and rice; poultry products; forage crops; wheat, barley; wool and mohair; sugar beets; dry beans and
peas; castor; safflower, and western oilseeds).

8. U.S. Congress. Senate. Committee on the Judiciary./ *Study of the Subcommittee on Patents, Trademarks, and Copyrights*. No. 1-. Washington, D.C.,
U.S. Govt. Print. Off. Feb. 7, 1957-.

9. U.S. Dept. of Commerce / *Publications Available from the Patent Office; Publications Available from Superintendent of Documents*. May 1969. 2 p.

10. U.S. Laws, Statutes, etc. / *Patent Laws*. Nov 1965. Washington, D.C., U.S. Govt.
Print. Off., 1965.

11. U.S. National Aeronautics and Space Administration./ *Significant NASA Inventions Available for Licensing in Foreign Countries*. Washington, D.C., NASA,
1971.

12. U.S. Patent Office / *Annual Report of the Commissioner of Patents*. Washington, D.C., U.S. Govt. Print. Off. 1836-1871, 1876-1919. (Superseded in 1920
by: U.S. Patent Office. *Index of Patents*).

13. U.S. Patent Office / *Annual Report of the Commissioner of Patents*. Washington, D.C., U.S. Govt. Print. Off. 1847-1871. [Ann Arbor, Mich., University
Microfilms. On Microfilm. 16mm. Poor copy].

14. U.S. Patent Office / *The Application of Random Access Techniques to Case
Law*, by D. D. Andrews. Symposium on Information Retrieval, American Bar
Association, St. Louis, Mo., Aug 6, 1961. [Reproduction of typewritten copy].

15. U.S. Patent Office /[*Class Definitions. 1-346]* Washington, D.C., U.S. Patent
Office. (Each class entitled: *Classification Bulletin. Class . . .* These classes, on
microfilm, supplement the later title U.S. Patent Office. *Classification Definitions. Class . . .* Numbers used are not consecutive).

16. U.S. Patent Office / *Classification Definitions*. Class[es 1-444] Washington,
D.C., U.S. Patent Office. (The run is not consecutive. Each class is revised and/
or abolished as necessary.)

17. U.S. Patent Office / Classification of Patents. (Section at end of: U.S. Patent
Office. *Annual Report of the Commissioner of Patents*) Washington, D.C., U.S.
Govt. Print. Off., 1916-1919.

18. U.S. Patent Office / Classification of Patents. (Section at end of: U.S. Patent
Office. *Index of Patents*) Washington, D.C., U.S. Govt. Print. Off., 1920, 1955-
1965.

19. U.S. Patent Office / Classification of Patents. (Running Title in: *Index of
Patents*. Part II—*Index to Subjects of Inventions*) Washington, D.C., U.S. Govt.
Print. Off., 1966-. (Received one to two years late)

20. U.S. Patent Office / *Concordance: United States Patent Classification to International Patent Classification*. 1st ed. [Washington, D.C.] U.S. Patent Office,
1969. (Use in conjunction with: Council of Europe . . . *International Classification of Patents*. v. 1-3)

21. U.S. Patent Office / Consolidated Listings of Recent Official Gazette Notices Re
Patent Office Practices and Procedures. (In: January issue of the U.S. Patent
Office. *Official Gazette: Patents*. Also issued as a separate).

22. U.S. Patent Office / *Cumulative Index to the Classification of Patents.* 1790/ 1968. (On microfilm in 16 reels. Rev. at irregular intervals. Patent numbers are arranged in consecutive order under each Class and Subclass. Updated by the Annual and/or Weekly cumulative listings. Both Original and Cross-Reference patent numbers, under each Class and Subclass, are included in annual cumulative listings. Omitted from weekly cumulative listings. Updated listings, however, available for both from Commissioner of Patents).

23. U.S. Patent Office / *Decisions of the Commisioner of Patents and of the United States Courts in Patent and Trademark Cases.* Washington, D.C., U.S. Govt. Print. Off., 1869-.

24. U.S. Patent Office / *Defensive Publication[s]* [Washington, D.C., U.S. Patent Office]. Nov 5, 1968-. (Included in: *Official Gazette* and *Official Gazette: Patents* in brief form. Also issued as separates. In a "T" numbered series where the first three figures indicate volume number of the U.S. Patent Office's *Official Gazette* and *Official Gazette: Patents* for that month, and the last three figures indicate item number for the month in consecutive order beginning with 001).

25. U.S. Patent Office / *Directory of Registered Patent Attorneys & Agents.* Arranged by States and Countries, as of Dec 1968. [Washington, D.C., U.S. Govt. Print. Off.] 1969. (Updated and corrected by irregular listings in *Official Gazette . . .* and the *Official Gazette: Patents* issued by the U.S. Patent Office).

26. U.S. Patent Office / *General Index of the Official Gazette and Monthly Volumes of Patents of the United States Patent Office.* Washington, D.C., U.S. Govt. Print. Off. 1872-1875.

27. U.S. Patent Office / *General Information Concerning Patents.* Rev. Mar 1972. Washington, D.C., U.S. Govt. Print. Off. (Rev. at irregular intervals).

28. U.S. Patent Office / *General Information Concerning Plant Patents.* May 1, 1961. [Washington, D.C., U.S. Dept. of Commerce].

29. U.S. Patent Office / "Geographical Index of Residence of Inventors (U.S. States, Territories, and Armed Forces, the Commonwealth of Puerto Rico, and the Canal Zone)": Georgia [No.] 10: May 18, 1965-Dec. 31, 1966; Georgia [No.] 13: Jan. 1, 1967-. Section In *Official Gazette,* and *Official Gazette: Patents.* (Coded numbers for each area. The Patent numbers are arranged weekly in ascending order for each).

30. U.S. Patent Office / *Guide for Patent Draftsmen.* 1971. Washington, D.C., U.S. Govt. Print. Off., 1971.

31. U.S. Patent Office / *How to Obtain Information from United States Patents.* Washington, D.C., U.S. Govt. Print. Off., 1962.

32. U.S. Patent Office / *Index of Patents.* Washington, D.C., U.S. Govt. Print. Off. 1920-1926. (Superseded, in part, by: U.S. Patent Office. *Index of Patents* and *Index of Trademarks*).

33. U.S. Patent Office / *Index of Patents.* Washington, D.C., U.S. Govt. Print. Off. 1927-1965. (Superseded by: U.S. Patent Office. *Index of Patents.* Part I—*List of Patentees*; Part II—*Index to Subjects of Inventions*).

34. U.S. Patent Office / *Index of Patents:* Part I—*List of Patentees Issued from the United States Patent Office*; Part II—*Index to Subjects of Inventions Issued from the United States Patent Office.* Washington, D.C., U.S. Govt. Print. Off. 1966-. (Parts I and II received two or more years late).

35. U.S. Patent Office / *Index to Classification.* [Apr. 1972. Washington, D.C., U.S. Govt. Print. Off.] (Index to: *Manual of Classification*).

36. U.S. Patent Office / *List of Patents for Inventions and Designs, Issued by the United States, from 1790 to 1847, with the Patent Laws and Notes of Decisions*

of the Courts of the United States for the Same Period. Compiled and published under the direction of Edmund Burke. Washington, D.C., J. & G.S. Gideon, 1847. (On Microfilm. 16mm. Ann Arbor, Mich., University Microfilms).

37. U.S. Patent Office / *Manual of Classification.* [Washington, D.C.] U.S. Patent Office. 1969-. (Loose-leaf. Updated quarterly).

38. U.S. Patent Office / *Manual of Patent Examining Procedure.* 3d ed. [Washington] U.S. Patent Office. Nov. 1961- (Loose-leaf. Updated quarterly).

39. U.S. Patent Office / *Obtaining Information from Patents, Patent Office Classification and Search Services.* Washington, D.C., U.S. Dept. of Commerce. Jun 1968. (Leaflet. Revised at intervals).

40. U.S. Patent Office / *Official Gazette.* v. 1-882. Washington, D.C., U.S. Govt. Print. Off. Jan 3 (i.e., Jan 2) 1872-Jan 26, 1971. (Superseded by U.S. Patent Office. *Official Gazette: Patents*, and its *Official Gazette: Trademarks*).

41. U.S. Patent Office / *Official Gazette: Patents.* v. 883-. Washington, D.C., U.S. Govt. Print. Off. Feb 2, 1971-. (Preceded by U.S. Patent Office. *Official Gazette . . .*).

42. U.S. Patent Office / *Patent Number Sequence Classification Record.* Including all patents issued through Apr 29, 1969, and all reclassifications through Jan 1, 1969. (On microfilm: 16 reels: PB-188600) [Washington, D.C., U.S. Dept. of Commerce. Office of Technical Services] (Updated Classification, in Numerical Sequence, Available in 1973 from U.S. National Technical Information Service (NTIS)).

43. U.S. Patent Office / *Patents.* No. 1-. [Washington, D.C., U.S. Govt. Print. Off.] Jul 13, 1836-. (Master copies only available of every complete U.S. Patent in U.S. Patent Office).

44. U.S. Patent Office / *Patents & Inventions; an Information Aid for Inventors.* rev. ed. Washington, D.C., U.S. Govt. Print. Off., 1964.

45. U.S. Patent Office / *Plant Patent[s]* No. 1-. Washington, D.C., U.S. Govt. Print. Off. Aug 18, 1931-.

46. U.S. Patent Office / *Q[uestions] & A[nswers] About Patents.* [Washington, D.C., U.S. Govt. Print. Off., 1971].

47. U.S. Patent Office / *Q[uestions] & A[nswers] About Plant Patents.* Washington, D.C., U.S. Govt. Print. Off., 1969.

48. U.S. Patent Office / *Reissue Patent[s]* Re. No. 1-. [Washington, D.C., U.S. Govt. Print. Off.] 1838-. (Reissues not separately numbered until 1838).

49. U.S. Patent Office / *Roster of Attorneys and Agents Registered to Practice Before the U.S. Patent Office.* [1965. Washington, D.C., U.S. Govt. Print. Off., 1966].

50. U.S. Patent Office / *Rules of Practice in Patent Cases.* Washington, D.C., [U.S. Govt. Print. Off.] 1970-. (Loose-leaf. Updated).

51. U.S. Patent Office / *Specifications and Drawings of Patents Issued from the United States Patent Office.* [Washington, D.C., U.S. Govt. Print. Off.] May 30, 1871-June 1912.

52. U.S. Patent Office / *The Story of the United States Patent Office.* Jan 1972. Washington, D.C., U.S. Govt. Print. Off. [1971].

53. U.S. Patent Office / *Supplement to the Manual of Classification.* Washington, D.C., U.S. Patent Office, Jul 1971. (This supplement uses several new terms which may be explained as follows. The Patent Examiners over the last decade or more have removed many patent numbers from their official subclass numbers and placed them in more specific appropriate 1) *unofficial subclasses* to facilitate their searches within the subject areas assigned to them. Each unofficial subclass is identified with a term or terms descriptive of the new specific

subject and cited with 2) an *alpha* designation following the official subclass
number. There are no explanations or definitions for these unofficial subclasses
and none will be compiled. Each term is to be interpreted from the titles used
and the explanations given in the U.S. Patent Office. *Classification Definitions.*
Those patent numbers which remain in the official subclass are identified by the
alpha designation "R" meaning 3) *residual.* Both the new alpha designated unofficial patent numbers and the residual patent numbers are the equivalent of
the earlier established official subclass and its patent numbers. The *Supplement*
was published July 1971; however, the first inclusion of the alpha designations
appeared in the U.S. Patent Office. *Official Gazette: Patents,* in the section entitled: "Classification of Patents," dated Jul 4, 1972.

The last term, 4) *Digest (DIG).*, may be defined as a collection of copies of
patents (U.S.) which may be found at the end of the unofficial subclasses for
that official class. These are identified by one or more terms for each. Some are
arranged by number in ascending consecutive order. This collection of patents
is based on a concept which may relate to many classes but not to any particular
subclass of any class. The present listings of published digests are associated
only with "Cross-referenced" patent numbers and not with patents classified as
"Originals." Digests were first included under class and subclass for the year
1971 in: U.S. Patent Office. *Index of Patents. Part II. Index to Subjects of Inventions,* in the section entitled: "Classification of Patents. Cross-Reference
Classification." These digests of U.S. Patents are in the Patent Examiners'
search files and have been gathered for their own use. For this reason, these
patents have been placed there without the designations: original, official cross-
reference, or unofficial cross-reference.

54. U.S. Patent Office. Office of Research and Development / *Reports.* [Washing-
    ton, D.C., U.S. Govt. Print. Off.] 1956–. (Issued in a numbered series).

55. U.S. Patent Office. Scientific Library / *Periodicals in the Scientific Library,
    U.S. Patent Office.* Washington, D.C., U.S. Dept. of Commerce, Patent Office,
    1962.

II. Foreign Patents

A. Guides, Aids, and Information Commercially Published.

1. Anderfelt, Ulf / *International Patent-Legislation and Developing Countries.* The
   Hague, Martinus Nijhoff, 1971.

2. Council of Europe. Committee of Experts on Patents. Working Party on Classification / *International Classification of Patents for Invention under the European Convention of 19th December 1954.* London, Morgan-Grampian Books
   Ltd., 1968. 3v. (Loose-leaf. Updated)

3. Finlay, Ian F. / *Guide to Foreign Language Printed Patents and Applications.*
   London, Aslib, 1969.

4. Grace, Herbert W. / *A Handbook on Patents.* London, Charles Knight & Co.
   Ltd., 1971.

5. Houghton, Bernard / *Technical Information Sources: A Guide to Patent Specifications, Standards, and Technical Reports Literature.* 2d ed. [Hamden, Conn.,
   London] Linnet Books & Clive Bingley, 1972.

6. Lang, William / *Foreign Patent Laws, with Comparative Analysis.* Worth Wade,
   ed. Ardmore, Pa., Advance House, Inc., 1968. (Loose-leaf)

7. Newby, Frank / *How to Find Out About Patents.* Oxford, Pergamon Press,
   1967. (British)

8. White, William Wallace / *Patents Throughout the World.* New York, Trade Activities, Inc., 1971. (Loose-leaf. Updated)

9. White, William W. and Byfleet C. Ravenscroft / *Patents Throughout the World.*
   New York, Trade Activities, Inc., 1973.

B. Guides, Aids, and Information Published in Foreign Countries.

1. Australia. Patent Office / *Australian Official Journal of Patents, Trade Marks,
   and Designs.* Melbourne, Australia, Patent Office. 1904-1930. (Superseded by:
   Title below)

2. Australia. Patent Office / *The Australian Official Journal of Patents, Trade
   Marks and Designs, with which Are Incorporated Particulars of Copyright Applications.* Canberra, Australia. Patent Office. 1931-.

3. Canada. Patent Office / *The Canadian Patent Office Record. La Gazette du
   Bureau des Brevets.* Ottawa, Canada, Queen's Printer . . . . Jul 12, 1960-Jun
   1969. (Patent titles in English and French. Superseded by: Canada. Patent
   Office. *Patent Office Record . . .*)

4. Canada. Patent Office / *The Canadian Patent Office Record and Register of
   Copyrights. La Gazette du Bureau des Brevets et Registre des Droits d'Auteur.*
   Ottawa, Canada, Queen's Printer . . . . Sep 21, 1954-Jul 5, 1960. (Patent titles
   in English and French. Superseded by: Canada. Patent Office. *The Canadian
   Patent Office Record . . .*)

5. Canada. Patent Office / *The Canadian Patent Office Record and Register of
   Copyrights and Trade Marks. La Gazette du Bureau des Brevets, Droits d'Auteur
   et Marque de Commerce.* Ottawa, Canada, Queen's Printer 1873-Sep 14,
   1954. (Patent titles in English and French. Superseded by: Canada. Patent
   Office. *The Canadian Patent Office Record and Register of Copyrights . . .*)

6. Canada. Patent Office / *Office Consolidation of Patent Rules Under the Patent
   Act.* Ottawa, Canada, Commissioner of Patents, 1970.

7. Canada. Patent Office / *Patent Office Record. Gazette du Bureau des Brevets.*
   Ottawa, Canada, Queen's Printer. Jul 12, 1969-. (Patent titles in English and
   French)

8. Germany (Federal Republic, 1949-) Patentamt / *Manual of Patent Classification.* 7th ed. 1958. Jerusalem, Israel Program for Scientific Translations, 1963.
   (Translated from German)

9. Great Britain. Patent Office / *Alphabetical Index of Patentees of Inventions,
   with an Introduction and Appendix of Additions and Corrections Compiled in
   the Patent Office Library.* [From Mar 2, 1617 (14 James I) to Oct 1, 1852 (16
   Victoriae) N.Y.] London. Augustus M. Kelley, Publishers [1854, 1969] (Bennet
   Woodcroft at head of title)

10. Great Britain. Patent Office / *Commissioners of Patents' Journal.* London,
    1854-1883. Printed for H.M. Stationery Off. (Superseded by: Great Britain.
    Patent Office. *The Official Journal of the Patent Office)*

11. Great Britain. Patent Office / *Group Allotment Index to Abridgments of Specifica-
    fications.* 340,001-720,000. London, Queen's Printer. (Patent numbers pub-
    lished in lots of 20,000 each. These are in numerical order followed by proper
    Group number for each. Location Index for patents)

12. Great Britain. Patent Office / *The Official Journal of the Patent Office.* London,
    1884-Jan 2, 1889. Printed for H. M. Stationery Off. (Superseded by: Great
    Britain. Patent Office. *The Official Journal (Patents))*

13. Great Britain. Patent Office / *The Official Journal (Patents).* London, Jan 9,
    1889-. H. M. Stationery Off.

14. Great Britain. Patent Office / *Patents for Inventions. Abridgments of Specifica-
    tions.* Class[es] 1-146. London H.M. Stationery Off. 1855/1866-1926/1930.

(Superseded by: Great Britain Patent Office. *Patents for Inventions. Abridgments of Specifications.* Group[s] 1–40)

15. Great Britain. Patent Office / *Patents for Inventions. Abridgments of Specifications.* Group[s] 1–40. London, H. M. Stationery Off. 1931–.

16. Moscow. Vsesoiuznaia / *Register of Inventions Published in the USSR, 1896–Jun 1963.* Class 45. Agriculture, including forestry; animal husbandry; hunting and animal trapping; fish breeding and fishery. 2d enl. and rev. ed. Translated from Russian. Jerusalem, Israel Program for Scientific Translations, 1968. (Information arranged under: Serial Number; Class, Subclass, Group, Subgroup; Designation of Invention)

III. U.S. Trademarks

A. Guides, Aids, and Information Commercially Published.
(See also entries in Section I. A. and I. B.: *U.S. PATENTS*)

1. Barach, Arnold B. / *Famous American Trademarks.* Washington, D.C., Public Affairs Press [1971].

2. Graham, John H., comp. and ed. / *Trade Mark Record for Perfumes, Toilet Preparations, Soaps.* New York, Beauty Fashion Drug and Cosmetic Industry, 1947.

3. Hague, Morton / *Hague's Trademark Thesaurus.* Illustrated. Calibrated-Word-Formation Computer Dials Included. Chicago, Ill., Mortons Press, Inc. [1964].

4. Haynes, Williams / *Chemical Trade Names and Commercial Synonyms, a Dictionary of American Usage.* New York, D. Van Nostrand Co., Inc. [1951].

5. Holcomb, Charles A. / *Trademarks.* New York, American Association of Advertising Agencies [1963].

6. Holub, Rand / *Signatures & Trademarks.* New York, Watson-Guptill Publications, Inc. [1956].

7. Leblanc, Robert E. / *Trademarks and Unfair Competition; Cases and Materials.* Washington, Lerner Law Book Co. [1967].

8. National Association of Credit Management, Inc. / *Patent Law & Practice; Trademarks Law and Practice.* New York, Oceana Publications, Inc. 1968– (Loose-leaf).

9. Praninskas, Jean / Trademark Names. *Trade Name Creation: Processes and Patterns.* The Hague, Mouton, 1968. p. 106–115.

10. Seidel, Arthur H. / *What the General Practitioner Should Know About Trademarks and Copyrights.* [2d ed.] Philadelphia, Joint Committee on Continuing Legal Education of the American Law Institute and the American Bar Ass. [1967].

11. *Trade-Names Index.* With definitions and sources from a card file in the Technology department of the Carnegie Library of Pittsburgh and a bibliography of sources of trade names and trademarks. New York, Special Libraries Ass., 1941.

12. *Trademark Register of the United States* / [Annual. Latest ed. cumulative: 1881/Jun 1 of preceding year. Includes current trademarks registered and all those renewed] Washington, D.C., Patent Searching Service.

13. *The Trademark Reporter.* New York, United States Trademark Ass. 1911–.

14. United States Trademark Association / *Trademark Management; a Guide for Businessmen.* 2d ed. New York, United States Trademark Ass. [1956].

15. Vandenburgh, Edward C. III / *Trademark Law and Procedure.* 2d ed. Indianapolis, Bobbs-Merrill Co., Inc. [1968].

B. *Guides, Aids, and Information Published by the U.S. Patent Office.*
(See also entries in Section I. A. and I. B.: *U.S. PATENTS*)

1. U.S. Patent Office / Alphabetical List of Registrants of Trademarks. In *Index of Patents Issued from the United States Patent Office.* Washington, D.C., U.S. Govt. Print. Off., 1920–1926. (Superseded by: *Index of Trade-Marks*).

2. U.S. Patent Office / Alphabetical List of Trade-Marks. In *General Index of Official Gazette and Monthly Volumes of Patents of the United States Patent Office.* Washington, D.C., U.S. Govt. Print. Off., 1872–1875.

3. U.S. Patent Office / *General Information Concerning Trademarks.* [Washington, D.C., U.S. Govt. Print. Off., 1966].

4. U.S. Patent Office / *Index of Trademarks.* Washington, D.C., U.S. Govt. Print. Off., 1927–.

5. U.S. Patent Office / *Official Gazette.* v. 1–882, Jan 3 (i.e., Jan 2) 1872–Jan 26, 1971. Washington, D.C., U.S. Govt. Print. Off. (Superseded by U.S. Patent Office. *Official Gazette: Trademarks*).

6. U.S. Patent Office / *Official Gazette: Trademarks.* Washington, D.C., U.S. Govt. Print. Off. Feb 2, 1971–.

7. U.S. Patent Office / *Q[uestions] & A[nswers] About Trademarks.* [Washington, D.C., U.S. Govt. Print. Off., 1967].

8. U.S. Patent Office / *Trademark Examining Procedure Directive(s).* [Washington, D.C.] U.S. Patent Office. 1971–.

9. U.S. Patent Office / *Trademark Rules of Practice of the Patent Office with Forms and Statutes.* 1966. Washington, D.C., U.S. Govt. Print. Off., 1967.

10. U.S. Patent Office / Trademarks: By Name of Registrants. In *Index of Patents.* Washington, D.C., U.S. Govt. Print. Off., 1920–1926. (Superseded by: U.S. Patent Office. *Index of Trademarks*).

11. U.S. Patent Office / Trademarks: By Name of Registrants and By Numbers. In *Annual Report of the Commissioner of Patents.* Washington, D.C., U.S. Govt. Print. Off., Oct. 25, 1870–1871. (Superseded by information in its *Official Gazette* . . . and its *Official Gazette: Trademarks*).

12. U.S. Patent Office / Trademarks: By Numbers. In *Official Gazette* . . . Washington, D.C., U.S. Govt. Print. Off., 1872–Jan 1971. (Superseded by its *Official Gazette: Trademarks*).

IV. Foreign Trademarks

A. *Guides, Aids, and Information Commercially Published.*
(See also entries in Section II. B.: *FOREIGN PATENTS*)

1. Caplan, David / *British Trade Marks & Symbols: A Short History and a Contemporary Selection.* London, Peter Owen [1966].

2. Gardner, William / *Chemical Synonyms and Trade Names, a Dictionary and Commerical Hand Book.* Containing Approximately 28,000 Definitions and Cross-References. 5th ed. rev. & enl. by Edward I. Cooke. London, Technical Press Ltd., 1948. (Registered Trademarks and Registered Trade Names).

3. Kamekura, Yŭsaku / *Trademarks and Symbols of the World.* New York, Reinhold Publishing Corp. [1965].

4. Kamekura, Yŭsaku / *Trademarks of the World.* New York, George Wittenborn [1965].

5. Offner, Eric D. / *International Trademark Protection.* New York, Fieldston Press, 1965.

6. Wildbur, Peter, comp. / *Trademarks: A Handbook of International Designs.*
London, Studio Vista, New York, Reinhold [1966].

B. *Guides, Aids, and Information Published in Foreign Countries.*
(For specific titles, consult entries in Section II. B.: *FOREIGN PATENTS*)

V. U.S. and Foreign Titles

Abstracting Journals Containing Patents.
(Selected titles with or without all changes in title)

1. *Airplane Patent Digest: Abridgments of Current U.S. Airplane Patents.* New
York, Manufacturers Aircraft Ass., Inc., 1930-.
2. *Airplane Patent Digest: British Supplement: Abridgements of Current British
Airplane Patents.* New York, Manufacturers Aircraft Ass., Inc. 1930-.
3. *Bibliography of Scientific and Industrial Reports.* Issuing agency varies.
Jan 11, 1946-Jun 1949. (Superseded by: *Bibliography of Technical Reports*
(varies slightly)).
4. *Bibliography of Technical Reports* (varies slightly). Issuing agency varies. Jul
1949-Sep 1954. (Superseded by: *U.S. Government Research Reports*).
5. *Biulleten' Izobretenii Itovarnykh Znakov.* Moscow, 1937-.
6. *British Patents Abstracts.* London, Derwent Publications Ltd., 1951-.
7. *Ceramic Abstracts.* [Easton, Pa., American Ceramic Society] 1922-. (Issued as
separately paged section of the Society's *Journal*).
8. *Chemical Abstracts.* Washington, D.C., American Chemical Society, 1907-.
9. *Chemical Market Abstracts.* New York, Chemical Horizons, Inc., 1950-.
10. *Chemisches Zentralblatt.* Berlin, Germany, Akademie-Verlag GmbH. (Ceased),
1830-1969.
11. *Derwent Belgian Patents Report.* London, Derwent Publications Ltd., 1955-.
[Chemistry and related fields].
12. *Derwent Japanese Patents Report.* London, Derwent Publications Ltd., 1962-.
[Chemistry and related fields].
13. *Derwent Netherlands Patents Report.* London, Derwent Publications Ltd.,
1964-. [Chemistry and related fields].
14. *French Patents Abstracts.* London, Derwent Publications Ltd., Jul 21, 1961-.
(Alternate issues include Indian and South African Patents. [Chemistry and
related fields] Preceded by: *Commonwealth Patents Gazette.* 1953-1961).
15. *German Patents Abstracts.* London, Derwent Publications Ltd., 1953-. (Covers
all subject areas).
16. *Government Reports Announcements.* [Springfield, Va., National Technical
Information Service] Mar 25, 1971-.
17. *Graphic Arts Patent Abstracts;* U.S. Patents related to printing, packaging, paper
and photography. Rochester, N.Y. Graphic Arts Research Center, Rochester
Institute of Technology, 1969-.
18. *Metal Finishing Abstracts.* Middlesex, Finishing Publications Ltd., 1959-.
19. *Paint and Resin Patents.* London, R.H. Chandler Ltd., 1964-.
20. *Patent Abstract Series.* Government-owned inventions available for license. 7
nos. [Washington, D.C.] U.S. Dept. of Commerce, Office of Technical Services.
1954. (Accompanied by: Supplement[s] issued: 1954/55-1962, and *Index to
the Patent Abstract Series*; Government-owned inventions available for license

through Dec 1961. Both titles published by [Washington, D.C.] U.S. Dept. of Commerce, Office of Technical Services).

21. *Patent Digest.* New York, Gas Appliance Manufacturers' Association, Inc., 1946-.

22. *Plastics Abstracts; a Comprehensive Abstracting Service Covering British Patent Specifications Dealing with the Science, Technology and Application of Plastics.* Welwyn, Herts., England, Plastics Investigations. 1959-.

23. *Plastics: RAPRA Abstracts.* [Shawbury, etc., England] 1945-1967 (Merged with: *Rubbers: RAPRA Abstracts* to form: *RAPRA Abstracts*).

24. *RAPRA Abstracts.* [Shawbury, etc., England] Rubber and Plastics Research Ass. of Great Britain, 1968-.

25. *Rubbers: RAPRA Abstracts.* [Shawbury, etc., England] 1923-1967 (Merged with *Plastics: RAPRA Abstracts* to form: *RAPRA Abstracts*).

26. *Russian Patents Abstracts: Chemistry and Chemical Engineering.* London, Technical Information Co., 1960-1961.

27. *Russian Patents Gazette: Chemistry and Chemical Engineering.* London, Technical Information Co., 1959. (Superseded by: *Russian Patents Abstracts. Chemistry and Chemical Engineering*).

28. *Science Citation Index/SCI.* Philadelphia, Pa., Institute for Scientific Information, 1963-. (Including: Source Index; Citation Index; Permuterm Subject Index).

29. Shirley Institute, Manchester, England / *Summary of Current Literature.* Manchester, England, Cotton Silk and Man-made Fibers Research Ass., 1921-1968. (Superseded by: *World Textile Abstracts*).

30. Society of Dyers and Colourists / *Journal.* Bradford, Yorkshire, England, 1884-.

31. *Soviet Inventions Illustrated.* London, Derwent Publications Ltd., 1961-. (Issued in 3 sections: I—Chemical; II—Electrical; III—Mechanical and General. Supersedes in part: *USSR Official Bulletin of Patents & Inventions* and *Derwent Russian Patents Report*).

32. *Textile Technology Digest.* Charlottesville, Va., Institute of Textile Technology, 1944-.

33. *U.S. Government Research & Development Reports.* Springfield, Va., Clearinghouse for Federal Scientific and Technical Information and National Technical Information Service, Jan 5, 1965–Mar 10, 1971. (Superseded by: *Government Reports Announcements*).

34. *U.S. Government Research Reports.* Issuing agency varies. Oct 1954–Dec 20, 1964. (Superseded by: *U.S. Government Research & Development Reports*).

35. U.S. National Aeronautics and Space Administration. Scientific and Technical Information Division / *NASA Patent Abstracts Bibliography: A Continuing Bibliography.* (PAB) May 1969/1971-. (NASA-SP-7039: Section 1: Abstracts; Section 2: Indexes).

36. *USSR Official Bulletin of Patents and Inventions.* no. 2. London, Derwent Information Service, 1959-1962. (Superseded, in part, by: *Soviet Inventions Illustrated*).

37. *Uniterm Index to U.S. Chemical and Chemically Related Patents.* Arlington, Va., IFI/Plenum Data Corp., 1950-.

38. *World Textile Abstracts.* Manchester, England, Shirley Institute, 1969-.

Journals Containing Patent Sections or References to Patents.
(Selected titles with or without all changes in titles. Current awareness aids. Patents may not appear in every issue)

1. Acoustical Society of America / *Journal*. New York, American Institute of Physics, 1929-.
2. *Aircraft Engineering*. London, Bunhill Publications Ltd., 1929-.
3. *American Dyestuff Reporter*. Devoted to textile wet-processing, dyeing, finishing, bleaching, etc., new product information, news of the industry. New York, SAF International, Inc., 1917-.
4. *Chemical Age*. London, Benn Brothers Ltd., 1917-.
5. *Coal Age*. New York, McGraw-Hill, Inc., 1911-.
6. *Drug and Cosmetic Industry*. New York, Drug Markets, Inc., 1914-.
7. *Food Technology*. Chicago, Ill., Institute of Food Technologists, 1947-.
8. Franklin Institute, Philadelphia / *Journal—Devoted to Science and the Mechanic Arts*. Philadelphia, Franklin Institute, 1867-. (The volumes from 1867 do not include mention of patents).
9. *The Franklin Journal, and American Mechanics' Magazine*. Devoted to the Useful Arts, Internal Improvements and General Science. Philadelphia, The Franklin Institute, 1826-27. (Two volumes a year. U.S. Patents from 1790 through Jul 2, 1836, are dated, but not numbered. The journal includes references to the U.S. Patents in the monthly issues dated, from May 1826 through December 1827, but these are not included in order by U.S. Patent Office date of issue. The unnumbered patents are identified by issue date and the information may include title, patentee, city/town/or county, and state. Superseded by: *Journal of the Franklin Institute of the State of Pennsylvania for the Promotion of the Mechanic Arts*).
10. *Gas Journal*. London, Walter King Ltd., 1849-.
11. *Geophysics*. Tulsa, Okla., Society of Exploration Geophysicists, 1936-.
12. *Glass Industry*. (Includes Annual Directory Issue) New York, Glass Publishing Co., 1920-.
13. *IBM Journal of Research and Development*. Armonk, N.Y., International Business Machines Corp., 1957-.
14. *Industrial Lubrication & Tribology*. A Technical Journal Devoted Exclusively to the Science and Practice of Tribology. London, United Trade Press Ltd., 1948-.
15. *Journal of the Franklin Institute of the State of Pennsylvania for the Promotion of the Mechanic Arts*. Devoted to Mechanical and Physical Science, Civil Engineering, the Arts and Manufactures, and the Recording of American and Other Patent Inventions (title varies) 1826-66. (Two volumes a year. U.S. Patents from 1790 through Jul 2, 1836, are dated, but not numbered. From Jul 13, 1836, patents were assigned consecutive numbers beginning with No. 1. The Journal includes many references to the U.S. Patents in the monthly issues dated, from May 1826 through September 1861, but these are not included in order by U.S. Patent Office date of issue. The unnumbered patents are identified by issue date. The numbered patents are cited in a numbering system the journal devised. References to these patents may be found in listings with title, patentee, city/town/or county, and state. Additional information may include abstracts, or brief statements, as well as a more detailed description beginning with: Specification [s] It is time consuming to identify the early patents in this title and its predecessor: *The Franklin Journal, and American Mechanics' Magazine*. — Superseded by: Franklin Institute, Philadelphia. / *Journal—Devoted to Science and the Mechanic Arts*).
16. *Light Metal Age*. San Francisco, Calif., 1943-.
17. *Lubrication Engineering*. Park Ridge, Ill., American Society of Lubrication Engineers, 1945-.
18. *Machine Design*. Cleveland, Ohio, Penton Publishing Co., 1929-.

19. *Manufacturing Chemist and Aerosol News.* London, Grampian Press Ltd., 1929-.
20. *Metal Finishing.* Devoted Exclusively to Metallic Surface Treatments. Westwood, N.Y., Metals and Plastics Publications, Inc., 1903-.
21. *Modern Plastics.* New York, McGraw-Hill, Inc., 1925-.
22. *Paper Maker* London, Phillips and Co. Ltd., 1891-.
23. *Papermaking, Converting, Allied Science & Technology: Bibliography and Patents.* [Atlanta] Technical Association of the Pulp and Paper Industry, 1970-.
24. Patent Concordance. In *Chemical Abstracts.* Columbus, Ohio, American Chemical Society, 1963-. (Identifies U.S. and/or foreign patents by number, if issued in another country).
25. Patent Index: Jan/Jun 1971. Patent Concordance: Jan/Jun 1971. In *Textile Technology Digest: Six Month Indexes: Jan.-June 1971.* [Charlottesville, Va., Institute of Textile Technology].
26. *Plating.* Electroplating, Finishing of Metals, Organic Finishing. East Orange, N.J., American Electroplaters Society, 1910-.
27. *Platinum Metals Review.* London, Johnson, Matthey & Co. Ltd., 1957-.
28. *Pulp and Paper Manufacture: Bibliography and Patents.* New York, Technical Association of the Pulp and Paper Industry, 1966-1969. (Superseded by: *Papermaking, Converting, Allied Science & Technology: Bibliography and Patents*).
29. *Pulp and Paper Manufacture: Bibliography and United States Patents.* New York, Technical Association of the Pulp and Paper Industry. 1931-1965. (Superseded by: *Pulp and Paper Manufacture: Bibliography and Patents*).
30. *Refrigeration and Air Conditioning.* Croydon, Surrey, England, 1898-.
31. *SPE Journal.* Greenwich, Conn., Society of Plastics Engineers, 1945-.
32. *Soap and Chemical Specialties.* (Chemical Specialties Manufacturers Ass.) New York, MacNair-Dorland Co., 1925-.
33. Society of Chemical Industry, London / *Journal.* London, 1882-1950. (Superseded by: *Journal of Applied Chemistry*).
34. *TAPPI.* New York, Technical Association of the Pulp and Paper Industry, *1949-*.
35. *Textile Manufacturer.* Manchester, England, Emmott and Co. Ltd., 1875-.
36. *Underwater Journal and Information Bulletin.* Guildford, Surrey, England, IPC Science and Technology Press Ltd., 1969-.
37. *Wire and Wire Products.* Devoted to the Production of Wire, Rod and Strip, Wire and Rod Products and Insulated Wire and Cable. New York, American Metal Market, 1926-.
38. *Wire Industry.* International Monthly Journal. Oxted, Surrey, England, 1934-.

Proprietary Company Publications

BERNARD E. PRUDHOMME

This presentation is based mainly on the author's individual handling and use of company documents, primarily in the chemical and food industries. Therefore, it will not cover many types of publications which a company library or information center may be called upon to store and retrieve. However, a great deal of the methodology discussed could well apply to other categories of proprietary information, such as business, medical, and legal records.

The types of documents covered include the following: 1) original research records, 2) progress and project reports, 3) internal memoranda and other correspondence, 4) minutes of company meetings and proceedings of seminars, 5) patent records, 6) papers for presentation or publication by company employees, 7) engineering drawings.

The handling of these materials will be set forth with reference to their selection and acquisition, organization, processing, referencing, and use. Before concluding, some comments will be directed at the retention, security, and public relations aspects of proprietary information.

Original Research Records

Laboratory Notebooks and Other Data

Written records of laboratory research can assume a multitude of forms, ranging from the initial data recorded in a laboratory notebook to various analytical or other tests which are conducted to evaluate certain properties of the material being prepared or investigated. Although it is customary for a researcher to retain the more current notebooks and other records in his office or laboratory, older records, especially those pertaining to completed projects, are usually transferred to

Bernard E. Prudhomme is manager, Technical Information Center, The Coca-Cola Company, Atlanta, Ga.
Additional material was supplied by Martha J. Bailey, Physics Library, Purdue University, West Lafayette, Ind. 47907.

another location; and this will often be a company library. There are
several reasons for this transfer. First, the scientists may not have the
space to house older records. Second, the library tends to be a safer
storage place than a laboratory. Third, and perhaps most important,
storing these records in the library will make them more available to
others in the company who may need to refer to them, and such users
will find their task considerably simplified, thanks to the retrieval system which the library staff will have provided. A recent paper by
Bailey (1) examines laboratory notebooks in detail.

The matter of selection does not apply here as it would in the case
of published material, since the director of research or someone else
at the technical management level usually formulates the policy as to
which records are to be retained and where they will be kept. Within
the framework of these guidelines, however, the library can and must
carry on a vigorous policy of acquisition. From the author's experience,
scientists tend to be remiss in turning their notebooks and files over to
the library, and so regular prodding and reminders are usually required.
There is another factor here which may tend to aggravate the problem:
the lack of confidence which some researchers display in the ability of
the library to produce the records when needed, once they have left
the laboratory. The same persons may be reluctant to admit that they
often had trouble locating a given piece of information in their own
files. I have found that such "Doubting Thomases" can usually be won
over, and even impressed, by having the library retrieve on a few occasions an elusive bit of information which was to have some bearing on
later work.

Various methods may be employed to house a collection of laboratory notebooks and other records. Since considerable time and money
will have gone into the laboratory work which the records represent, it
is mandatory that adequate protection be provided to store these
records. In a smaller organization, where the volume of files and notebooks is limited, one or two fireproof filing cabinets will serve the purpose. If the nature of the material is particularly confidential, the cabinets should be equipped with a double-locking device. In some libraries,
a special room is set aside for this purpose, and is often designated as
the "technical files" area. If the volume of research records warrants it,
a fireproof vault with built-in shelves may be employed. This offers the
advantage of permitting the storage of binders, large format documents,
and other materials which do not lend themselves to filing in a conventional file cabinet.

In some libraries, it may not be possible or practical to store large
quantities of records in hard copy form. If such is the case, microfilm or
microfiche offer an excellent means of protecting the information,
while at the same time making it readily available to the user. Depending upon the size of the collection, the number of potential users, and
the frequency of use, one or more readers and at least one reader-printer

will, of course, have to be available. Microforms offer a further important advantage—the relative ease of duplication. This is especially useful in organizations carrying on research in various locations, particularly overseas. Some companies may be reluctant to have their confidential research records microfilmed elsewhere by a commercial firm. In this case, the library will have to acquire its own camera.

Samples and Test Data

Another source for original data is the sample which the technical people prepare for testing and analysis. The laboratory management should devise a clearly understood method for numbering samples so that all of the work on a project may be traced from inspiration through analysis and final production. Probably few companies establish such elaborate schemes, with the result that samples, test information, and other material are scattered in desks, attics, filing cabinets, and storage areas. Some chemical and pharmaceutical companies retain a sample of each compound upon which work is performed. The bottles are kept in a central storage area for a specified length of time. Eckermann (6) outlines a method for accessioning samples and maintaining detailed records. Benson (3) provides an example of a master record for compounds.

The analytical data or test data which are obtained by the chemistry laboratory or the metallurgical laboratory may not be entered in laboratory notebooks. Usually there are standard forms for recording this information, which may be filed in looseleaf notebooks or bound volumes. Since the records must be cross-referenced to the samples and to the projects, they may be kept in the library also.

AV Materials

There are often photographs, slides, or movie films which are sources for original research or test information. For example, in wind-tunnel experiments, it is common practice to film the tests. The various visuals may be arranged by type of material and then linked to the appropriate project through coordinate indexing or other methods.

Processing of Records—Classification and Indexing

Thus far, what could be termed "the custodial aspects" of laboratory records have been discussed. Next, the intellectual processing of these records, i.e., their classification and indexing will be taken up. This is a task which requires the most careful planning and execution, for as is well-known, the quality of the input will determine that of the output. Here are several possible approaches to indexing and retrieval.

The simplest is the standard card catalog. One or more subject cards are typed for each experiment or project in the notebook; reference is made on the card to the book number and page. If desirable, a one or two sentence abstract may be included. The method will probably suffice for a small collection, but for a larger collection, or one in which

the nature of the material is such that a coordination of subject headings is often required, a coordinate card index may be preferable. In
this case, it might be necessary to number each experiment or project
sequentially, so that each one has its own unique identification. These
numbers are then posted on 3" x 5" or 4" x 6" cards containing 10
vertical columns numbered from 0 to 9. The last digit of the number
posted determines its position on the card. These are the familiar Uniterm cards. Each represents a single term or subject heading. Subsequent searching of the card file is accomplished by selecting the appropriate terms, juxtaposing the cards vertically, and scanning the various
columns for identical numbers. Coordination exists wherever the latter
occur.

A few words should be said at this point regarding the subject
headings used in either of the above indexes, as well as in those discussed afterwards. Unless an effort is made to develop a thesaurus of
terms, or to control the vocabulary in some way, the entire retrieval
system will inevitably come to a bad end. This comment is especially
applicable in the field of chemistry where it is quite common for a
given compound to possess two or more names. Since it is most un-
likely that the name used by the scientist will happen to be the pre-
ferred or recommended one, the library will have the responsibility of
assigning the correct name, while at the same time making sure that
variations are indicated by means of appropriate cross-references. Needless to say, this task requires a sound background in the library's subject specialty, as do many of the activities in a special library or information center.

A somewhat more elaborate method of indexing, but still based on
concept coordination, is found in the optical coincidence or "peek-a-
boo" systems, the best known being Termatrex. Like the Uniterm card
index, this technique also requires that documents be serially numbered.
The individual subject cards, in this case, are larger in size, usually made
of plastic, and so arranged that a hole can be drilled at a precise position on the card, representing a certain document number. Such a deck
of cards will accommodate a collection of 10,000 documents, beyond
which a second or third deck would be required. For larger collections,
the method tends to become rather impractical. In searching the file,
selected cards are superimposed and placed in a specially designed
reader or light box. The holes or document numbers through which
light shines indicate coordination. Equipment costs may prove to be an
obstacle to libraries operating on a restricted budget, but I understand
that less mechanized systems are available which are equally satisfactory.
Mount discussed the use of Termatrex for reports some years ago (12).

Another retrieval method which has proved to be a convenient way
of indexing a large number of documents in relatively short time, is the
Key-Word-in-Context or KWIC Index. We are presently using this method to index the 1,000 or so abstracts of articles, patents, and books

appearing in each issue of the Coca-Cola Company's *Information Bulletin.* KWIC indexing consists of permuting by means of a computer every keyword in a title or every descriptor in a string of keywords into a single alphabetical sequence. The resulting printout lists all of these descriptors as in a dictionary catalog, but in context with the other descriptors pertaining to a given document, together with each document number. Although there is a tendency here to use a less controlled vocabulary, certainly if document titles alone are the source of the descriptors, there is no reason why more descriptive and appropriate terms could not be chosen from a standard listing. Besides convenience, a KWIC index offers two further advantages—the ease of updating or integration of new materials and the ability to reproduce multiple copies of the index for use in other locations. Other techniques have been described by Chamis (*4*) and Moran (*11*).

Referencing or use of laboratory records filed in the library is usually done by the library staff, and this is only logical since it is they who originally classified and indexed the records, and presumably, they should be more skilled at retrieving information when needed. Notwithstanding, some researchers prefer to do their own searching, and this should be perfectly acceptable. If this is the case, the library should be prepared to assist and guide them in any way possible.

Progress and Project Reports

Having discussed the handling of laboratory notebooks and related research records, let us now move on to the next category of proprietary information, progress and project reports. These are perhaps the most important documents that the library may be called upon to handle. First, they represent a distillation or refinement of all the laboratory work which preceded. Second, they generally include a discussion of the implications of the results obtained, conclusions, and recommendations for the future. I have no doubt that in some organizations, perhaps in many, the basic laboratory records which have already been discussed in some detail are not deemed to be suitable for the time-consuming processing suggested, and that interim and final reports are indeed the documents which merit the library's careful attention. It is admittedly difficult to argue with this contention, particularly if the library or information center is heavily burdened with other work. If the company is blessed with scientists who are prompt and conscientious in the matter of writing reports, there may be little need to devote much time to the processing of notebooks and other records. Every effort should then be made to ensure that the reports are promptly and adequately indexed once they reach the library. On the other hand, in some companies, the policy on report writing tends to be lax. It is in such instances that the indexing of original research documents takes on some urgency, for these are then in effect the only records of work performed. The library must be guided here by circumstances existing within that particular company.

As a rule, the library should be in a position to receive all reports when issued, probably even more automatically than might be the case for various other research records. As a matter of fact, the library may even have the responsibility of disseminating reports, in which event it will be assured of having at least one copy. Reports issued at one or more of a company's remote or overseas locations may represent an acquisition problem, but this can be avoided if a good liaison is established between those locations and the library. In this connection, reports written in foreign languages could also be a source of difficulty, were it not for the probability of at least one library staffer or someone else in the organization assisting in the report's processing.

As noted earlier for notebooks and other records, reports may be organized in various ways, the method of choice often depending on the retrieval system employed. In some organizations, every project is assigned a certain number, and consequently, all reports later issued under that project will bear the same number. It may, therefore, be advantageous to file the reports according to these project numbers. By the same token, if a coordinate indexing system is to be used, the library will want to assign accession numbers to the reports and file them in that order. Regardless of how the reports are classified, it is of the utmost importance that they be kept in a safe and secure location. There should exist a clear policy stating who may have access to the reports, and whether they may be copied or borrowed from the library. Carelessness in this regard could easily spell disaster for a company's new product, process or venture, and the harm done thereby to the company, not to mention the library's stature, could be irreparable.

Most of the comments made earlier concerning the processing of notebooks and laboratory records will also apply to reports. The latter, however, will often contain two additional features which should facilitate the task of the library indexer. Most reports include a summary or abstract which hopefully has captured all the salient points in the report. The other feature is a list of suggested indexing terms which the author has appended to his report. I use the word "suggested" advisedly, for considerable editing may be required by the library. When included, these terms are nevertheless a useful guide, in particular for reports whose content is quite complex.

Referencing of the reports is normally done as discussed earlier, with one important exception. Whereas in the case of laboratory records, the collection is consulted only when the need arises, company reports, representing as they do the cumulation of weeks or months of effort, deserve to be brought to the attention of all persons within the company who are permitted access to such information. Granted that it would be neither practical nor desirable to place complete copies of all reports in the hands of these persons, the library will be performing a splendid service if it regularly notifies the latter of all new reports received and added to its collection. Depending upon the volume, this may be done by means of monthly or quarterly alerting bulletins as described by McKenna (9), consisting of the titles, and preferably brief abstracts as well, of all reports received during the interim period. This service will be especially appreciated by persons who do not have ready access to the library, or who, for one reason or another, may not be in the mainstream of corporate communication.

Internal Memoranda and Other Correspondence

The next category of company information is internal memoranda and other correspondence. Material of this type can easily become a veritable quagmire and librarian's nightmare if not handled effectively. Many companies screen incoming correspondence and select items for the files. The items are then logged in in some manner and sometimes filmed or photocopied before being forwarded to the recipient. Devlin described a system used at Esso involving filming and indexing correspondence (5).

Some organizations prefer to use the "central files" approach to house this material; and if this is the case, the library should breathe a collective sigh of relief. It is possible, however, that the organization may have neither the facilities nor the personnel to maintain a central files department, and so it may befall the library to administer this collection of correspondence. The library's task will be greatly facilitated if it can manage to relate the memoranda and letters which it receives to existing reports or other records in its collection. Doing so may avoid, or at least lessen, the need for additional indexing. Also, it is necessary in this case, perhaps more than for any other category of information, to establish a regular program of weeding obsolete material. Deciding what is obsolete and what is not may turn out to be a tricky affair. Thus, it may be preferable simply to microfilm all correspondence older than a certain year and destroy the originals.

Meetings and Seminars

The minutes of meetings and proceedings of seminars held within the company will now be dealt with. These publications, representing as they do reviews of the organization's activities, new developments, and future plans, constitute a highly valuable source of information. Their acquisition depends upon the extent of management's willingness to allow access to such materials. For example, it may be felt that a report of a policy meeting may be simply too sensitive for inclusion in the library collection, even in its confidential files. However, there undoubtedly will be other documents of this type which are not restricted, and which the library will be expected to handle.

Organization of such documents could be chronological, by subject, or perhaps by department or division. If the collection is small, it may not be necessary to do any formal indexing since the respective tables of contents may suffice for referencing purposes. A larger collection may be cataloged by means of a simple card index. If the library has already adopted some form of a coordinate indexing system, it might then be preferable to transform a set of the meeting reports into unit documents or blocks of information, and to index them according to the characteristics of the system. To reiterate earlier words of caution, subsequent use and duplication should be closely controlled, as dictated by the library's established rules.

Patent Records

Now a special category of proprietary information, i.e., patent applications and related correspondence will be touched upon. Assuming that a company is moderately active in filing patent applications, the company's patent department may be the one to decide whether copies of these documents are to be available in the library. If the company is so organized that the patent department is located at some distance from the library and the research or engineering groups who have contributed most to the products and processes for which patent protection is being sought, this may be a good argument in favor of maintaining a set of applications in the library. These patent applications, incidentally, could be those filed with the U.S. Patent Office, as well as corresponding ones filed thereafter in foreign countries. Furthermore, in the course of prosecuting patent applications, a sizable dossier of correspondence is inevitably created on each application. This usually consists of letters and memoranda back and forth between the patent attorneys, the patent offices and the individual inventors or assignors, to use the correct expression. Here again, a decision will have to be made as to whether the library should receive copies of this voluminous correspondence. There would seem to be less compelling reasons for this, yet there are some instances where it is done, possibly because the research and engineering groups have become so involved in the patenting process that they must have ready access to every piece of pertinent information.

Arranging a collection of patent applications, with or without related correspondence, is subject to several approaches. The author has found, from his experience, that the simple expedient of using the patent attorney's unique docket numbers, appearing on every application and letter, is an effective means of classifying all related documents in order. If docket numbers are not assigned, a good alternative is the application number, equally unique, and also prominently displayed on all documents.

As mentioned earlier for minutes of meetings, the nature and extent of indexing of patent applications should be dictated, at least in part, by the size of the collection. Regardless of size, however, further detailed indexing is not advantageous since most if not all of the information contained in these applications may also be found in research reports and other records already indexed by the library. It might even be suggested that a brief addendum to the respective reports, stating that an application has been filed and identifying the latter by number, would be quite acceptable.

As to the eventual use of this material by company employees for information purposes, I suspect that the patent department will harbor very strong feelings in this regard, at least until the application has been accepted or published. As soon as an application has been made public in any one country, a certain "declassification" of the remaining corresponding applications is possible, but this should be done with caution since the subject matter and patent claims are not necessarily identical in all countries.

Papers for Presentation or Publication

The next type of proprietary information discussed is manuscripts of talks and articles by company employees. At first glance, these would appear not to be proprietary in nature; and indeed, they no longer are to the same extent, once the talk has been presented or the article published. Before these events take place, however, the documents are generally not available to persons outside the company. Accordingly, they must be regarded as restricted items. If, as it sometimes happens, the manuscript is not accepted and therefore does not become public knowledge, it continues to maintain a proprietary status.

It is only natural that the library should become a depository for these manuscripts. There, not only can they be classified and indexed according to subject matter, but they are then readily accessible to others in the company who may be contemplating related papers, and who may benefit from them. After the manuscripts have been made public, either through presentation or publication, a stock of preprints or reprints may be received by the authors. It is not unusual for the library to maintain and handle the distribution of these documents, and thus a certain continuity has been established. Pawlikowski and Tucker discuss unpublished manuscripts in a recent paper (*14*).

An allied area is the slides, tapes, films, transparencies, and other visuals which are utilized in presenting papers either within the company or to outside groups. These may be filed with the speech or paper to which they refer. Often, however, the speaker wishes to use the material again, or present it in slightly different form. The librarian, therefore, must develop some type of system for, or index to, the visuals. Some suggestions in these areas have been given by Baker (2).

Engineering Drawings

Since they are housed in the drafting room or engineering office, engineering drawings may not be considered as part of the library's responsibility in the area of technical information. The librarian may become involved in them only through his expertise in microfilming or indexing.

Depending upon the subject interests of the company, the drawings may be considered as part of the project records or research activities. For example, in the development and engineering of welding equipment, the schematics of the various components or designs must be noted in some way in the laboratory notebooks and progress reports. In the food and beverage or pharmaceutical industry a company may build its own equipment for producing a product. The designs must be linked to the corresponding research reports or pilot plant records.

Many companies merely arrange their drawings by size. They file the "A" size drawings in numerical order, "B" size in numerical order, etc. To reduce the bulk of the files, companies use the aperture card system as described by Southard (16) and Parker (13). The aperture cards greatly facilitate the indexing of the collection of drawings.

Retention

The retention of much proprietary information is based on whether or not the items are related to patents. Since the lifetime of a U.S. patent is 17 years, many company patent attorneys retain material 25 years. Other types of publications may be retained for 5, 10, or 15 years depending upon management's inclination. Through the use of microfilm and microfiche, companies may keep original material a specified number of years and then retain the filmed copies forever.

Security

The distribution of reports may be limited by the subject matter of the reports. All company personnel cannot see all of the reports that are prepared. For example, summaries only may be given to the Vice-President of Research or to the Planning Committee because they are not interested in the full technical details. The complete reports are distributed to the Director of Research, the patent group, the project supervisor, and the project members. Sometimes copies are circulated to analytic groups or other persons who are interested in the work but do not require copies permanently; after circulation these copies are returned to the central files.

The company management, in conjunction with the patent attorneys, establish categories of information which may be restricted, much in the same way that the Department of Defense has established security classifications for reports. An example in industry would be an employee's medical and personnel files which are considered highly confidential.

A paper which was published a number of years ago in Weil's *The Technical Report* discusses this topic (*15*). Lura Shorb and Jack Barsha, of Hercules Company, suggest a security classification system for a technical reporting system, as follows: Classification 1—(Confidential Company); Classification 2—(Private Company); Classification 3—(Commercial Technical); Classification 4—Information (of Other Organizations); Classification 5—(Unrestricted).

Jermy suggests the categories of Strictly Confidential, Confidential, Restricted, and Open (*8*) while Gerrard mentions the classifications of Highly Confidential, Confidential, and Ordinary (*7*).

Employees may be asked to sign contracts or patent agreements stipulating that the work they perform belongs to the company. The agreements also restrict them from revealing proprietary information while currently employed or in the future employment of other companies.

The handling of proprietary information sometimes is in direct opposition to the librarian's inclination to make information available to everyone who wants it. Due to company security stipulations, the librarian must restrict access to research information to employees who are authorized to receive it. On the other hand, the librarian is attempting to obtain cooperation from employees in securing complete files of documents to put into his system. He must devise methods for advertising within the corporation that the information is there in one place, conveniently indexed, and ready to be used.

Conclusion

Having now reviewed the handling of several categories of proprietary company information, the important role which these documents have in the overall collection of the company library or information center should be reemphasized. This author suggests that all other publications in the collection are really auxiliary in nature. From a corporate point of view, these are one of the means to an end; that end or goal is the realization of successful research efforts and their further implementation. The proprietary materials examined here are the documented results of these achievements, and yes, of the occasional failures.

Literature Cited

1. Bailey, Martha J. / The Laboratory Notebook as a Research and Development Record. *Special Libraries* 63 (no. 4): 189–194 (Apr 1972).

2. Baker, Walter S. and Alexander G. Hoshovsky / The Storage and Retrieval of 'Visuals' *Graphic Science*: 22–24, 26–27 (Mar 1968).

3. Benson, Frederic R. and Roger A. Walck / The Atlas Chemical Research Information System *Journal of Chemical Documentation* 8 (no. 2): 88–93 (May 1968).

4. Chamis, Alice Y. / Variety of Records Calls for a Variety of Techniques and Tools *Information and Records Management* 4 (no. 4): 18–19, 30–31 (Apr/May 1970).

5. Devlin, T. J. / Use of Microfilm in Internal-Mail Control *Journal of Chemical Documentation* 10 (no. 1): 22–25 (Feb 1970).

6. Eckerman, E. H., J. F. Waters, R. O. Pick, and J. A. Schafer / Processing Data from a Large Drug Development Program *Journal of Chemical Documentation* 12 (no. 1): 38–40 (1972).

7. Gerrard, S. A. and D. F. Lyle / Handling Industrial (Scientific and Technical) Confidential Report Material *Aslib Proceedings* 18: 206–217 (Aug 1966).

8. Jermy, K. E. / Control of Commercially Confidential Information Reports *Aslib Proceedings* 18: 218–223 (Aug 1966).

9. McKenna, F. E. / An Abstract Bulletin for Corporate R&E Reports *Special Libraries* 56 (no. 5): 318–322 (May/June 1965).

10. Matt, Richard J. / Engineering Project Reports *Machine Design*: 157–160 (Nov 7, 1968).

11. Moran, Marguerite / Indexing of Metal and Thermit Corporation Research Records on Keysort Cards *American Documentation* 11: 222–228 (1960).

12. Mount, Ellis / Information Retrieval from Technical Reports Using Termatrex Equipment *Special Libraries* 54 (no. 2): 83–89 (Feb 1963).

13. Parker, F. M. / Engineering Drawing Processing System *Special Libraries* 51 (no. 8): 429–432 (Oct 1960).

14. Pawlikowski, Nancy J. and Robert G. Tucker / The Untapped Resource—Unpublished Manuscripts *Journal of Chemical Documentation* 11 (no. 4): 215–217 (1971).

15. Shorb, Lura and Jack Barsha / Distributing the Company Technical Report *In* Weil, B. / *The Technical Report*. New York, Reinhold, 1954. p. 244–245.

16. Southard, W. P. / Managing and Using Engineering Drawings *Chemical Engineering* 78 (no. 1): 117–129 (Apr 19, 1971).

Company and Trade Literature

RICHARD JOHNSTON

The selection, acquisition, organization, processing, and referencing of company and trade catalogs, publishers' catalogs, business reports, financial reports, pamphlets, advertising material, and campaign literature are discussed. The procedure will be to discuss standard, and some non-standard, operational methods used for each type of publication.

Probably the single most important step in developing a collection is the determination of the objectives of that collection. This should be done before any literature is gathered. Determine the objectives of both the parent organization and the planned library. Then determine who will be using the collection and for what reasons. Once the objectives, the users, and their library needs are known, a selection policy can be written to insure orderly development of the collection rather than ending up with a hodge-podge of miscellaneous catalogs and pamphlets of no real use to anyone. Since conditions change, these objectives and selection policies should be reviewed periodically to determine the need for possible changes.

For this paper the definition of each type of publication is as follows.

1. Trade catalogs are a "book or pamphlet issued by a manufacturer or dealer illustrating and describing his goods or products and sometimes including or accompanied by a price list."
2. "Consolidated or union trade catalog is a compilation of catalog data from several manufacturers in a single industry or group of allied industries. These may be published for sale or rent by commercial publishers or more often as advertising ventures, in which case they are usually free to libraries whose clients are potential purchasers of products included. Sometimes the catalogs are published by trade periodicals, either free to subscribers as a special

Richard Johnston is research scientist, Industrial Development Division, Engineering Experiment Station, Georgia Institute of Technology, Atlanta, Ga.

or supplementary issue, or at an additional fee" (*1*).
3. Publishers' catalogs are catalogs supplied by publishers that list their available publications and include pricing information and shipping instructions.
4. Business reports are those reports which provide information, either general or specific, about a certain industry, specific company, or a general business outlook.
5. Financial reports are those reports which reveal financial conditions about a specific company, an industry, or general financial conditions.
6. Pamphlets are unusual publications that are produced in many different sizes, shapes, forms, and types, and in this discussion they are book-like publications that require special housing conditions such as vertical file folders or boxes.
7. Advertising materials are those publications which are designed to motivate a person to acquire a product or service.
8. Campaign literature is a collection of myths, fiction, propaganda and occasionally facts produced to motivate voters to support a particular candidate, party, or issue.

Trade Catalogs

The publication *Acquisition of Special Materials* by Isabel H. Jackson (*2*) has an excellent section on trade catalogs; much of this section is quoted from her work.

"Trade catalogs form an important body of reference material in any technical organization. They are of value when anything is to be purchased . . . Additionally, catalogs have a utility to the engineer or designer that sometimes goes beyond the obvious. Often a piece of specialized equipment is available from a manufacturer and it can be used or adapted to the job without having to be designed and built from scratch.

"Frequently an engineer needs to know the properties of a particular material. Sometimes the properties of a material, particularly if it is a relatively new one, are not to be found in the conventional literature but only in catalog literature issued by a manufacturer."

Some directories which can be used to locate manufacturers are
1. *Thomas Register of American Manufacturers*. New York, Thomas Publishing Co., Annual.
2. *MacRae's Blue Book*. Chicago, Annual.
3. *Conover-Mast Purchasing Directory*. New York, Conover-Mast Publications, Inc., 1965. 2150 p.
4. Klein, Bernard, ed. / *Guide to American Directories: A Guide to the Major Business Directories of the U.S.* 5th ed. New York, Prentice-Hall, 1962. 428 p.

5. *National Trade and Professional Associations of the United States.* Washington, Columbia Books, Inc., Annual.

Although these directories are good primary sources, often excellent regional or local directories exist which list and describe manufacturers not listed in the national publications. Examples of these are listed below:

1. *Directory of Georgia Manufacturers 1971.* Georgia Department of Industry and Trade, Atlanta, Annual.

2. *Maine Metal Industry Handbook 1971.* Department of Economic Development, Augusta, Me.

3. *Wichita Manufacturers Directory.* Division of Economic Development, Wichita Area Chamber of Commerce, Wichita, Kan.

To keep aware of new products, services, and catalogs, regular and systematic examinations must be made of trade journals and periodicals which often have articles about new catalogs and developments. They also have "reader service cards" by which further information can be obtained.

Each month, there appears in the magazine *Industrial Marketing* a feature entitled "Guide to Special Issues of Business Publications." A typical entry is one listed under the heading "Chemical, Processing," *Environmental Engineering Deskbook*, which includes a list of pollution control equipment manufacturers. In the section "Machinery and Equipment" of *Modern Plastics* there are such listings as "Polyether Foam Molding Machine" on which additional information can be obtained by mailing a completed "reader service card" to the publisher. Many of the trade journals have a similar service.

Trade shows are excellent for obtaining a great deal of new material. In addition, there are several compilations of trade catalogs which are available as aids to manufacturers and others interested in their wares. Some of them are listed below.

1. *Sweets Catalog File.* Sweets Catalog Service, New York, Sweets Division, McGraw-Hill Information System, Annual.

"This is a nicely bound annual set of books made up from the catalogs and brochures of several hundred major manufacturers, arranged in broad product classifications. The titles of the various volumes of Catalog Files are, *Interior Design File, Light Construction Catalog File, Industrial Construction File,* and *Plant Engineering File.* In addition, there is a special series, the *Architectural File in Ten Volumes.*"

2. *(Vendor Specs. Micro File) VSMF*, Information Handling Services, Inc., Los Angeles, Calif.

This expensive service, about $5,000 per year, claims to have about 3,000 subscribers. Through regular updating of 11 microfilm services, it keeps contact with over 18,000 vendor-manufacturers. The standard services provide cartridges of film read on a Recordak Lodestar reader-printer. These cartridges contain "Military Specifications," "Vendor Catalog Data," "Design Engineering Service" for persons concerned with component selection and coordination.

3. Thomas Marketing Information Center (TMIC) is a division of Thomas Publishing Company. TMIC has the information from the *Thomas Register* and *Industrial Equipment News* registered in a data bank and available through a computer for quick retrieval for users. Other similar systems are *MPS Library File Product Index.* Micro Publishing Systems, Inc., Brooklyn, N.Y., $250.00; and *ASCAM* (Aero Space Catalog Automated Microfilm). Engineering Affiliates, Palo Alto, Calif.

When the needed information concerning a manufacturer is not available from a directory, there is nearly always an association which will have the directory information required. The particular association of manufacturers representing the manufacturer in question may be listed in a publication with national coverage, such as the *Encyclopedia of Associations*. 5th ed. (Detroit, Gale Research, 1968, 2v.), or on a local or regional level in a publication such as the *Directory of Statewide and Regional Associations in Georgia 1970–71*. 2d ed. Kay C. Rogers, ed. (Industrial Development Division, Engineering Experiment Station, Georgia Institute of Technology, 1971. 108 p.)

International trade information can be obtained directly from embassies and consulates. An example is the bulletin mailed from the British Consulate General's Office—*New Products and Processes*—which describes in detail the new products and lists the addresses of the manufacturers in England and their American representative, if there is one.

Dun & Bradstreet's international services publishes many books, reports, and guides concerning trade affairs in foreign countries. Some examples of these are their *Argentina Reference Book, International Reports, International Market Guide—Continental Europe,* and *International Market Guide—Latin America*.

The Bureau of International Commerce, U.S. Department of Commerce, provides many publications and much information concerning international trade. An example is their publication, *International Marketing Information Service*. This series provides information and statistical data on forthcoming foreign exhibitions, market profiles by country and market profiles by commodity. "Electronic Data Processing Equipment" and "Food Processing and Packaging Machinery" were two sections in a recent report of this series, *World Markets for U.S. Exports*.

If a person wants to do business in a foreign country, the U.S. Department of Commerce, for $2.00, will prepare a fairly detailed *World Trade Directory Report* for almost any business in the world with whom one might wish to trade.

An additional publication dealing with international trade is the UNIDO *Guide to Industrial Directories*. (Vienna, Austria, United Nations, 1971. 137p.) "This publication is designed to provide information to the developing countries on the sources of supply, the cost, and the quality of equipment needed for their development. This publication is not an exhaustive catalog of recommended directories, but comprises rather a representative selection of directories to assist developing countries in locating sources of supply of industrial equipment. Fifty-nine different directories are listed from twenty-nine different countries."

Business and Financial Reports

Business and financial reports are similar; sometimes it is difficult to determine whether the report is business or financial. Publications concerning these two subjects will often include information that seems to overlap. The publications showing sources tend to use "business" in the overall context with "finance" as a lesser term.

There are many publications giving sources of business information. Some of these are listed below.

1. Harvard University. Graduate School of Business Administration, Baker Library. / *Business Literature: An Annotated List for Students and Businessmen.* Boston, 1968. 139p.

"This publication provides students and businessmen with a highly selected list of books and magazines in the principal areas of business. The descriptive notes indicate the scope or audience for which each book is intended."

2. Hunt, F. E. / *Public Utility Information Sources.* New York, Gale, 1966. 200p.

"An annotated guide to literature and bodies concerned with rates, economics, accounting, regulation, history, and statistics of electric, gas, telephone, and water companies."

3. Janezeck, Elizabeth G. / *Basic Library Reference Sources.* Small Business Bibliography No. 18. Washington, D.C., GPO, 1970. 11p.

"The purpose of this bibliography is to acquaint the small business-man with the wealth of business information available through library research. The list contains the most basic business directories, guides, and reference sources available in many libraries."

4. Janezeck, Elizabeth G. / *A Survey of Federal Government Publications of Interest to Small Business,* 3rd ed. Washington, D.C., GPO, 1969. 58p.

"This booklet is intended to help small business owners in selecting publications from the many publications which are issued each year by the various departments, bureaus, offices, commissions, and other administrative arms of the Federal Government."

5. Johnson, H. Webster / *How to Use the Business Library with Sources of Business Information.* 3rd ed. Cincinnati, Southwest-

ern Publishing Co., 1964. 160p.

"This manual provides a guide for training in the use of the business library. Sources cited, listings made, and methods described are abundant enough to permit anyone to tap large areas of information."

6. Wasserman, P. / *Sources of Commodity Prices.* New York, Special Libraries Association, 1960. 159p.

This publication covers periodicals "that provide regular or seasonal price information." It is a source for locating current commodity prices. "The body of the work is an alphabetical list of commodities which lists the name of the commodity, title of periodical publishing the price, market or markets in which price is effective, and the frequency with which prices appear in the periodical."

7. Woy, J. B. / *Business Trends and Forecasting Information Sources.* New York, Gale, 1965. 152p.

An annotated guide to theoretical and technical publications, and to sources of data.

8. *1971 Business Statistics.* Washington, D.C., Office of Business Economics, U.S. Department of Commerce, Biennial.

A biennial statistical supplement to the monthly *Survey of Current Business.* The most recent edition provides, for the past 25 years, historical data for approximately 2,500 series and lists its sources of data.

9. *Statistical Abstract of the United States.* Washington, D.C., Bureau of the Census, U.S. Department of Commerce, Monthly.

"This *Abstract*, published annually since 1878, is the standard summary of statistics on the social, political, and economic organization of the United States. It is designed to serve as a convenient volume for statistical reference and as a guide to other statistical publications and sources. The latter function is served by the introductory text to each section, the source notes appearing below each table, the "Guide to Sources," the section on "Publications of Recent Censuses," and the "Guide to State Statistical Abstracts."

Baker Library, Graduate School of Business Administration of Harvard University has produced the guide *Selected Business Reference Sources.* This guide lists sources of financial information under six headings—Investment Manuals; Investment Data, Opinions, Forecasts, Recommendations; Financial Newspapers; Financial Periodicals; Indexes to Financial Publications; Company Reports of Six General Types: Annual Report to Stockholders, Annual Reports to SEC, Registration Statements, Proxy Statements, Prospectuses, Indentures.

Investment data, opinions, forecasts, and recommendations can be found in many fine publications, such as:

Standard & Poor's—Industry Surveys
United Business Service
Value Line Investment Survey
Predicasts

Moody's Investors Service, Inc.
Industrial Manual
OTC Industrial Manual
Industrial News Report
OTC Industrial News Report
Dun & Bradstreet—Reference Book
Reports
Million Dollar Directory
Reference Book of Corporate Managers
Reference Book of Manufacturers.

The financial newspapers publish information concerning stocks, bonds, commodity prices, shipping news, and business gossip. The leading ones are *The American Banker, Journal of Commerce, The New York Times, Wall Street Journal.* Financial and business reports also appear in the financial periodicals, some of which are *Journal of Finance, Barrons, Forbes, Financial World.* There are, of course, business and financial periodical indexes such as the *Funk & Scott Index of Corporations and Industries, Wall Street Journal Index.*

In addition to these types of publications, there are other sources available. Nearly every community has a credit bureau organization that sells a publication which lists the items of public record as recorded in the Clerk of the Court's Office in that county. These include suits filed in the JP courts—the defendant, plaintiff, amount, date, and nature of the suit as to whether it is a garnishment or suit on account. It will also list the bankruptcies, liens and foreclosures, chattel mortgages, equipment mortgages, automobile mortgages and registrations, deeds to secure debt, warranty deeds, quit-claim deeds, canceled mortgages, business registrations, and other information. These local credit associations have foreign affiliations to provide information to foreign companies wanting to do business in the United States.

Each county government designates a newspaper to be its official notification newspaper. Here are published annual reports of local governments, notices of action on estates, and disclaimers of credit responsibility for spouse's debts.

Dun & Bradstreet has a commercial service, generally unavailable to non-company libraries, that provides in-depth historical and financial reports on business firms. These credit reports usually provide sufficient information for a seller to decide if the firm is able and willing to pay a debt. The reports also list any unusual damages or losses from fires, floods, and other disasters. The Dun & Bradstreet reports provide a very fine service to the business community, but because the company will sometimes supply unaudited information to Dun & Bradstreet, one should be careful in accepting at full face value what is printed in the report.

Microfiche copies of the annual reports, current and semi-annual reports, SEC disclosure filing, proxy statements, registration statements, final prospectuses, N1-Q quarterly reports of registered management investment companies, and the N-1R annual reports of registered management companies are available on several thousand companies from Leasco Information Products, Information Products Division, Leasco Systems & Research Corporates, Bethesda, Md.

Copies of annual reports may be acquired from the company itself, stockholders, and stockbrokers.

Any company, large or small, that decides to go public by offering shares of stock for sale comes under the jurisdiction of the Securities and Exchange Commission and must issue an annual report. In addition, individual states have their own laws governing corporations, some of which require an annual report.

These annual reports are more easily obtained from the larger companies than from the smaller, closely held local companies which tend to keep their financial condition a secret. Occasionally, these local companies will disclose financial information when they print legal notices in their newspaper of legal notifications. They may also print "brag sheets" on historical occasions, and some print and distribute an annual statement of conditions. Clippings from the local newspaper are probably the best published source for these closely held local companies.

Investment manuals usually include a brief history of the company and its operation, subsidiaries, plants, products, officers, and directors, comparative tables of income account, balance sheet, earning record over several years, description of outstanding securities, ". . . and sections providing useful data including ranges of outstanding stock" (3).

Examples are Standard and Poor's Corporation, *Standard Corporation Records* and Moody's Investors Services: *Moody's Bank & Financial Manual, Moody's Industrial Manual, Moody's Municipal Utility Manual, Moody's Public Utility Manual,* and *Moody's Transportation Manual.*

Pamphlets

Often pamphlets are the only sources of information available in certain subject areas. Many publications in the field of industrial development are produced in the pamphlet form. Many government publications are in pamphlet form. In fact, pamphlet-type publications are produced by organizations in business, commerce, science, technology, and practically all groups. However, it is not always easy to obtain them.

There are standard sources of information concerning pamphlets such as the *Vertical File Index: A Subject and Title Index to Selected Pamphlet Material* (New York, Wilson, Monthly). The trouble with such indexes is that the literature supply is sometimes depleted before or soon after being listed.

Newspaper and periodical articles describing publications just issued are a constant source of acquisition for pamphlets and reports.

Staff members and other personnel of your organization can be trained to be aware of and bring in pamphlets for your collection from fairs, conventions, and meetings of various sorts.

Some other published sources of pamphlet acquisitions are

1. Alexander, Ralph / *Business Pamphlets and Information Sources.* New York, Exceptional Books, 1967. 72p. "A guide to currently available pamphlets, reprints and paperbacks in the field of business, and to organizations and government agencies which are sources of business information."
2. DeVolder, A. L. / Selected Sources to Free and Inexpensive Materials. *New Mexico Libraries* 3:83-86 (Fall 1970).
3. Berner, R. C. / On Ephemera, Their Collection and Use. *Library Resources and Technical Services* 7:335-339 (Fall 1963).

Publishers' Catalogs

Bowker annually binds a collection of publishers' catalogs into one volume entitled *Publishers' Trade List Annual.* (New York, Bowker, Annual). These catalogs list the books in print for each publisher.

If this publication is not available or does not include the catalog of a certain publisher, it may be necessary to find a publisher's listing in a directory such as: *American Book Trade Directory* (New York, Bowker, Biannual); or *Publishers International Yearbook* (London, Alexander P. Wales, Annual).

If the publisher is not listed in any of the published directories, a letter to the publisher requesting a catalog would be the easiest way to acquire it.

Campaign Literature

Campaign literature really fits the description of short-lived or ephemeral literature.

A primary source of campaign literature is the candidate's publicity office. Ask that your name be included on their mailing list to automatically receive the standard mail-outs. Contrive to make a small contribution and you will receive bushels of literature. Staff members with differing political views should be good sources of this type of literature.

The Democratic National Committee maintains a library in the Riddle Building in Washington, D.C. This library has five professionals and the library is open to the public. The Republican Party also has a library in Washington, D.C., and use of the library for reference may be requested. This library publishes their accessions list.

The Fair Campaign Practices Committee Library in New York City collects election campaign literature. In addition, each party and each candidate has local offices in various cities, and you are most welcome to their give-aways.

Organization of Holdings

Now that this special material has been acquired, how should it be handled? No matter what the type, size, or subject interest of your library, it is probable that another library has already crossed most of the bridges you now face. A letter to the director or a visit to such a library should be very rewarding. In the directory edited by Anthony T. Krusas, *Directory of Special Libraries and Information Centers* (2d ed. Detroit, Gale, 1968. 1,048p.), there are listed many different types of special libraries. For example, in the subject index under: Advertising and Marketing—145 libraries are listed, Banking and Finance—95 libraries are listed, Business and Business Management—294 libraries are listed, Politics—7 libraries are listed, Publishing—53 libraries are listed. A 3d edition of the *Directory* is in preparation. Surely some of these existing libraries have proven answers to many of your questions. The publications of the Special Libraries Association are also especially helpful.

You may want to use a classification scheme such as Dewey, Library of Congress, or one listed in the bibliography compiled by Barbara Denison, *Selected Materials in Classification*. New York, Special Libraries Association, 1968. 142p. In this bibliography, a list of titles in the Bibliographic Systems Center (BSC) at Case Western Reserve University library school, there are citations to classification schemes, subject heading lists, and specific citations for the various types of activities. Classification schemes are available on loan from the BSC. Under "Advertising" on page 14, there are 19 entries such as the following three examples: Ten Basic Classifications; Extension of Dewey Decimal Classification for Advertising; Suggested List of Subject Headings for Use in File Clippings and Pamphlets on Advertising and Merchandising. Under "Business" there are 20 citations; under "Finance," 13 citations; under "Pamphlets," 5 citations; and under "Trade Catalogs," 9 citations which have additional citations such as "Dewey Decimal Numbers Assigned to Trade Catalogs. Subject Headings and Classification Outline."

In *Library Literature* under the heading "Ephemeral Materials" there are potentially useful references. You might also want to check the publication by Collison, Robert L. / *Commercial and Industrial Records Storage* (New York, John DeGraff, 1969. 183p.). The book contains information on the more common items handled by commercial and industrial organizations. It also considers ideas for obtaining more value from the material in a collection.

If you have several hundred trade catalogs, these could be arranged on the shelves alphabetically by company. Suitable subject headings could be typed at the top of photocopies of the title page and these sheets then filed alphabetically. There may be other simple, effective, pragmatic systems.

It is the author's belief that the central principle to follow in organizing, classifying, and cataloging special materials and the operation of special libraries is to keep the system simple.

Circulation Policies

Special collections are often irreplaceable. So the general rule is to restrict the use of the materials to in-house use and arrange any exterior circulation not to conflict with the needs of the designated users of the special library.

Weeding

Weeding is difficult. For each type of publication, catalog, report, and pamphlet, set a policy for its expected useful shelf life. Develop a procedure for non-professionals to screen one-half of the collection each month. The professionals can then spot check some or check all of the discards. Each special library will have its own time-limit needs, but through experience and consultation with other librarians, one can develop suitable policies. In *Acquisition of Special Materials,* Jackson suggests three years as a sufficient time to keep catalogs. Where newspaper clippings are used to show the economic climate, maturity or growth of a community, it might be wise not to weed too harshly. Business reports, especially predictions and projections, sometimes become jokes, but a file of business reports can provide an historical basis for projections. A long run of financial reports can be fascinating reading, and these reports can also provide needed information for market analyses and feasibility studies.

With the references given here plus those in the bibliography, it is hoped that initial involvement with trade catalogs, business and financial reports, pamphlets, advertising material, and campaign literature will have been facilitated by this exposure to information about the selection, acquisition, organization, and referencing of these materials to develop a useful collection.

Literature Cited

1. *Contributions Toward a Special Library Glossary.* New York, Special Libraries Association, 1950. p. 21–22. o.p.
2. Jackson, Isabel H., ed. / *Acquisition of Special Materials.* San Francisco, Special Libraries Association, San Francisco Bay Region Chapter, 1967. 220 p.
3. Harvard University, Graduate School of Business Administration, Baker Library / *Selected Business Reference Sources.* Boston, 1963. p. 17–23.

Maps

BARBARA WALKER

The importance of maps in the library has often been underestimated. Contrary to popular belief, their usage is not restricted to geographers and historians. In this complex and interesting world, almost every field of human enterprise and activity has problems which are best solved by information presented on maps. And, like other library holdings, they are being consulted more and more by library users today. Librarians, too, have finally realized the importance of maps and are relying on them more heavily in their search for additional sources of information. They are discovering that maps are as necessary for reference purposes as the books: They clarify and supplement the written word, graphically illustrate the trend of current events, and by employing combinations of diverse symbols, also visualize many other important topics such as ethnic relationships, physical, social and economic conditions, and historical, artistic, and literary development.

Acquisition

The acquisition of maps is often a major problem for the map librarian. Aside from the limitations of the amount of money available to spend on these materials, there is always the question of what to purchase. It should be kept in mind that maps are of two basic classes and the map librarian should acquire both for his collection. One is the general map which is either physical or political or a combination of the two; the other is the thematic map which serves some special purpose.

In selecting materials for his collection, the map librarian must keep his clientele in mind. They fall into three categories: small, with limited needs; medium, with broader needs; or large, with a much broader and wider range of needs. They may be the collections in the high school,

Barbara J. Walker is map librarian, Price Gilbert Memorial Library, Georgia Institute of Technology, Atlanta, Ga.

college, university, public, or special library. The map librarian must also consider the type of geographical maps and/or aids, such as atlases, which will meet the needs of his library's patrons. These include, in addition to the physical, political, and thematic maps, those maps which are products of special interest groups, e.g., the oil companies, advertising groups, and government agencies (which are free or inexpensive), and also atlases (within a limited price range).

Regardless of clientele or the purpose for acquiring maps, there are certain guidelines which need to be established for evaluating them. Current lists six criteria for selection (1):

1. Visibility: Maps summarize and give a pictorial representation of materials. Therefore, good visibility is a must.

2. Size: The map usage is of primary importance. Whether it will be designed to serve a group or an individual, the important thing is to make sure that the map to be purchased will meet the needs of the user.

3. Amount of Detail and Suitability for Grade Level (or your particular clientele if you are not in a school situation): Maps are often unsatisfactory because they contain too much or too little information. Thus the maps to be purchased should relate to the needs and abilities of those who will be using them.

4. Color: It is the use made of color and not the presence or absence of it which indicates its value. Good use of color in maps not only makes them more attractive but also shows relationships and emphasizes contrasts.

5. Durability: The main concern here is with potential rather than initial quality.

6. Accuracy: A must for any map. The authority of the geographer, the precision of scale, the projection, the clarity of symbols used, and the date of publication are all factors to be considered whether the map is simplified or highly detailed.

Other factors to consider in acquiring maps for your collection are noted in a catalog on *Business and Reference Maps, Atlases, Guides* published by Rand McNally (2). They are as follows:

1. For what purpose are you going to use the map?
2. What area do you want your map to include?
3. How large a map do you want? (You should consider both the size of the map sheet and the scale)
4. What specific data do you want shown on the map?
5. Do you need an index?
6. Do you want a colored or black and white map?

These factors may be used to assist in tailoring your collection to meet the needs of your clientele as well as in acquisition and selection.

Sources

In discussing the sources of map information, the map librarian, again, must consider his patron, because the sources for map information vary with the purpose or needs of the library's users.

For small collections, free or inexpensive materials may provide answers. Use local resources if available. If there are none, make use of a nearby large library or visit a collection of the size needed. Usually the medium-sized collection, and always the large collection, will have basic reference tools which can provide sources of information about maps.

Among the periodicals which can be of aid in the procurement program are *Current Geographical Publications, Geographical Journal, Geographical Review, The Military Engineer* (which has a section on "Geodesy, Mapping, Oceanography"), *National Geographic Magazine,* the *Bulletin* of the Geography and Map Division, Special Libraries Association (which has a section on "New Maps"), and *Surveying and Mapping* (which has two sections on maps: 1) "Map Information," and 2) "Distinctive Recent Maps").

United States Governmental Agencies which are sources for maps include the U.S. Geological Survey's *New Publications of the Geological Survey,* section, "Maps"; U.S. Superintendent of Document's *Monthly Catalog,* (see section in the Index "Maps and Charts"); the Library of Congress, Copyright Office, *Catalog of Copyright Entries—Maps, Atlases*; and the Library of Congress, Processing Department, *Monthly Checklist of State Publications.*

The price lists on various subjects issued by the Superintendent of Documents provide some help as to the existence of particular specialized maps and some information on the nature of the map publications of certain agencies. *Price List 46, Soils and Fertilizers,* has a complete list of the counties and areas for which soil maps are available. *Price List 53, Maps,* lists maps from several special map issuing agencies.

Among the state agencies are the lists which may come from the various Departments, such as the Departments of Conservation, Geology—Mines and Mining, Fish and Wildlife, Forest Service and Highway Department.

You may also include local city planning departments, and chambers of commerce, as well as the oil companies, as sources for maps.

Problems

There are three major problems in the acquisition of maps: 1— the lack of well-established bibliographic aids, thus the problem of scattered sources and of getting the information needed; 2) the greater number of sources of map materials as compared with those of books; and 3) the ephemeral and documentary nature of maps.

The processing of these important cartographic materials entails many considerations. Clara LeGear in her manual, *Maps—Their Care, Repair and Preservation in Libraries,* states that "the care of maps in a library begins upon their arrival, and unwrapping them carefully cannot be stressed too emphatically" (3).

Maps may be received in rolls, in envelopes, or in boxes, or by hand as gifts. When opening a roll of maps, it is necessary to observe how it has been wrapped before removing the covering, that is, whether the maps are rolled inside or outside of a tube, whether the paper is wrapped around the tube, or partly under the maps (4). This is important because many maps have been slashed or torn by careless unwrapping.

After the maps have been unrolled or unfolded, they should be flattened for easier processing. We flatten our rolled maps by reversing them, and placing the unfolded maps under heavy weights for a few hours. If the creases are tight, the maps can be dampened with a wet sponge along the folds, or over the entire surface before placing them under the weights.

After the maps have been flattened, they should then be given some mark of ownership. In most libraries, maps are given a mark of ownership by embossing or rubber stamping the name of the institution on the face or verso of each map. At Georgia Tech the maps are given the mark of ownership by stamping the name of the institution and date of receipt on the face of each map. This stamp is affixed in the lower right corner of each map sheet, or as near it as possible. If there is no blank space in the margin, the stamp may be placed as near the lower right corner as possible, where it will not obliterate any part of the map. Try to be as consistent as possible about placing the stamp of ownership in the same general position on each map sheet, and to take care that the impression is clear and unsmudged.

Record keeping is also a phase of map processing. It is a necessary phase because it shows growth and accomplishment. Counting maps as they are received, according to Clara LeGear (5), should be done in a manner to satisfy the objective of keeping this statistical record. One library may be interested in the number of map titles it holds, whereas another may want to know how many actual map sheets it houses. This more impressive figure, maintained in some large libraries, may be useful to show growth in relation to personnel and to storage equipment. A small map library does not have to keep elaborate statistics, but they would give a more adequate picture of its growth and actual holdings by the time it has grown large. At the Georgia Tech Library each map is counted as it is received and the number is recorded in the statistics notebook. There are two counts taken, one of the maps received and the other of maps added. Maps that are to be cataloged are counted as "maps received," but are counted as "maps added" by the map cataloger.

After the acquisitions records have been completed, there is a preliminary sorting. Those maps that do not need special attention (cataloging, etc.) are arranged in alphabetical order, by state and sheet name, or by series and sheet number, then checked off on the various indexes or recorded in the serials record file. The maps to be cataloged are routed to the map cataloger.

Organizing the Collection

Another important aspect of the map librarian's work is the arrangement and organization of his collection. The materials should be arranged so that they are readily available and the users can help themselves when necessary.

The Library of Congress classification system is used in organizing and arranging the Georgia Tech collection. There are instances, however, when it is necessary to deviate from the standard arrangement. At such times the maps have been arranged so that they are more accessible for our particular patrons. The state topographic maps are arranged alphabetically by state and quadrangle name at the end of the LC classification scheme. The sets of maps and single maps from the U.S. Army Topographic Command* are filed by "sets" of maps and "single" maps, beginning with G7000–G9999. The trays are clearly marked to show their contents. The call number, along with other distinguishing marks, is given. For example, the trays for "sets" of maps are labeled G7000s, set of maps; and "single" maps—G7000, single maps. The trays for the state topographic maps bear the name (or names) of the state.

The use of chemically pure paper and map covers are recommended to protect maps from dust and friction. Individual jackets are recommended to give added protection to rare or fragile maps.

A necessary chore in map work is that of filing materials in their correct location. It is necessary because it may save hours of searching as well as professional embarrassment; a chore because it can be time-consuming. In the filing of maps, there are a few precautions which will insure neat looking files and protection for the maps. The drawers should not be overcrowded because this will cause damage to the maps. No part of a map should protrude from the drawers. Edges left hanging out are likely to tear or fray. Sheet maps should lie face up and be aligned to the front and to the corner that has the classification designation. Maps of uniform size should be neatly stacked as they are handled. No paper clips should remain on maps in the files (6).

Use

In addition to the selection, processing, and general upkeep of his collection, the map librarian is also responsible for its use. He determines

---

On Jul 1, 1972, the U.S. Army Topographic Command became part of the newly formed Defense Mapping Agency and its designation is now the Defense Mapping Agency Topographic Center (DMATC).

which maps will circulate, if any, and to whom; what the loan period will be; and whether they will be available on interlibrary loan. Some libraries circulate virtually all maps freely; others permit no circulation at all. The Georgia Tech policy is "to make materials as freely available to the patron as reasonably as can be done," all maps, except the depository maps from the U.S. Army Topographic Command, circulate. These maps do not circulate because of certain restrictions that have been placed on them by TOPOCOM.

There are some map librarians, however, who disagree with the policy of circulating maps. Robert C. White, former map librarian, University of Illinois, in an article on map librarianship, states that "the risk of damage or loss of maps is very high when the map files are open to the public. When you restrict access to the map files, you place a greater burden on yourself, because you then take on greater responsiblity in selection of maps for use" (7).

Maps that circulate need a protective covering. The tubes in which many maps are shipped are suitable for this purpose. All of the maps that circulate at Georgia Tech are checked out at the library's circulation desk and those in charge there are asked to place the maps in such tubes. A sufficient number of tubes are kept at the desk. The loan policies for the maps are the same as those for books and other library materials.

The Patron

All librarians have a responsibility to assist users in the selection of materials. But the map librarian has to go beyond this service of selection (8). Most of the questions directed to him will concern the determining of geographic location. Therefore, he needs all the necessary tools at hand to perform this service, gazetteers, postal and shipping guides, map indexes, etc. The gazetteer or place name list is one of the most valuable types of reference materials in the map library. A great many places can be located by consulting some of the world atlases, but there are many questions that can be answered only by consulting gazetteers of small places or specific sets of maps. The large world atlases, which offer the most extensive general lists of names and have the added advantage of having maps in the same volume for quick reference, are frequently the first reference tools searched (9).

Of great value also are atlases of special countries which have gazetteers in them, and the publications from the U.S. Board on Geographic Names.

Other reference aids which may supplement the atlases and gazetteers are the census reports, postal guides, road guides, guidebooks, etc. Then there are the pamphlets and brochures that may come from your travel bureaus, state agencies, and foreign embassies. The various indexes that accompany certain map series or sets of maps are valuable reference aids in that they show the extent of mapping done for certain areas and may even assist you in locating a given sheet. The *Index to Topographic Mapping in the [States]* is also used to show holdings.

In addition to helping the patron select his materials and locate certain geographical areas, the map librarian has a responsibility to help him buy maps, i.e., advice on what to buy and where to buy them. A file of publishers' and dealers' catalogs should make it very easy to render this kind of assistance.

Finally, make a periodic check of map files for curled, badly wrinkled, or torn maps, and pull them for mending. Clara LeGear's manual (3) is an excellent source for the care and preservation of maps.

Literature Cited

1. Current, Charles E. / The Acquisition of Maps for School (and Other Small) Libraries, *Wilson Library Bulletin* 45:578-583 (Feb 1971).
2. Fetros, John G. / Developing the Map Collection in Smaller Libraries, SLA *Geography and Map Division Bulletin* 85, 24-25 (Sep 1971).
3. LeGear, Clara / Maps—Their Care, Repair, and Preservation in Libraries, rev. ed. Washington, D.C., Library of Congress, Division of Maps, 1956.
4. Ref. (3) p. 1-3.
5. Ref. (3) p. 5.
6. Ref. (3) p. 13-15.
7. White, Robert C. / Map Librarianship, *Special Libraries* 61 (no. 5): 233-235 (May/ Jun 1970).
8. Ref. (7) p. 234.
9. Irish, Kathleen / What About Gazetteers? *Library Journal* 447-449 (Mar 15, 1950).

Map Cataloging

FRANCES K. DREW

At the Georgia Tech Library, the Library of Congress system of classification is used. The Georgia Tech Library follows the cataloging and classification of the Library of Congress in its book catalog so as to take the fullest advantage possible of the services of the MARC II format of cataloging. Georgia Tech has participated in this project from its beginning; because Machine Readable Map Cataloging is also available, advantage is also taken of that program.

Some brief note of varying opinions concerning map cataloging should be made: Most librarians agree that some cataloging is necessary, but they disagree on a classification. The problem is that the Library of Congress classification and the Anglo-American Cataloging Rules for maps are based on an author–title type of entry, as in book cataloging, and others, represented by the American Geographical Society, feel that area is of primary importance.

Actually, most maps are asked for by area, but the subject catalog and the call number are adequate to take care of this. Then too, in a computerized system, as used by the Library of Congress and Georgia Tech, a map citation can be found quite easily under any number of headings.

So, Georgia Tech uses the geographical section of class "G" of the LC classification scheme, and we accept all modifications as they are issued. This schedule also includes atlas cataloging, but since atlases are part of the book collection, they are not considered here.

In the LC classification, *Area* is considered most important, and this is shown in the call number. The *subject* of the map is secondary, and this is indicated in the subject headings. In the class "G" volume, the schedules assign the area numbers; the tables at the end of the map numbers assign the subject subdivisions.

Frances K. Drew is catalog librarian, Price Gilbert Memorial Library, Georgia Institute of Technology, Atlanta, Ga.

Area Number

Each geographical area for maps has five numbers assigned to it,
e.g., Georgia's call numbers are G3920–3924. These five numbers are
divided according to a specific plan.

1. *General Area.* This is shown by a zero at the end of the call number. This usually indicates a base map or outline map. It does not
   use a Cutter number, e.g., G3920 1959 .U5. This is a map of
   Georgia (see Figure 1).

G3920
1959   U. S. Geological Survey.
.U5   Georgia. Compiled in 1932; ed. of 1933.
Reprinted in 1959. Washington, 1959.
    map 43 x 37 in.

    Scale 1:500,000.
    "Lambert conformal conic projection; North
American datum."
    1. Georgia—Maps.
    I. Title.

Figure 1.

2. *Subject* is indicated by a 1 at the end of the call number. The
   Cuttering is 1 time only. The number, G3921 .G52 1955 .G4,
   denotes a map of the state parks of Georgia. Refer to Figure 2.

G3921
.G52   Georgia. Dept. of State Parks, Historic Sites
1955   and Monuments
.G4   Official map of the Dept. of State Parks, in
conjunction with the Roadside Parks Division of
the State Highway Dept. [Atlanta, 1955]
    col. map 30 x 25 in.

    Scale ca. 1: 950,000.
    Includes table of locations and facilities.
    Text and illus. on verso.
    Title on outside, when folded: Official State
parks map.

(a)

```
G3921
.G52    Georgia, Dept. of State Parks, Historic Sites and Monuments.
1955       Official map of the Dept. of State Parks. [1955] (Card 2)
.G4
           1. Parks—Georgia—Maps.
           2. Georgia—Maps.
           I. Georgia. State Highway Dept.
           II. Title: Official State parks map.
           III. Title.
```

(b)

Figure 2.

3. A *Region* or *Natural Feature* is shown by a 2 at the end of the call
   number, e.g., G3922 .C5 1960 .U5, a map of the Chattahoochee
   National Forest in Georgia. The Cuttering is 1 time only. (See
   Figure 3.)

```
G3922
.C5     U.S. Forest Service. Southern Region.
1960       Chattahoochee National Forest, Georgia, 1960.
.U5     Reduced photographically, assembled and traced at Regional
           Office, Atlanta, Georgia, 1938, by F. F. Claflin. Rev. and
           traced by Helen D. O'Neill, 1953. [Washington?] 1960.
           col. map 23 x 49 in.

           Scale ca. 1:127,500.
           "Polyconic projection, 1927 North American datum."
           "Class D map."
```

(a)

```
G3922
.C5     U.S. Forest Service. Southern Region. Chattahoochee
1960       National Forest, Georgia, 1960. (Card 2)
.U5
           1. Chattahoochee National Forest—Maps.
           I. Title.
```

(b)

Figure 3.

4. *Political Division* is denoted by a 3 at the end of the call number,
   e.g., G3923 .D5 1961 .D6. A map of De Kalb County, Georgia (as
   seen in Figure 4). The Cuttering is 1 time only.

```
G3923
.D5      Dolph Map Company, Inc., Fort Lauderdale, Fla.
1961       Dolph's map of De Kalb County, Georgia. Fort Lauderdale,
.D6      Fla. [1961?]
            col. map 23 x 36 in.

            Scale ca. 1:250,000.
            Includes: "Secondary Schools," "Places of Interest," and
         "Street Index."

            1. De Kalb Co., Ga.—Road Maps.
            I. Title: Map of De Kalb County, Georgia.
            II. Title.
```

Figure 4.

5. *City* or *Town* is denoted by a 4 at the end of the call number. If necessary, 2 Cutter numbers may be used; e.g., G3924 .A8 1965 .A83 denotes a map of Atlanta, Georgia (see Figures 5 and 6).

```
G3924
.A8      Atlanta Convention Bureau
1965       Map of Atlanta, Georgia. [Atlanta, 1965?]
.A83       col. map 15 x 11 in. on sheet 23 x 11 in.

            Scale ca. 1:58,000.
            Locates 63 "Points of Interest."
            Inset: [Downtown Section]
            Descriptive text and illus. on verso.

            1. Atlanta Metropolitan area—Maps.
            2. Atlanta—Maps.
            I. Title.
```

Figure 5.

```
G3924
.A8P2    Atlanta Region Metropolitan Planning Commission.
1967       Detailed base map, Atlanta region: major street names.
.A82     Atlanta, 1967.
            col. map 41 x 43 in.

            Scale ca. 1:102,000.
            Base map from Feb. 1967 aerial photography (ARMPC)
            Location sketch, "Five county Metropolitan planning dis-
         trict," includes Fulton, Cobb, Gwinnett, DeKalb, Clayton,
         Douglas, Rockdale and Henry counties.
                              (Continued on next card)
```

(a)

```
G3924
.A8P2   Atlanta Region Metropolitan Planning Commission.
1967        Detailed base map, Atlanta region: major street names.
.A82        1967. (Card 2)


            1. Atlanta metropolitan area—Road maps.
            2. Atlanta—Maps.
            I. Title.
```

(b)

Figure 6.   G3924 .A8P2 1967 .A82 denotes a street map of Atlanta, Georgia.

Date

Maps always have a date in the call number. The date may have various meanings. It may indicate 1) the imprint date (see Figure 7), 2) the date of the information given, or 3) the historical period.

```
G3701
.C3     U.S. Geological Survey.
1963        United States: Water resource development. Ed. of Jan.
.U6         1963. [Washington, 1963]
            col. map 50 x 40 in. on 2 sheets 50 x 25 in.

            Scale 1:2,500,000; 1 in. equals approx. 40 mi.
            "Albers equal area projection, based on standard parallels
            29½ [degrees] and 45½ [degrees]. North American datum."
            Shows flood control, irrigation, navigation and power
            development activities of Dept. of the Army, Dept. of the
            Interior and Tennessee Valley Authority.
            Insets: Alaska.—Hawaii.—Major Drainage areas.—Puerto
            Rico and Virgin Islands.
            1. Water resources development—U.S.—Maps.
            2. U.S.—Maps.
            I. Title.
```

Figure 7.

Point 2, the date of the material depicted, is examined in Figure 8. Figure 8 shows one finding of the 1960 census, though not published until several years later.

G3701
.E68   U.S. Bureau of the Census.
1960   Population with high school education or more, by counties of
.U5   the United States: 1960. Prepared by Geography Division, Bureau
         of the Census. U.S. Dept. of Commerce. Washington, U.S. Govt.
         Print. Off., 1966.
              col. map 24 x 36 in. (Its United States maps, GE-50, no. 9)
              Scale: 1:5,000,000.
              "Albers equal area projection: standard parallels 29½
         [degrees] and 45½ [degrees]"

(a)

G3701
.E68   U.S. Bureau of the Census. Population with high school education
1960   or more, by counties of the United States: 1960. 1966. (Card 2)
.U5
              "Educational data from the 1960 Census of population."
              Insets: [Hawaii] – [Alaska]

         1. Education–U.S.–1945–   –Maps.
         2. Education, Secondary, 1945–   –Statistics.
         3. U.S.–Maps.
         I. Title. II. Series

(b)

Figure 8.

Figure 9 shows a condition covering a period of time, 1939-1964,
which would take the beginning date of its information, even though
the imprint date is considerably later.

G3701
.J15   U.S. Bureau of the Census.
1939   Percent change in the value of farm products sold per acre of
.U5   land in farms, by counties of the United States: 1939-1964.
         Prepared by Geography Division, Bureau of the Census, U.S.
         Dept. of Commerce, Washington, U.S. Govt. Print. Off., 1970.
              col. map 26 x 39 in. (Its United States maps, GE-50, no. 32.)
              Scale 1:5,000,000.
              "Albers equal area projection; standard parallels 29½
         [degrees] and 45½ [degrees]"
              Includes 3 tables.
              Inset: [Hawaii]

         1. Field crops–U.S.–Maps.
         2. U.S.–Maps.
         I. Title.

Figure 9.

Point 3, a modern map of an historical period or event needs two dates in the call number: the original date, and the imprint date. For example, G3924 .A8 1864 .G41 1964 would depict a map concerned with the Siege of Atlanta in 1864, but printed in 1964. The card is in Figure 10.

```
G3924
.A8      Georgia. State Highway Dept.
1864        Civil War Centennial, City of Atlanta, showing the area of
.G41     the three major engagements and deployment of Union and
1964     Confederate forces during the summer of 1864. Prepared by
         State Highway Dept. of Georgia, Division of Highway Plan-
         ning. [Atlanta, 1964]
            col. map 54 x 84 in.

            Scale ca. 1:24,000.
            Indexed for points of interest.

         1. Atlanta Campaign, 1864—Maps.
         2. Atlanta—Maps.
         I. Title.
```

Figure 10.

Entry

Maps are ordinarily entered under the person or organization responsible:

1. Individual cartographer, e.g., L'Enfant, Pierre Charles, 1755–1825 (see Figure 11).

```
G3921
.E75     Andrews, Ernest M.
1966        Georgia's fabulous treasure hoards: 71 authentic locations
.A4      based on factual information, by Ernest M. Andrews.
         Hapeville, Ga. 1966.
            col. map 35 x 40 in.

            Scale ca. 1:1,470,000; not "1/500,000."
            Includes illus. and 2 inset maps.
            Issued also with text of same title.

         1. Treasure-trove—Georgia—Maps.
         2. Georgia—Maps.
         I. Title.
```

Figure 11.

2. Governmental agency, e.g., U.S. Geological Survey (Figure 12).

```
G3921
.C5      Georgia, Dept. of Mines, Mining, and Geology.
1939       Geologic map of Georgia. Prepared by the Georgia Division
.G3      of Mines, Mining and Geology in cooperation with the U.S.
         Dept. of the Interior, Geological Survey. [Atlanta] 1939.
           col. map 20 x 30 in.

           Scale 1,500,000.

         1. Geology—Georgia—Maps.
         2. Georgia—Maps.
         I. U.S. Geological Survey.
         II. Title.
```

Figure 12.

3. Commercial agency, e.g., General Drafting Company (note Figure 13).

```
G3851
.P2      Rand, McNally and Company
1958       Touring map of metropolitan Washington, D.C.
.R3      [Prepared for] Texaco. [Chicago? 1958?]

           Scale ca. 1:69,696; 1 in. equals approx. 1.1 mi.
           Title on outside when folded: Texaco Street map of
         Washington, D.C.

         1. Washington, D.C.—Maps.
         2. Washington metropolitan area—Maps.
         I. Title: Street map of Washington, D.C.
         II. Title.
```

Figure 13.

4. Society, e.g., National Geographic Society (Figure 14).

```
G3300
1952     National Geographic Society, Washington, D.C.
.N3          Cartographic Division.
             North America. Compiled and drawn in the Cartographic
         Section of the National Geographic Society, James M. Darley,
         chief cartographer. Washington, 1952.
             col. map 40 x 50 in.

             Scale 1:11,000,000 or 173.6 mi. to the in.
             "Chamberlin trimetric projection."
             Issued with the National Geographic magazine, v. 101,
         no. 3, Mar. 1952.

             1. North America—Maps.
             I. Title.
```

Figure 14.

Call Number

The call number on a monographic map may have three or more elements.

   a. G3920 A general map of Georgia,

       1959   Imprint date,

       .U5   Cutter number for author (see Figure 15).

```
G3920
1959     U.S. Geological Survey.
.U5          Georgia. Compiled in 1932; ed. of 1933. Reprinted
         1959. Washington, 1959.
             map 43 x 37 in.

             Scale 1:500,000.
             "Lambert conformal conic projection; North American
         datum."

             1. Georgia—Maps.
             I. Title.
```

Figure 15.

  b. As seen in Figure 16:

    G3841 A subject map of Maryland,

    .C5   Cutter from table for subject (geology),

    1968   Imprint date,

    .M3   Cutter number for author.

G3841
.C5   MARYLAND. Geological Survey.
1968   Geologic map of Maryland. Compiled and edited by Emery T.
.M3   Cleaves, Jonathan Edwards, Jr., and John D. Glaser; prepared
            under the supervision of Kenneth N. Weaver. [Baltimore] 1968.
              col. map 35 x 50 in. fold. in envelope 11 x 8 in.

            Scale 1:250,000.
          Includes 2 col. cross sections, and "Inferred stratigraphic
          and facies relationship in the Maryland Piedmont."
          Insets: Metamorphic zones in the Maryland Piedmont.—Source
          map: Data other than county geological maps [with bibliography]

            1. Geology—Maryland—Maps.
            2. Maryland—Maps.
            I. Title.

Figure 15.

c. As in Figure 17 (a)—(c):
  G3701 For a subject map of the United States,
  .S524 Cutter from table for Siege of Atlanta,
  1865   Date of information depicted,
  .U2   Cutter number for author,
  1891   Imprint date.

G3701
.S524   Ulffers, Herman A.
1865   Map illustrating the Siege of Atlanta, Ga., by the United
.U2   States Forces under Command of Maj. Gen. W. T. Sherman
1891   from the passage of Peachtree Creek, July 19, 1864 to the
            Commencement of the movement upon the Enemy's lines of
            Communication South of Atlanta August 26, 1864. Surveyed
            and compiled under the direction of Capt. O. M. Poe. Drawn in
            June, July, August and Sept., 1865, by Capt. H. A. Ulffers.
            [Washington? 1865]
              col. map 16 x 17 in.
                                              (See next card)

(a)

```
G3701
.S524   Ulffers, Herman A. Map illustrating the Siege of Atlanta, Ga.
1865      [1865] (Card 2)
.U2
1891      Scale ca. 1:50,000.
             "Accompanying report of Capt. O. M. Poe, Corps of Engin-
          eers, U.S. Army. Series 1, Vol. 38, Part 1, Page 137."
             From U.S. War Dept. Atlas to accompany the Official
          Records of the Union and Confederate armies 1861–1865.
          Washington, 1891–1895. Plate 88, no. 1.
                                              (See next card)
```

(b)

```
G3701
.S524   Ulffers, Herman A. Map illustrating the Siege of Atlanta, Ga.
1865      [1865] (Card 3)
.U2
1891      On same sheet: Brooks, A. F. Map illustrating the Operations
          of the Army under Com'd of Maj. Gen. W. T. Sherman in
          Georgia. 1864.

          1. Atlanta Campaign, 1864—Maps.
          I. Title: The Siege of Atlanta.
```

(c)

Figure 17.

Serials

Monographic maps make up only a small portion of the map collection. The most numerous maps are issued in serials or sets. According to
Dr. Walter W. Ristow, Chief of the Map Division at the Library of Congress, that library receives about 90,000 maps annually, which includes
some 20,000 monographic maps. Though on a much smaller scale, this
proportion is roughly represented in the map collection at Georgia
Tech. The majority of maps are serials or sets and, as each succeeding
one arrives, the map librarian needs only to check it on its index map,
add it to the Map Serial Record File, and affix the call number for it to
be ready for use. Hence, this discussion will only include those that are
handled in cataloging.

Serial maps are issued either annually or at some regular interval
and are intended to be continued indefinitely. Figure 18 is an example.
An explanation follows:

G3921   This represents the call number for Georgia state transpor-
.P2   tation maps issued annually.
year   The word "year" is used in the call number on the cards
.G4   to show its frequency, and so that new cards will not have
           to be made each year as new maps are issued.

G3921
.P2   Georgia. Division of Highway Planning.
year   Georgia State highway system and connections. Prepared by
.G4   State Highway Dept. of Georgia, Division of Highway Planning,
          in cooperation with U.S. Dept. of Commerce, Bureau of Public
          Roads. [Atlanta] 1921-
             col. maps on sheets 34 x 32 in. or smaller, fold. to 9 x 4 in.

          Scales vary.
          Titles and subtitles vary.
          Title on outside, when folded, varies, but each indicates
       that it is the official state highway map.

       1. Georgia—Road maps.
       I. U.S. Bureau of Public Roads.
       II. Title: Official highway map: Georgia.

Figure 18.

The maps belonging to this serial are marked with the actual "years"
that they represent, e.g., the latest Georgia transportation map would
be: G3921 .P2 1972 .G4.
    Another example is Figure 19:
    e.g., G3923 This represents a map of Chatham County, Georgia,
         .C45   reissued at set intervals.
         year   The call number of each map takes the year of its issue.
         .G4

G3923
.C45   Georgia. Division of Highway Planning.
year   Chatham County, Georgia.
.G4   [Atlanta?] 19
             maps 33 x 37 in.

             Scale ca. 1:63,360.
             Includes 3 insets of unincorporated settlements, including
          Bloomingdale and Isle of Hope.

          1. Chatham Co., Ga.—Road maps.

Figure 19.

Maps issued in *sets* may be a number of maps issued at the same time, under the same general heading, or it may be a number of maps issued at irregular intervals, under the same general heading (see Figure 20).

G3932s   The "s" here means "set": This is for a set of maps of the
.E9   Florida Everglades.
63   The set has a scale of 1:63,000
.U5   Author Cutter

G3932s
.E9   U.S. Soil Conservation Service.
63   Florida: Everglades drainage district, physical land conditions
.U5   [by] U.S. Dept. of Agriculture, Soil Conservation Service [and]
           University of Florida Agricultural Experiment Station. Wash-
           ington, 1946.
              38 col. maps 22 x 18 in.

              Scale ca. 1:63,000.
              Accompanied by Index map 22 x 18 in.
              Library has sheets 2–7, 9–34, 36–38.

              1. Land—Florida—Maps.
              2. Everglades, Fla.—Maps.
              I. Florida. Agricultural Experiment Station, Gainesville.
              II. Title.

Figure 20.

The maps belonging to this set are marked: G3932s .E9 63 .U5 no. 1, etc.
   Another example of this kind of marking follows.
   G3971s   This indicates a set of geological maps of Alabama having
   .C5   a different scale on each map.
   var.   "Var" means "various" scales.
   .A5   Author Cutter

G3971s
.C5   Alabama. Geological Survey.
var.   Map[s]
.A5   Montgomery, Geological Survey of Alabama.
              col. maps 20 x 26 in. or smaller.

              Scales vary.
              Alabama. Geological Survey. Map series.
              Prepared by U.S. Geologic Survey in cooperation with the
           Geological Survey of Alabama.

              1. Geology—Alabama—Maps.
              2. Alabama—Maps.
              I. Alabama—Geological Survey. Map series.

Figure 21.

The maps belonging to this set are marked: G3971s .C5 var. .A5 no. 1, etc.

Map Cards

All map cards have certain elements that are also common to book cards: the call number, author, title, and imprint, with which we are all familiar.

However, some note should be made in regard to the title. If two titles are given on the same map, the more appropriate one is used, and the variant title is given in a note, and traced.

Other elements pertaining specifically to maps need some explanation. These include the following.

1. Collation: This tells the number of maps and gives the size. (col. map 32 x 48 in.; or, map 10 x 14 in.). Georgia Tech measures its maps to the nearest inch; the Library of Congress uses centimeters to measure its maps. Maps are measured, first by height, then by width.

2. Scale: This is the ratio of the distances and areas shown on the map to the corresponding distances and areas on the earth's surface. For example, if the card reads scale 1:25,000, the scale is given on the map. However, if the entry on the card appears as scale ca. 1:25,000, the scale is measured by the cataloger.

3. Projection: If stated on the map, this is put in a quoted note, e.g., "Mercator projection."

4. Notes: As in book cataloging, these mention identifying features. "Blue line print," "Relief shown by contours and spot heights," "Text and illus. on verso," etc.

5. Insets: These are smaller maps relating to the main map and inserted around its edges. If small or unimportant, they may be covered by a general note. If they are to be listed, the cataloger begins in the upper left corner and proceeds in a clockwise sequence.

6. Subject Tracings: Because the call number of a map, except in those numbers ending with a 1, e.g., G3961, usually indicates the area, the tracings indicate the subject material of the map. The subject tracings for a geological map of Tennessee would be, as in Figure 22:

1. Geology—Tennessee—Maps.
2. Tennessee—Maps.

```
G3961
.C5      Hardeman, William D.
1966        Geologic map of Tennessee, by William D. Hardeman, assisted
.H3      by Robert A. Miller and George D. Swingle. [Nashville] State
         of Tennessee, Division of Geology, 1966.
             4 col. maps 45 x 36 in. or 45 x 24 in. fold. in envelopes
         11 x 8 in.

             Scale 1:250,000.
             "Contour interval 100 ft., with supplementary contours at
         50-ft. intervals."
```

(a)

```
G3961
.C5      Hardeman, William D. Geologic map of Tennessee.
1966        1966. (Card 2)
.H3
             Each sheet includes "Map showing sources of geological
         information," and index map of sheets.

         1. Geology—Tennessee—Maps.
         2. Tennessee—Maps.
         I. Tennessee. Division of Geology.
         II. Title.
```

(b)

Figure 22.

7. Added Entries: A title entry is usually given, but other added entries are used sparingly. Added entries for co-cartographers or joint compilers are traced by the Library of Congress but Georgia Tech does not usually trace them, since area is more important in the questions asked by the library's clientele.

Management and Administration of Special Materials

ARTHUR T. KITTLE

Before discussing the management and administration of special materials, the terms *management* and *administration* will be defined within the framework of this particular paper. The term *special materials* also will be defined. Then a look will be taken at the functions of planning as an element of administration, including some program planning methods with particular reference to special materials in a library operation.

Personnel is another element of the management function that deserves serious attention in the special materials area. This includes the selection of specialists to deal with these materials, the practices of personnel administration, the orientation and training of these specialists, as well as their job motivation and evaluation, and their status in the organization.

A fourth topic to be considered is library organization and communication with reference to special materials. This will be followed by brief references to fiscal management as it relates to special materials. Then measurement and evaluation as functions in the management of special materials will be considered with a suggestion concerning library automation and its implications in the special materials area.

MANAGEMENT AND ADMINISTRATION OF SPECIAL MATERIALS

Authorities in the management field define the activity of managing in numerous ways. Terry defines *management* as that "activity which plans, organizes, and controls the operations of the basic elements of men, materials, machines, methods, money, and markets, providing direction and coordination, and giving leadership to human efforts, so as to achieve the sought objectives of the enterprise" (1).

Dr. Arthur T. Kittle is associate director, Price Gilbert Memorial Library, Georgia Institute of Technology, Atlanta, Ga.

Davis refers to management as the function of executive leadership. He says: "Its organic subfunctions are the creative planning, organizing, and controlling of the organizational activities for which the executive is responsible. They have to do with accomplishment of the group and project objectives of the organization" (2).

Using the term administration rather than management, Newman states that "administration is the guidance, leadership, and control of the efforts of a group of individuals toward some common goal. Clearly, the good administrator is one who enables the group to achieve its objectives with a minimum expenditure of resources and effort and the least interference with other worthwhile activities." (3).

Special Materials

Special materials include government publications, technical reports, maps, proprietary company publications, company and trade literature, patents and trademarks, audiovisual, and related miscellaneous materials.

From a management, or an administrative, point of view, it seems reasonable to look at special materials as a category of library resources for which a set of general policies might be formulated. These policies should relate to those set forth for standard book resources in the form of monographs and serials.

Looking at these materials administratively, or from a managerial or functional point of view, we might categorize them in three ways as follows:

1. materials requiring special access control and circulation,
2. materials requiring special equipment for their use,
3. materials for which special bibliographic controls are needed, or materials requiring special organization by a specialized staff which can likewise devise or interpret whatever special bibliographic controls are needed.

In the first group, those requiring special access control, we find those textual or illustrative materials that are unusually susceptible to mutilation or theft as well as those which must be restricted because of governmental security classification or company proprietary regulations. These items include archives, manuscripts, fine prints, incunabula and other rarities, company or governmental and military technical reports.

In the second group requiring special equipment, we find the extensive and rapidly growing area of microtexts, sound recordings, motion pictures, slides, punched cards, video and computer tapes.

In the third group requiring special bibliographic control we find photographs, prints, vertical file materials, technical reports, sheet maps, sheet music, government documents, as well as a variety of ephemera or fugitive miscellaneous items. Materials may fall into this category

because of a particular library's policies on physical storage or bibliographic treatment. They may be organized in hard bindings and freely
cataloged as if they were important monographs or serial literature. To
some extent the quantity involved, i.e., the size of the collection, will
determine how this category is treated. This may, indeed, be a budgetary
problem of considerable magnitude. Some materials in this category
may involve special use controls as well as special bibliographic controls.
Examples are phonorecords, manuscripts, and fine prints.

In larger academic libraries these three types of special materials may
occupy 10%-15% of the total square footage for library materials. They
generally require larger reading spaces per reading station, and they
usually demand greater staff effort to acquire, organize, control, and
service. On a unit cost basis, they usually constitute the most expensive
part of the library collection. Thus their place in the library program
should receive careful evaluation.

Because of the expense of acquiring and processing, it is desirable to
develop general statements of policy for handling of some special materials,
such as government documents, technical reports, and maps. For other
materials, the information contained in these sources would be acquired
as a natural extension of general selection policies irrespective of
whether or not the item is issued in microform, or published as a government document, or restricted in any way in its use. In other words,
if a library collects in depth in a particular subject area, the item will be
acquired regardless of its physical format or specialized nature. Again,
because of the costs involved in building special collections, be certain
that there is a definite need for the material by the library users.

Special materials should be given adequate attention in the overall
cataloging policies of the library. It is likewise necessary to find a compe-
tent person to manage a program in one of these specialized fields. The
job market for rare specializations is slim, and recruiting and training require a great deal of effort. Special physical housing and equipment for
many of these special materials are also essential. Before launching into a
program to build and service any collections of special materials, consider
all these factors, visit other libraries where similar materials exist, and consult with recognized authorities in order to find the best possible advice.

A final general policy decision one might need to make is the degree
of physical centralization to be achieved. For some special materials,
there is little need to centralize. The need for a staff specialist, special
equipment, or special physical or environmental facilities, however, may
make it desirable for others.

Planning with Reference to Special Materials

Needless to say, any institution or group should define its goals, not
only with an understanding of what these goals or objectives are but

also knowing the speed with which such aims can be achieved. A general view of library goals must be maintained, and all individual decisions involved in numerous complex issues should be directed toward the long-range objective. Any program planning to formulate specific goals leading toward the overall objective should include participation of the staff as well as participation of the user whose needs and interests are of primary concern in setting goals and target dates.

Do not overlook the program relationships with officials in the institutional environment of the library. Cultivate and educate the trustees or regents, the president, the controller, and other administrative officers. This is not only appropriate, it is necessary in order to create an understanding of and support for the place of the library in the scheme of things.

There are numerous other program planning methods worth mentioning. Remeber that the use of standards or objective measures is both effective and impressive. The use of consultants and outside survey teams can be beneficial. Libraries in general have failed to utilize the techniques of more specialized planning and operational research.

PERSONNEL

The term *administration* has been defined as the art of getting things done through people. Surely nothing in the personnel area is more important than finding the best possible person for every position, regardless of the importance of the job. This is true to an even greater extent when dealing with the selection of more highly specialized personnel needed to work with special materials.

Personnel classification, now widely applied in libraries, can be helpful in staffing the special materials area. There is today an increasing need for specialized skills in libraries, including linguistic skills, subject specialists, and numerous technical specializations, such as computer programmers, and systems analysts. Personnel classification is a constantly evolving matter, just as a progressive library organization is a constantly evolving entity. Any complex operation needs reexamination and possible reorganization.

In passing, the author would like to mention other applicable facets of personnel. Salary administration is one. Salary alone does not, of course, determine a person's happiness on the job, but it is indeed a most sensitive and significant factor.

As libraries grow and become more complex, an orientation and training program is decidedly worthwhile. Orientation is essentially generalized instruction, but more formalized training classes may also be considered worth their time and effort.

With reference to personnel, administrators should be concerned with three objectives: 1) job productivity; 2) advancement of the overall library program; and 3) the individual's personal development and satisfaction on the job. These can be achieved through a program of personnel development with suitable training and supervision. This development is measured by formal performance reviews and achievement ratings. Without good supervisors who can train, direct, encourage, sympathize, and review, the best of policies have no effect.

Staff motivation is difficult to achieve, but it is as important as salary and fringe benefits. A good supervisor can convey a sense of purpose. He can show how each task is important in the overall scheme of things. He not only shows interest in the individual's job problems, but he also seeks suggestions from the employee for improving the organization.

The supervisor should also review regularly the contribution of the individual as well as his professional development. Employees want to know where they stand, and if conducted honestly and fairly, the performance rating can be a valuable tool.

Keep in mind that today all of us, while perhaps not status seekers per se, are ever conscious of our status within our own particular environment. The librarian in the academic community is increasingly interested in his academic status or faculty rank. Library staff members have been encouraged to move toward unionization for reasons other than wages or working conditions. Librarians today participate more than ever before in professional associations at local, regional, national, and international levels.

LIBRARY ORGANIZATION AND COMMUNICATION

Today's modern library structure deals with an ever increasing volume of the traditional forms of information contained in monographs and serial literature. It also provides for greater numbers of special materials—the microforms, phonorecords, films, computer programs, digitally stored data banks, etc. Staff growth, like the nature of these materials, is likewise characterized by greater diversity and specialization. To this mass of specialized materials and specialized staff, new techniques of operation are now being added, including increased use of mechanization and automation. All of this together quite naturally affects the organization, requiring reassessment, reorganization, and restructuring to meet swiftly changing needs. These factors of change demand new patterns of administrative organization. They require coordination and improved methods of communication.

Successful communication is a keystone of good administration, and yet communication is one of the most difficult of all functions to achieve. It should flow upward and horizontally across the organization, just as much as it should flow downward. Failure to communicate causes misunderstanding of objectives, feelings of isolation, and working at cross-purposes. Failure to communicate is expensive, and it has an adverse effect on morale. The reason good communication is hard to achieve is the absence of a single formula that can be applied to it. Nothing contributes so much to good communication as a library-wide awareness of its importance and a constant effort to inform the right people when something important occurs, when a new policy is being formed, or when a decision is reached. Such a general spirit is necessary for successful communication. The mere existence of certain communication machinery likewise helps to achieve the communication objective.

Budget

Budget administration, or fiscal management, is a year-round operation, not only with reference to special materials but also with reference to the entire library program. In passing it should be mentioned that there is the regular and continuing procedure of preparing, presenting, and negotiating the budget. The budgetary process becomes more complex as sources of funds multiply, as institutions become larger, and as the organization proliferates. No library should operate without a set of goals with projections that clearly forecast well in advance of a fiscal year.

Measurement and Evaluation

Libraries have a long way to go in the use of statistics, or other quantitative measurements, for the purpose of management. Measurement is one of the techniques used in surveys, time and motion studies, simulation, operations research, the critical path method, most qualitative studies, standards of support and standards of use, as well as cost accounting. Indeed, it is an important aspect of accreditation methodology. These techniques of management can be of assistance to the administration of special materials. They can provide objective data which can serve as definitive evidence of need, efficiency, or accomplishment. Remember, however, that measurement techniques only help to solve the problem. They do not provide the solution.

LIBRARY AUTOMATION

Some of the administrative considerations of library automation will be discussed in this section. After defining this subject from a library management point of view, some background with reference to automation's challenge to librarians as well as some practical problems of application will be included. Then a brief look will be taken at four major administrative areas involved in library automation and how it affects them: 1) personnel, 2) organization, 3) costs, and 4) control.

In the area of personnel, the concern is with educating librarians for change. Our current attitudes toward automation need considerable attention. The library administrator, like the business manager, will find himself involved with the selection and organization of a data processing staff as well as the education and training of that staff. There are special data processing personnel problems not found in other aspects of personnel work. Consideration must be given by the librarian to the use of consultants, and his attention ultimately will be devoted to the possibility of a library data processing manager. These are some of the factors included in the first of the four major administrative areas— personnel.

In the second area we shall consider, organization, there is, of course, the first and perhaps terrifying decision of whether or not to automate; what to do, once the decision is made; and then what to do first. Indeed, there is no doubt that automation has a profound effect upon your library organization.

Cost, our third administrative consideration, is an ever present factor in any undertaking, whether it is a business, an industrial money-making enterprise, or an endeavor to render professional service. The costs and economies of mechanization are major administrative concerns. The librarian, like the businessman, must weigh automation in terms of his library budget, and any program he chooses must be developed within the framework of that budget. These considerations include such cost elements as services and software, as well as equipment.

The fourth consideration is control as associated with library administrative policy and its relation to mechanized systems. Several library administrative control procedures should be mentioned. They include control forms, the audit, and other checks and balances. Responsibility and accountability go hand in hand, and the administration of any library considering automation must concern itself with the overall management of systems analysis, systems design, and the implementation of the particular system that is chosen.

Defining the Subject: A Library Administrative View

Diebold has said that, "Automation is more than a series of new machines and more basic than any particular hardware. It is a way of thinking as much as it is a way of doing. Automation is a new concept— the idea of self-regulating systems—and a new set of principles. Only when our political, industrial, and labor leadership understand this shall we gain the full benefits from automation. But this kind of understanding is still so rare in policy-making levels as to be almost an isolated phenomenon" (4).

In the world of business and industry today, top management personnel readily admit that machine technology has far outreached man's ability to utilize this new capability. During the past 25 years in which all major data processing machine developments have taken place, management's understanding of its uses and applications has increased little. If this is true in the business and industrial world, to what an even greater extent must it be true of the administrator in the profession of librarianship. True, like those in business and industry, librarians too have been busy in a traditional way with other important tasks, such as trying to satisfy the ever increasing demand for more materials and better service to readers. There seems to be too little time to consider new methods; too little time to cope with the problems of mechanization; too little time even for exposure to what automation can do. This is true in all types of libraries—academic, school, public, and special.

Certainly the need to focus attention on library automation has become critical. Some administrators feel it may already be too late. Today almost every issue of every professional journal speaks loudly of activities in this area. Librarians everywhere are experimenting with computerization.

Brief History

To look at the history and development of data processing equipment is to see the computer as an amalgamation and expansion of the capabilities of many common office machines that more than ever require direction and management by man. Without electric accounting machines, it is doubtful that World War II could have been won. While this equipment ground out the mundane tasks of the business world, the computer was also playing its role in the war. It came into being along with the atomic bomb. Which has made the greatest impact on civilization—the bomb or the computer—indeed remains a moot question.

In the business world the computer was first used as a scientific calculator, and human imagination was slow to catch up with its potentialities. Input/output capability was a major technical problem during the formative years. But very slowly business and industry began to accept the idea of automatic data processing. There was suspicion, distrust, and a lack of comprehension. And surely the same is true today in the library world.

Machine Effect on Library Management

Automatic data processing has been defined as "an organized way of thinking—not simply a machine process but an application of human knowledge within the bounds of machine capability" (5). Logic capabilities are built into modern computers with almost unlimited flexibility.

What the machine performs depends on what it is asked to do. The amount of human knowledge put into the system is in direct ratio to the payoff. Sometimes we forget that the machine is inanimate. It performs only as instructed. It takes no responsibility for its actions. This is perhaps one of the reasons why automation has presented the administrator with a new major problem.

Library Automation Needs

The basic motive behind the librarian's decision to begin, or to continue, if he has already begun, to use data processing equipment is no different from that which leads him to acquire additional resources or plan a new building. Need is established on the basis of sensible criteria. Does it, or will it, improve library service? Can it do the job more efficiently, more effectively, and at the same time more economically?

How, you may ask, does one determine whether or not automation is needed? There is no set formula, but there is a rule that applies in every case. Before buying, retaining, or replacing equipment, first determine the library needs. What must the library have in order to thrive and grow? Answer this question and then decide whether or not automatic equipment is required to satisfy your needs. If it is needed, then what is the equipment necessary to do the job?

In most instances, there is a need for conservatism in making the decision to use or expand a data processing capability. In some business and industrial enterprises the rule has been that estimated savings on new projects (that is, additions to an existing program of data processing) must be five to one. Although not strictly interpreted, management has decided that the five-to-one ratio prevents excess optimism and in fact produces savings closer to two-to-one. Data processing machine applications can and do save considerable money. Avoid the common mistake, however, of assuming that the machine is always the solution to a problem. Librarians, like business managers, will avoid the costs of such misconception only by thorough study and complete understanding.

Automation's Challenge to Library Administration

There is no question that the accelerated pace of change in technology creates in itself a serious challenge to library administration. Considerable attention must be devoted to the problems of putting new innovations to work. Indeed, technology is having a profound effect on the very processes of management itself. The basic concepts of administering a library must be reexamined in terms of new tools and new techniques available for managing any kind of enterprise.

Recent technological changes in themselves appear to be overwhelming. It is the rate of change, however, that seems to be a more significant phenomenon. Many factors are producing change in the future of libraries: population increases; education on a massive scale unknown before; mobility of a more educated population; and communication in every possible form.

An increasing emphasis upon science must be mentioned at this point. There is likewise greater motivation, especially government sponsored motivation, that affects this rate of change. Needless to say, numerous problems are created. But the point is that they are fundamentally administrative problems. They are primarily managerial in nature. And yet librarians have hardly begun to recognize them as problems at all.

Practical Problems of Application

Some librarians have begun to think about solutions in a fragmentary manner, let us say, as if the problem required a one-time solution. However, recognition and discussion of these administrative problems must be within the framework of a continuum of change that affects the foundations of library philosophy. Just as in business and industry, the planning process will play a more significant role in library operations. It is becoming increasingly more important that administrators exert positive influence on professional personnel, service operations, and creative activities. As suggested earlier, many accepted concepts of librarianship must change, and the new technologies themselves are altering the processes of effective library administration.

At the present time in libraries, the new technologies of information handling are beginning to be applied to the mechanization of work that is already performed manually. Most of what is being done is applied rather crudely. This application, however, contains within it the basis for substantial changes in the process of library management. To an even greater degree it serves as a foundation for extending the range of our capabilities. As librarians we have not yet begun to grasp the significance of this potentiality.

Literature Cited

1. Terry, George R. / *Principles of Management.* Homewood, Ill., Richard D. Irwin, Inc., 1953, p. 8.
2. Davis, Ralph C. / *The Fundamentals of Top Management.* New York, Harper, 1951, p. 785.
3. Newman, William H. / *Administrative Action.* Englewood Cliffs, N.J., Prentice-Hall, 1950, p. 1.
4. Diebold, John / *Beyond Automation: Managerial Problems of an Expanding Technology.* New York, McGraw-Hill, 1964, p. vii.
5. Smith, Paul T. / *How to Live with Your Computer: a Nontechnical Guide for Managers.* New York, American Management Association, 1965, p. 24.

Miscellaneous Special Materials

FRANCES E. KAISER

The five types of special materials brought together in this paper each justify separate treatment, in a longer presentation than the present chapter affords. Therefore, each will be treated in overview form, with references both to bibliographic tools and background readings which will lead the reader to further information.

The five types of materials to be examined follow:

1. reference materials, considered as a class, with special emphasis on specialized files, indexes, and collections within the jurisdiction of the reference department;
2. standards and specifications;
3. translations;
4. conference and symposium records;
5. dissertations and theses.

Despite the diversity of subject and format in these materials, they have at least five elements in common. First, they all pose problems in acquisition. Second, they often require special indexing and classification. Third, because of format they often require special housing separate from the regular book collection. Fourth, they usually require the use of bibliographic tools not normally found in small or medium-sized libraries. Fifth, for all of the above reasons, as well as their internal complexity, they are difficult for the reader to locate or use efficiently without the help of a reference librarian. Bearing these factors in mind, we will present each material in turn, considering selection and acquisition, housing, bibliographic control, and use problems where appropriate.

Frances E. Kaiser is head of the Department of Library Instruction, Price Gilbert Memorial Library, Georgia Institute of Technology, Atlanta, Ga.

I. REFERENCE MATERIALS

Reference materials are treated here as a class of specialized material, rather than individually by title or subject. Furthermore, the reference department often has jurisdiction over a variety of materials, both book and nonbook, requiring different types of bibliographic controls. It does so because the public often needs professional guidance in locating and using them.

A. Special Files Within the Reference Department

The following special files illustrate typical examples of such materials likely to be found in a large university library. They may be physically located in the reference department or bibliography area, or, in some cases, located elsewhere in the building but directly supervised by the reference staff.

1. *Ready Reference Collection:* In any library, it is usually necessary to keep a certain number of traditional reference tools adjacent to the reference desk. The collection serves the dual purpose of answering questions from the academic users and providing quick access to information for telephone requests. In a school which specializes in a given subject area, such as science and technology, the ready reference collection may be heavily slanted to tools in the subject disciplines of the university, with less emphasis on liberal arts and humanities. Each library must determine which titles are most necessary for its clientele. For example, in an engineering library, the collection would contain the following types of tools: subject directories, biographical directories, scientific and engineering handbooks, statistics sources, both general and special-subject encyclopedias, scientific and technical dictionaries, foreign language dictionaries (both general and scientifically oriented), buyer's guides, guides to the literature of various subject fields, yearbooks, and compendia of scientific and technical data.

If the ready reference collection is large, a small desk-top card catalog may be maintained by subject, giving the author and title of the tool in abridged form, as well as the call number. This catalog will also afford an analysis of key reference tools in greater depth or in more specific subject terms than the main card catalog, pinpointing chapters or sections within a given tool that contain special information not immediately obvious from the mere title of the book.

2. *Telephone Directories:* Out-of-town telephone directories constitute a valuable reference source. Depending upon the size of the library and its mission, the collection may be limited to the state in which the library is located, to all major cities, or may include a combination of both, plus directories of major foreign cities, such as London and Paris. The *International Yellow Pages* is another valuable tool in this connec-

tion. The collection may be filed alphabetically by the name of the city.

3. *Newspapers:* Microfilm files of local and national newspapers are often kept in or near the reference department. In the case of national papers, such as the *New York Times*, the *Wall Street Journal*, and the *National Observer*, the bound volumes of the indexes to such journals would be shelved adjacent to the microfilm files. Where the local newspaper does not provide an index, some libraries either maintain a clipping file of articles of local importance, or compile a card index to such articles. On a university campus, a useful project is to index all major institutional, faculty, alumni, and student organization news from the campus newspaper.

4. *Standards and Specifications:* Since this topic is one of the five types of special materials to be discussed in detail, it will not be covered at this point, other than to point out that special collections of standards and specifications are sometimes housed in or near the reference department. The reason for this is the frequency with which the user needs help in using standards.

5. *Miscellaneous Vertical Files:* Among the miscellaneous vertical files that may be kept under the jurisdiction of the reference department are the pamphlet file, the file of corporate annual reports, the file of annual reports from directors of libraries and presidents of universities, and the trade catalog file.

6. *Miscellaneous Files on Microfiche and Microfilm:* Still another type of special material that may be kept under the jurisdiction of the reference department is microform, either microfiche or microfilm. Examples of such files are as follows: 1) microfiche copies of annual reports to the Securities and Exchange Commission, by corporations listed on the New York Stock Exchange, the American Stock Exchange, and the Over-the-Counter Market; 2) conference papers on microfiche, such as papers of the American Institute of Aeronautics and Astronautics, or the Society of Automotive Engineers; 3) special sets of microfilm in cartridges, containing military specifications, military standards, and trade catalogs. In addition to the above types of files, which come on a subscription basis, there may be occasional copies of single dissertations ordered from other universities, or back files on microform of out-of-print periodicals. The largest collection of microfiche and microfilm, usually housed in a separate department of technical reports, is the technical reports collection of Atomic Energy Commission, National Aeronautics and Space Administration, and other U.S. Government research reports.

7. *College Catalogs:* Last, the reference department may be responsible for maintaining a collection of college catalogs from other universities. In some areas, cooperative agreements exist between university libraries to maintain permanent archival files of such catalogs in the subject specialty of the university, such as engineering, life sciences, or agriculture. Otherwise, the latest edition of the catalog is placed on public display in an area convenient to students and faculty.

B. Bibliographic Tools for Selecting and Using Reference Materials

The scope of this paper precludes coverage of individual reference books; but it may be well to call attention to a few important bibliographic tools for selecting and using reference materials. These aids are listed in Section 21 of the Bibliography, Refs. 1–30.

Most of the following titles need no introduction. For example, there is Constance Winchell's *Guide to Reference Books* (*27*), which has gone through eight editions and which is kept up-to-date by supplements compiled by Eugene P. Sheehy (*22, 23*). Attention is also called to its British counterpart, *Guide to Reference Material*, edited by Albert J. Walford, in three volumes (*25*). A recent compilation is *American Reference Books Annual* (*2*), published for the first time in 1970, under the editorship of B. S. Wynar. Another new title of interest is *Government Reference Books* (*8*), compiled by S. Wynkoop and to be published biennially beginning with the 1968/69 edition. Still another recent compilation is *Fundamental Reference Sources*, edited by Frances Neel Cheney and published by the American Library Association in 1971 (*5*).

Guides to Special Subject Areas: A frequently overlooked and neglected source of valuable information about reference materials is the guide to the literature of a specialized subject field. The author has noted more than a hundred such guides in recent years, some of which are listed at the end of this section and in the Bibliography, Section 21, Supplement. Many others have come from the press since this paper was compiled.

At least three publishers are issuing series of guides. The Gale Research Co., Detroit, Mich., lists 27 titles in its "Management Information Guide" series in the current catalog. Pergamon Press has published 31 titles in its "How to Find Out" series. The Information Resources Press, a division of Herner & Co., has a new series of "Brief Guides to Sources," most of which are still in press or in preparation. Nine titles are currently projected, and at least two have already been published. Besides the above series, many similar guides are published sporadically by other publishers and university presses.

Some subject guides cover more than one subject field. Typical examples of those covering a broad spectrum are:

Jenkins, Frances B. / *Science Reference Sources.* (5th ed. Cambridge, Mass., MIT Press, 1969);

Malinowsky, Harold R. / *Science and Engineering Reference Sources; a Guide for Students and Librarians.* (Rochester, N.Y., Libraries Unlimited, 1967);

Herner, Saul. / *A Brief Guide to Sources of Scientific and Technical Information.* (Washington, D.C., Information Resources Press, 1969).

II. STANDARDS AND SPECIFICATIONS

The second type of special materials includes standards and specifications. These publications are very important in an engineering library. A typical working collection might include approximately 15,000 items, not including bound sets in loose-leaf or other binders. Many standards are issued in pamphlet format, to facilitate updating of individual standards at irregular intervals. A collection of this size would represent the standards of approximately 300 organizations.

A. Definitions

To understand standards and specifications better, a few definitions are in order. According to the *Nuclear Standard News,* a standard is:

> The result of a particular standardization effort, approved by a recognized organization, which has been achieved by general consent, or common use, and establishes a definite level, degree, material, quality and the like as that which is proper and adequate for a given purpose.*

C. Douglas Woodward says:

> Standards are documents containing a set of conditions to be fulfilled. They are technical publications which state how materials and products should be made, measured, tested or described.†

Standards are established by companies; by trade associations representing an entire industry; by federal government departments; and by national and international standards organizations. An example of a trade association producing standards is the American Society of Tool and Manufacturing Engineers. This society is in turn a member of a national standardizing organization, the American National Standards Institute. The Federal Government issues military standards through the U.S. Department of Defense and civilian standards through the U.S. General Services Administration, Federal Supply Service. At the international level, the International Organization for Standardization (ISO) coordinates the activities of the various national standards organizations.

By contrast with standards, which are largely voluntary, specifications are statements which are legally binding in a contract agreement between the purchaser and the vendor of a product.

According to *Nuclear Standards News,** a specification is:

> A concise statement of a set of requirements to be satisfied by a product, a material or a process indicating, whenever appropriate, the procedure by means of which it may be determined whether the requirements given are satisfied. A specification may be a standard, a part of a standard, or independent of a standard.

Nuclear Standard News p. 3 (Aug 1971).

†Woodward, C. Douglas / *Standards for Industry.* London, Heinemann, 1965, p. 2.

Another definition is given by E. H. MacNiece‡ as follows:

> Specification is the definite, particularized, and complete statement of qualities, characteristics, and requirements of materials, processes, and procedures.

MacNiece points out further that large purchases of items by federal, state, and local governments, as well as by large nongovernmental institutions, must be based upon specifications, because such purchases are the result of competitive bidding. He says:

> Specifications serve as the reference standards that protect governmental agencies from accepting goods and services of inferior quality and protect suppliers in their competition for business since each must bid on and supply exactly the same items under the terms of specifications included with invitations to bid.§

B. Selection Tools for Standards and Specifications

Having established the nature and importance of standards and specifications to the engineering library, let us see how to go about selecting and acquiring them. Several basic tools exist. They are listed at the end of this paper and in Section 14 of the Bibliography, References 1–17.

1. *General Guides:* Struglia, E. J. / *Standards and Specifications Information Sources.*

The most comprehensive general guide to the literature of public and private agencies is by Erasmus J. Struglia, *Standards and Specifications Information Sources* (Section 14, *12*). Struglia gives names and addresses of the standards-producing agencies, and a checklist of the types of standards published.

□ *Directory of United States Standardization Activities*

Another excellent source is the *Directory of United States Standardization Activities,* by Joan E. Hartman (Section 14, *5*). This alphabetical directory of 486 American associations gives the complete address of each group, a brief history of its activities, a statement of its purpose and services, an outline of its relationships with other standardizing agencies, and a description of its publications.

2. *Catalogs and Indexes of Specific Organizations:* Even if the library is not large enough to warrant establishing a collection of standards, the librarian should have certain basic catalogs and indexes for patrons to use in locating a desired standard. The following publications constitute a working collection of such tools.

□ American National Standards Institute

The *Catalog* of the American National Standards Institute (Section 14, *1*), published annually, is a must. The Institute serves as the national clearinghouse for standards. It is a nonprofit organization composed of members from national trade, technical, and professional groups, firms from commerce and industry, government agencies and departments,

---

‡ MacNiece, E. H. / *Industrial Specifications.* New York, Wiley, 1953, p.1.
§ MacNiece, p.105.

consumer groups, and similar organizations. As such, it "provides the machinery for developing and approving standards which are supported by a national consensus" (5, p.232). The *Catalog* lists ANSI Standards alphanumerically in broad categories, with a complete subject index. It also includes a partial listing of such international standards as those of the ISO, IEC, COPANT, and CEE.

The American National Standards Institute publishes two serials which the library should have for updating the information given in the *Catalog*. These are the *ANSI Reporter* (Section 14, 2), a biweekly news magazine, and *Standards Action* (Section 14, 2), a biweekly listing of the text of new and revised standards, and for proposed new standards. They supersede its earlier publication, the *Magazine of Standards* (Section 14, 9), published from 1930 to 1970.

Libraries interested in purchasing a complete set of American National Standards may do so at a cost of $4,300.00, plus $200.00 for binders to house the complete set. Forty rod binders and sixteen three-post telescopic binders are required to house a complete set. Some libraries may find it easier to house the American National Standards in vertical files, because of the frequency of interfiling new standards and removing superseded ones. Discounts of 33 1/3% are available to company members of the Standards Institute. No discounts are given to libraries and educational institutions except on standing orders to keep complete sets or series on a current basis. Such discounts are computed on a graduated scale, according to the dollar value of the order. For orders totaling $100 or over the charges are 4% of the dollar value of the order.

□ British Standards Institution

The *Yearbook* of the British Standards Institution (Section 14, 3) is another important reference tool for the engineering library. It costs $6 per copy, and contains information about BSI and the services it offers. It lists the British Standards and other BSI publications, and gives a brief description of each. The *Yearbook Supplement,* complete to Mar 31 each year, contains a table showing British Standards and international standards on related subjects, and an alphabetical index. It also contains a Universal Decimal Classification (UDC) index to both British Standards and ISO recommendations.

A complete set of the BSI Standards costs approximately $2,000; the annual updating service, $250. Most BSI publications may be bought by libraries at a 40% discount, and there are special terms for purchasers of complete sets. This also applies to overseas purchasers.

The BSI issues a monthly periodical, *BSI News* (Section 14, 4), which updates the information given in the *Yearbook* and its *Supplement.* It is issued free to subscribing members. The *Annual Report* of the BSI is also free to subscribing members.

□ International Organization for Standardization

A third selection tool which the engineering library needs is *ISO*

Catalog (Section 14, 7), published annually by the International Organization for Standardization. Copies may be purchased for $6.00 from the American National Standards Institute, or from the ISO, Geneva, Switzerland. ISO Standards are partially listed in the *ANSI Catalog* and the *BSI Yearbook*, previously described.

□ American Society for Testing and Materials.

The fourth important set of standards which should be found in an engineering library is the *Book of ASTM Standards,* revised annually, of the American Society for Testing and Materials. The ASTM, founded in 1898, is a scientific and technical organization formed for "the development of standards on characteristics and performance of materials, products, systems, and services; and the promotion of related knowledge."‖ It is the world's largest source of voluntary consensus standards.

The 1973 *Annual Book of ASTM Standards* consists of 33 volumes, containing over 32,000 pages and over 4,700 ASTM standards and tentatives. Volume 33 is a combined index. The 1973 subscription to the set costs approximately $1,000 (prepaid $900).

□ U.S. National Bureau of Standards

We now come to the first of three U.S. Government agencies which play a large role in standardization. The National Bureau of Standards (NBS) was established in 1901 "to strengthen and advance the Nation's science and technology, and facilitate their effective application for public benefit."# The Institute for Applied Technology, one of the five divisions of the NBS, "cooperates with public and private organizations leading to the development of technological standards (including mandatory safety standards), codes and methods of test."# It also monitors NBS engineering standards activities, and serves as a liaison between NBS and national and international standards bodies. Typical examples of standards series issued by the NBS are Federal information processing standards, and product standards.

□ U.S. Department of Defense / *Index of Specifications and Standards*

The U.S. Department of Defense standardization program is the largest and most comprehensive in the world—either governmental or nongovernmental. The specifications and standards developed by the program are widely used within industry. The purpose of the program is to give uniform definitions of the technical requirements for parts, equipment, and systems in which the Department of Defense has an interest. The system comprises nearly 40,000 specifications and standards (Section 14, 5, p.245-246).

The *Index of Specifications and Standards* (Section 14, *14*) is issued annually, with cumulative bimonthly supplements, in two parts, one

---

‖Foreword. *Annual Book of ASTM Standards*. Part 1. 1973, p. iii.
U.S. National Bureau of Standards / *Publications of the National Bureau of Standards*. Washington, D.C., U.S. Govt. Print. Off., Spec. Publ. 305, Suppl. 2, 1970, cover II.

alphabetical and the other numerical. Requests for copies of specifications, standards, and qualified products lists should be sent to the Naval Supply Depot, 5801 Tabor Avenue, Philadelphia, Pa. 19120. To facilitate rapid handling of requests, one should obtain copies of DD Form 1425, which includes space for a self-addressed mailing label.

In addition to the officially published DOD specifications and standards, microform sets are available upon subscription from commercial sources. These sets will be discussed under *Microform Systems.*

□ U.S. General Services Administration. Federal Supply Service. *Index of Federal Specifications and Standards.*

The civilian counterpart of the Department of Defense in government standardization activities is the Federal Supply Service of the General Services Administration. Its mission is "to provide for the Government an economical and efficient system for (a) the procurement and supply of personal property and nonpersonal services . . . , (b) the utilization of available property, (c) the disposal of surplus property, and (d) records management" (Public Law 152, 81st Congress, 1949). Its standardization activities cover real and personal property as well as certain management practices and procedures (Section 14, *5*, p.246ff.).

The *Index of Federal Specifications and Standards* (Section 14, *15*) is published annually on January 1, and kept to date by supplements. It provides both alphabetical and numerical listings of Federal specifications, standards, and handbooks. Complete sets are available for reference use at General Services Administration Business Service Centers and at some U.S. Government depository libraries. The price of a complete set is $225, while the subscription price for continuous distribution of current Federal standards and specifications is $14 per year. Orders should be addressed to Specification Sales (3FRSBS), Bldg. 197, Washington Navy Yard, General Services Administration, Washington, D.C. 20407.

C. Microform Systems

At least two companies provide complete sets of Military and Federal specifications and standards on cartridges of 16 mm microfilm: Information Handling Services, Englewood, Colo., and Global Engineering Documentation Services, Inc. of Newport Beach, Calif. The advantages of such files on microfilm are obvious: 1) saving of storage space, 2) ease of use and duplication, and 3) saving of clerical time in filing new material and removal of superseded material. Another advantage is that these files are updated more quickly than the individual user could update his own files, and superseded material remains in the file for historical purposes. It should also be noted that both firms have available on microfilm a complete set of vendor trade catalogs.

1. *VSMF (Visual Search Microfilm File):* The microfilms available from Information Handling Services are called the VSMF, or Visual Search Microfilm Files (Section 14, *17*). The annual subscription price for the VSMF Standards File is $560; for the VSMF Specifications File, $3,350; and for the VSMF Documentation File, $3,125. Standards and specifications are updated on a 15-day cycle, while vendor trade catalogs are updated on a 60-day cycle.

2. *Global Engineering Documentation Services, Inc.:* Global Engineering provides 16 mm microfilm cartridge files of Military and Federal Specifications and Standards, with updating of Specifications on a 30-day cycle and of Standards on a 60-day cycle. The address is: Global Engineering Documentation Services, Inc., P.O. Box 2060, Newport Beach, Calif. 92663.

D. Organization and Servicing of the Collection

Because of the diversity of forms in which standards and specifications are published, no one system will suffice for housing them. It is usually necessary to use a combination of vertical files and library shelving. The collection need not be cataloged in the public catalog, although full cataloging would be desirable. To alert the user to the existence of a set of standards from a given organization, a guide card may be placed in the author section of the card catalog, under the name of the issuing organization, with the following type of statement: "Library maintains current file of Standards issued by this organization. Please consult Librarian on duty for assistance."

Marginal notations on the guide card would indicate whether the set is filed in the vertical file or on the shelf. The collection may be arranged alphabetically by issuing agency in both places.

For internal control, the reference department may keep a small card index containing a duplicate set of the guide cards found in the public catalog. U.S. Government standards and specifications, it should be noted, may be shelved in the Government Document Depository Collection, if desired, along with the appropriate indexes of the issuing agencies.

Standards and specifications pose problems in the library, because they are expensive to purchase; difficult to house, organize, and service; and complex to use. Nevertheless, they are vital to the engineering library, and are well worth the trouble and expense.

Before leaving this topic, a word should be said about the need for retaining superseded standards. Where space and filing help are a problem, it may be necessary to discard all but the latest edition of a given standard. However, experience has shown that requests are made for older editions by users who have equipment manufactured at the time the older edition was in effect. Sometimes even the issuing agency no longer has a copy of the superseded standard. The engineering library is under increasing pressure to retain, if not all standards, then at least the superseded editions of major sets, like the American National Standards Institute.

III. TRANSLATIONS

One of the more difficult problems that arises in a library is to help a user find a translation of a foreign language publication. This need arises frequently in the use of scientific and technical periodical literature, but it may also develop in any other subject field.

The librarian generally goes through a three-stage process in solving the problem. First, he searches published lists of translations. If this search fails to yield the desired item, he then writes to, telephones, or teletypes the nearest national translations center. Third, if the translation is still not located, he refers the user to a professional translator. Let us explore these three steps in greater detail.

A. Bibliographic Tools

Published lists of translations, the major ones, that is, are listed in the Bibliography, Section 19, References 1-20.

1. *Index Translationum:* For translations of monographs, the main tool to use is *Index Translationum* (Section 19, *18*), an annual bibliography published by UNESCO since 1948. Each volume is indexed by author, and is arranged alphabetically by the country in which the book was published. Under each country, the list is arranged by the Universal Decimal Classification. The 1970 volume indexed 41,322 translated books published in 73 countries.

2. *Translations Published in the Form of Journals:* Many foreign, especially Russian, scientific and technical journals are published in cover-to-cover English translation. Others are translated on a selective basis, and still others bring together in one journal excerpts from several foreign journals in a given subject discipline. The smaller library will not be able to afford subscriptions to many of these journals because of their expense. However, single copies of the issues containing the desired article may be purchased from the publisher. An excellent tool for identifying such journals is, *A Guide to Scientific and Technical Journals in Translation* (Section 19, 7).

For those who have access to a large library, similar lists may be found in some journals from time to time, notably in the *World Index of Scientific Translations*, to be discussed more fully below. Another such list appeared in the five-year cumulative index to *Transatom Bulletin*, Part II: Original Source Index. 6-10 (1966-1970).

3. *Translations Register-Index:* The *Translations Register-Index*

(Section 19, *19*) is the only continuing American bibliographic tool
solely devoted to announcing and indexing translations into English
from the world literature of the natural, physical, medical, and social
sciences. Each issue contains two sections. The first is the "Register Section," which announces new accessions of the National Translations
Center. The second is the "Index Section," which lists both these
accessions as well as translations listed in *Government Reports Announcements* (Section 12, 7), reported by commercial translating agencies, and by other sources. The Register Section is arranged in 22 subject categories according to the COSATI subject classification. The
"Index Section" lists journals, reports, standards, newspapers, and other
serial publications alphabetically by title. Separate index sections are
provided for patents, monographs, and conference papers. The "Index
Section" cumulates quarterly, for all entries to date in a given volume.

4. *Consolidated Index of Translations into English:* In 1969, *Consolidated Index of Translations into English* (Section 19, *15*), was published, which brought together in one list all of the holdings of the
National Translations Center as well as all of the items previously listed
in the various publications of the Special Libraries Association and the
Federal Government between 1953 and 1969. The *Consolidated Index*
is an extremely valuable tool, listing 142,000 translations by journal
title, volume number, and page number.

5. *World Index of Scientific Translations:* The European counterpart of the *Translations Register-Index* is the *World Index of Scientific
Translations and List of Translations Notified to ETC*, published by the
European Translations Centre, Delft, The Netherlands. As the title
would indicate, this publication is arranged in two parts. The *World
Index* portion, arranged alphabetically by journal title, lists translations
of serial articles, patents, and standards relating to science and technology, with some social science translations. The *List of Translations*
portion, arranged in broad subject categories, announces the monthly
acquisitions of translations, giving author; title of the original article,
patent, or standard; and further bibliographical data. This publication,
which began in 1967, is essentially a finding list for translations from
nonwestern languages, both Slavic and Oriental, into western languages,
primarily into English, French, or German. The index cumulates quarterly and annually. A five-year cumulative volume, covering 1967–1971,
has been published by the Centre.

The European Translations Centre also publishes an annual list of
Translations Journals, giving a complete bibliography of cover-to-cover
translations journals. This is available separately from the *World Index*,
and may be ordered from the Centre. It includes not only cover-to-
cover translated periodicals, but also abstracted publications and
periodicals containing translations of selected articles.

B. Translations Centers

If the desired translation is not found in a published bibliography, the next step is to get in touch with the nearest national translations center. At any given moment, the translations center is processing several hundred new translations which have not yet been listed in the published lists. Therefore, a manual search of their current files is in order, and often productive.

Most of the major western European countries have a national translations center, as does the United States and Canada. For brevity, only two will be considered: the National Translations Center, located at the John Crerar Library, Chicago, Ill., and the European Translations Centre located at Delft, Netherlands, which is multinational.

1. *National Translations Center:* The National Translations Center, to quote from the *Translations Register-Index*, is "a depository and information source for unpublished translations into English from the world literature of the natural, physical, medical, and social sciences." It is a cooperative, nonprofit enterprise, organized in 1953 by the Special Libraries Association, which collects and indexes translations donated by scientific and professional societies, government agencies, industrial libraries, universities, and other institutions in the United States and abroad. It also indexes, but does not collect, translations reported to it by commercial translators and other collections.

Files are maintained by author, journal or other citation, report number, patent number, issuing agency, and similar headings. The center will search its files, without charge, in response to mail, telephone, or teletype inquiries. It will supply photocopies, or, in some cases, interlibrary loans, of translations in its collection. The center is housed in the John Crerar Library, 35 West 33rd St., Chicago, Ill. 60616. As of 1973, its holdings totaled 202,770 translations.

2. *European Translations Centre:* The European Translations Centre, located at 101 Doelenstraat, Delft, Netherlands, serves as a clearinghouse and depository for translations from nonwestern languages, chiefly Slavic and oriental languages, into western languages, primarily English, French, and German. It cooperates with the national translations centers of England, France, and West Germany, which in turn report their holdings to the E.T.C. Listings of items indexed by the E.T.C. are published in its serial publication, previously described, and translations into English are also reported to the National Translations Center in the United States, for listing in the *Translations Register-Index*.

C. Directories of Translators

The third step in the librarian's search for a translation occurs if no existing translation can be found in either published bibliographies or translations centers. It is then necessary to put the user in touch with a professional translator, who can prepare a custom translation for him.

Many libraries maintain a card file, listing names, addresses, telephone numbers, language proficiencies, and subject specializations of local translators. On the university campus, it is well to keep a record of foreign-born faculty and students. One can usually get a list of the foreign students from the Dean of Students. If registration files are computerized, this list may be issued each quarter or semester as a computer printout, arranged by country of origin. From the name of the country, one can usually deduce the mother tongue; however, one should keep in mind that many foreign students are proficient in several languages besides their mother tongue. This is an added dividend to the librarian. One difficulty in using foreign students for translating work is that their student visas prohibit them from engaging in gainful employment without a work permit. It is the author's understanding that work permits are difficult to obtain. The student may do work for pay, if he is working for someone on the university campus; however, if he is working for an off-campus employer, the work permit is required.

If the library has no file of local translators, consult the yellow pages of the local telephone directory, under "Translators," or those of the directories of such major cities as New York, Washington, Chicago, and San Francisco. Care should be taken in choosing names from the telephone directory if a scientific or technical translation is needed. Most translators listed there have no science-technology training, unless specifically indicated in the listing; they are primarily equipped to handle commercial correspondence.

Still another, and perhaps more reliable, source of translators' names is the published directory of translators. Three such directories are listed here.

1. *The International Directory of Translators and Interpreters.* London, Pond Press, 1967.
2. Kaiser, Frances E. / *Translators and Translations: Services and Sources in Science and Technology.* 2d ed. New York, Special Libraries Association, 1965.
3. Millard, Patricia / *Directory of Technical and Scientific Translators and Services.* London, Crosby Lockwood & Son, 1968.

Another good source of translators' names is the *Professional Services Directory* (Section 19, *1*) published by the American Translators Association, which lists by language, subject specialization, and geographical location those members of the association who wish to be included. For each member listed, the *Directory* gives name, address, telephone, languages translated from and into English, and a brief biographical sketch giving degrees held and subject specialties. Copies of the *Directory* may be obtained from the Association at P.O. Box 129, Croton-on-Hudson, N.Y. 10520.

The library user in search of a translator sometimes asks what rates he should expect to pay for the service. This is a difficult question to answer, because rates fluctuate and no two translators seem to employ the same method of computing them. Typical translating rates for European languages (both Eastern and Western) vary according to the kind of translator employed. Freelance translators charge $0.015 per English word (Free-lance linguist or subject specialist with some language facility, usually three or more years of college training in the language.) Commercial translators charge $0.011 per word of the original language. Typical rates for Far Eastern and Oriental languages are higher. In this case, charges range from $0.025 to $0.03 per word, and sometimes as high as $0.04 per word. These prices are based on estimates given to the author in 1972 by an experienced translator and should be taken as merely indicative of the range of rates at that time and not as an absolute guide.

When working with a free-lance translator who is an employee of one's own firm or a colleague on the same university campus, it is sometimes easier for both parties concerned to let the translator dictate his translation into a tape recorder. If secretarial help is available, the tape can be transcribed into a rough draft. The person requesting the translation can then meet with the translator personally and review the transcript. Sometimes the desired information can be obtained from the rough draft, without going to the time and expense of producing a letter-perfect typed copy. In this case, it is sometimes possible to negotiate payment of the translator on an hourly basis, rather than on a per word basis, at a possible saving in expense.

IV. CONFERENCE AND SYMPOSIA LITERATURE

One of the thorniest problems faced by the reference librarian in a scientific and technical library is to locate preprints, papers and proceedings of conferences and symposia. There is no easy solution to this problem; only a series of methods for living with it. And live with it one must, because the conference or symposium has become one of the primary announcement mechanisms for new scientific and engineering research.

A. Acquisition and Maintenance of Conference Records in the Library.

What form do conference records take in the library? The answer is: every conceivable form—books, serials, technical reports, preprints and microforms. How are they acquired? By individual order and by subscription, by purchase and by depository agreement. How does one deal with them? In a variety of ways, which we shall review briefly.

1. *Acquisition:* There is no one simple way to acquire conference records, because of the multiplicity of forms in which they are published. The library may use standing orders for continuing series, where

the dealer or agent will accept them. However, most conference proceedings are either one-time-only meetings or, if annual, are held in a
different country each year and hence issued by a different publisher. A
few technical societies publish conference papers individually, either in
full-size printed copies or on microfiche. For example, the American
Institute of Aeronautics and Astronautics publishes its meeting papers
on microfiche, at a standard charge of 75¢ per paper. The cost of the
microfiche received in 1971 came to approximately $700. Such series may
be ordered on a subscription basis. A large number of conferences are
sponsored by U.S. Government agencies, such as branches of the Department of Defense, the National Aeronautics and Space Administration, or
the Atomic Energy Commission. These conference proceedings are generally published on microfiche, which is supplied free of charge to
depository libraries, and sold on a subscription or an individual item
basis to non-depository libraries and to the general public.

2. *Processing, Cataloging and Housing:* The method used to process,
catalog, and house conference and symposium proceedings varies with
the form of the publication. One-of-a-kind conferences are usually classified and cataloged fully and placed in the general collection. Proceedings which are published in serial format are sometimes cataloged
and classified as a series, but are not always analyzed in the card catalog
individually. It is felt that published bibliographic tools usually provide
sufficient access to the series by subject area. (The deciding factor on
whether or not to analyze a given series of proceedings in the card catalog is what the Library of Congress had done with it. However, the
Library of Congress is quite inconsistent in policy on such matters.)
Individual papers issued in printed form in a numbered series may be
cataloged as a series, without analysis. Papers or preprints issued on
microfiche may be filed numerically by paper number, in a vertical file
in the reference department, and the set listed in the card catalog.
Patrons who find references to such papers usually consult the reference
librarian for help in locating them, and are directed to the microfiche
file accordingly. Proceedings issued on microfiche as *technical reports*
are usually filed by report number in a separate Technical Reports Collection, and are located by using the major abstracting services which
index technical report literature.

B. Bibliographic Tools for Locating Conference Records

If the card catalog does not yield a reference to a given conference
proceedings, what should the librarian do next? The search should be
continued in two steps, as follows: 1) He should try to locate the
desired proceedings in various bibliographies of published proceedings
and, having done so, should locate the publication in another library
through searching the *National Union Catalog* and/or *New Serial Titles*.

2) If step one does not yield results, he should search for the conference in various indexes of scientific meetings, and should give the patron the name and address of the conference sponsor or organizer. The bibliographic tools needed for these two steps are listed in Section 24 of the Bibliography. Let us consider them briefly now.

1. *Indexes to Published Proceedings: Proceedings in Print* (Section 24, 7) is "an index to conference proceedings in all subject areas and all languages" (Introduction). Part 1 contains Current Entries, those published within the last two years, while Part 2, Retrospective Entries, covers those published prior to the last two years. Conferences are listed under the significant words of the title, not under "Conference on" or "Symposium on." The index, covering both current and retrospective entries, gives in a single alphabet corporate authors, sponsoring agencies, editors, and keywords. A list of acronyms and abbreviations accompanies each issue and is cumulated annually, as are the indexes. Prices and order information are given when available. *Proceedings in Print* began publication in 1964, as a project of the Special Libraries Association, but is now commercially published. The frequency is bimonthly. The subscription price is $60 per year.

The *Directory of Published Proceedings* (Section 24, 3, 4), another useful tool, comes in two series: Series SEMT (for Science, Engineering, Medicine, Technology), and Series SSH (for Social Sciences and Humanities). It covers both preprints and published proceedings held on a worldwide basis from 1964 to date. Series SEMT is published monthly, ten times a year, with an annual cumulation, while Series SSH is quarterly, also with an annual cumulative index. Each issue is arranged chronologically, with indexes by keyword, sponsor, and title. The publishers, InterDok Corporation, provide an acquisition service for subscribers. Subscription rates are $65 per year for Series SEMT, with an additional charge of $84.50 for annual cumulative indexes. Series SSH costs $60 per year.

For the period of time from September 1969, through February 1972, there is a series of publications issued by the CCM Information Corporation which indexes individual conference papers. Unfortunately, this series has ceased publication. However, for retrospective search, it is still valuable. The series includes the following titles, shown chronologically:

Current Index to Conference Papers in Chemistry. Sep 1969–Aug 1970;

Current Index to Conference Papers in Engineering. Sep 1969–Aug 1970;

Current Index to Conference Papers in Life Sciences. Sep 1969–Aug 1970;

Current Index to Conference Papers: Science and Technology. Jan 1971–Feb 1972. (Supersedes the three titles above).

By taking its information from conference programs before the con-

ference was held, CCM Information Corp. claimed that it could report
new research and development "well over a year before services based
on the journal literature . . ." (Introduction).

The first three titles above are arranged in three sections: 1) subject
index, 2) author index, and 3) meetings information. The fourth title,
which supersedes the first three as of January 1971, is arranged in four
sections: 1) main entry, 2) subject index, 3) author index, and 4) meeting
title and sponsor index. The "main entry" section is divided into 18
broad subject categories. Order information is given, including addresses
of preprint authors.

In addition to the above publications, the librarian often uses a number of other bibliographic tools to locate and identify conference papers
or proceedings. Many professional societies publish monthly announcement bulletins in which they give the programs of forthcoming meetings,
with instructions for ordering preprints. An example is the *AIAA Bulletin*. Many indexing and abstracting journals, such as *Engineering Index,
International Aerospace Abstracts,* and *Electrical and Electronics Abstracts*, regularly index preprints and proceedings after the meetings
have been held. Also, one should not overlook the obvious though general tools, like the *National Union Catalog* and *New Serial Titles*.

2. *Indexes to Meetings:* If, after consulting all of the services previously mentioned, one is still unable to locate a given conference proceedings, the only remaining alternative is to search indexes to meetings,
in the hope of finding the name and address of the meeting organizer or
sponsor. Several bibliographic tools exist for this purpose.

Scientific Meetings (Section 24, *8*), published quarterly since the
Spring of 1957 by the Special Libraries Association, is one such source.
It lists future national, international, and regional meetings in the fields
of science, technology, medicine, health, engineering, and management.
The arrangement is in four parts: Part I is an alphabetical list of names
and addresses of sponsors. Part II is an alphabetical list of meetings. Part
III is a chronological listing. Part IV is a subject index. Subscriptions
are $17.50 a year.

World Meetings (Section 24, *10*) is actually three separate publications: *World Meetings, United States and Canada; World Meetings Outside
U.S.A. and Canada;* and *World Meetings: Social and Behavioral Sciences,
Education, and Management.* The first two are limited to future medical, scientific, and technical meetings. All three are published quarterly
by CCM Information Corporation. Details of arrangement vary slightly,
but all contain a data section, followed by five indexes organized by
date of meeting, by keyword, by location, by deadline for abstracts of
papers, and by sponsor. The subscription price is $35 per year for each
title.

A third title is *International Associations* (Section 24, *5*) published
by the Union of International Associations. It regularly includes a list of
proceedings received. The December issue contains an Annual Interna-

tional Congress Calendar, covering meetings projected for five years in
advance, with geographical, subject, and organizational indexes. This
feature is supplemented in the other issues throughout the year.

From the preceding discussion, one can see that the problem of
finding conference and symposium literature is complex. While bibliographic control is far from complete, several publishers are making a
conscientious effort to ameliorate the situation. With increasing use of
computer-based services, this effort should prove successful in the years
ahead.

V. ACADEMIC DISSERTATIONS AND THESES

The last of our five types of miscellaneous materials is the academic
dissertation, submitted for the PhD degree, or the thesis, submitted for
the Master's degree. The method of handling such "unpublished publications" varies from one university to another, but is essentially the
same in principle.

A. Processing, Storage, and Servicing in the Library

Two or more copies of theses and dissertations are usually submitted
to the library of the university by the degree candidate. The original,
or first typed copy, is placed either in the archives or in the special
collections of the university for permanent safe-keeping and is not
allowed to circulate. The second copy is used for circulating purposes.
Some libraries also require a third copy, which is sent to the dean or
director of the school or department in which the degree work was completed, for permanent retention in departmental files. Most large universities have offset printing facilities which the graduate student can use to
have multiple copies of his dissertation printed, so that all copies are, in
effect, "originals" of top printing quality and legibility. This is preferable to the older custom of typing originals with multiple carbon
copies.

Dissertations are generally classified and cataloged completely, and
are listed in the main card catalog of the library by author, title, and
subject. Many libraries publish a master bibliography of all their theses
and dissertations, cumulated annually. It is often arranged by departments, listing dissertations and theses in chronological order within each
department, and in alphabetical order by author within each year.

B. Bibliographic Control

Bibliographic control of graduate theses and dissertations is complex. Bibliographic tools for this topic are listed in Section 13 of the

Bibliography.

1. *American Dissertations:* By far the most important single agency for bibliographic control of dissertations is University Microfilms, Ann Arbor, Michigan. This publisher has issued a monthly announcement service, *Dissertation Abstracts International* (Section 13, *5*) since 1938. Most universities of any size participate in *Dissertation Abstracts International,* by depositing their doctoral dissertations with University Microfilms. A lengthy abstract is published in the *Abstracts,* and readers may purchase microfilm or Xerox copies from the publisher at a standard rate of $4 for microfilm and $10 for Xerox copies regardless of length of the dissertation. Most universities who participate in this program decline to lend their dissertations on interlibrary loan, referring the inquirer to University Microfilms for copies. Approximately 290 universities now participate in the program.*

In 1969, University Microfilms published a 15-volume cumulative index to *Dissertation Abstracts International,* covering the years 1938–1969. This Retrospective Index (Section 13, *6*) is divided into eight major subject fields; each volume is indexed by author and subject. Volume 9 is a master author index to the set.

Dissertation Abstracts International is a computer-based publication. The publisher provides a Datrix searching service to interested readers who wish a computer printout of all dissertations in a given subject area. Both retrospective searches and current awareness services are available.

Before the advent of University Microfilms, the bibliographic control of dissertations and theses was somewhat skimpy. For many years, from 1933 to 1955, the H. W. Wilson Co. published an annual author-title listing, *Doctoral Dissertations Accepted by American Universities* (Section 13, *7*). While adequate for locating dissertations in rather broad subject categories, it provided no abstracts. To obtain a copy of the dissertation, one had to write to the university in question for an interlibrary loan or, often at considerable expense, for a photostat or microfilm copy. This annual publication was incorporated into *Dissertation Abstracts* as a special issue from 1955/56 until 1964/65. Finally, starting in 1965/66, it emerged as a separate title, *American Doctoral Dissertations* (Section 13, *1*), from University Microfilms, and is still so published. The advantage of this list is that it includes all doctoral dissertations in the U.S., regardless of whether they are included separately in *Dissertation Abstracts International.* While some 290 universities

---

*Xerox University Microfilms has announced the publication, in late 1973, of its *Comprehensive Dissertation Index (CDI),* replacing the *Retrospective Index.* The new title, indexing by author and subject more than 400,000 dissertations accepted in the United States between 1861 and 1972, from over 380 institutions, will be available in two formats: a library bound edition and a computer-generated microfiche edition. Annual supplements will be available in both formats.

participate in the latter, this by no means represents all of the universities producing dissertations.

From 1912 to 1938, the Library of Congress published a *List of American Doctoral Dissertations Printed in 1912-1938* (Section 13, *11*). This list, it should be noted, covered only *printed* dissertations. Since very few universities required printing at that time, the coverage of total output of dissertations was limited. However, it served a useful purpose at the time, and is still the only national list extending back as far as 1912.

2. *Foreign Dissertations:* Considerable interest is developing in doctoral research done outside the United States. For British output, one should refer to the *Aslib Index to Theses Accepted for Higher Degrees in the Universities of Great Britain and Ireland*, which began publication in 1950/51 (Section 13, *2*). A recent (1969) article in *Libri* (Section 13, *10*) discusses microfilming and bibliographic control of European dissertations. Starting in 1969, University Microfilms broadened its coverage in *Dissertation Abstracts* to include Canadian and a few European universities. It is expected and hoped that this program will continue to expand in the future.

Ordering copies of foreign dissertations is often a time-consuming and frustrating experience for the librarian. Assuming that one has located the author and title of a desired dissertation and found that it was submitted to a given foreign university, it is often necessary to obtain written permission from the author before a microfilm or photocopy can be made by the university. Sometimes the university no longer knows the author's address. Sometimes the author neglects to answer his mail. In addition, most British universities require payment in advance, so the American librarian must send for a price estimate before the order can be placed, and forward a check in advance. All of this does not even take into account further delays and complications resulting from calculation of exchange rates, overseas air mail shipment, postal strikes, etc.

The Florida State University Library, Tallahassee, is attempting to become a national depository for foreign dissertations. When seeking a foreign dissertation, the librarian should contact Florida State before going to the time and expense of writing directly to the university overseas.

Some foreign universities issue their dissertations in printed form, as part of a numbered series. Such a series can be obtained, for example, by an exchange agreement with the Federal Technical Institute in Zurich, Switzerland. Since this set is a numbered series, with a printed cumulative index, it can be cataloged as a set, bound, and placed in the main collection. The series is complete back to 1909.

Another series of printed dissertations in engineering is available on exchange from the Tekniska Högskolan, Stockholm, Sweden. The *Avhandling*, as the series is called, dates back to 1928 and is issued in

Swedish, English, German, or French. Other Technische Hochschule, such as those in Munich and Stuttgart, are willing to enter into exchange agreements for their printed dissertations.

3. *Masters' Theses:* At the present time, bibliographic control of masters' theses is at the same stage of development as was the control of doctoral dissertations thirty years ago. In other words, there is no control. Perhaps this is because the master's thesis is considered below the level of original research. However, some master's theses represent a solid contribution, and deserve to be more widely known. There are two bibliographic tools which serve this purpose.

Masters Abstracts (Section 13, *9*), published since 1962 by University Microfilms, abstracts masters' theses from some 25 universities. The small number of participating universities seriously limits its value.

Masters' Theses in the Pure and Applied Sciences, compiled and edited annually since 1955 by the Thermophysical Properties Research Center, Purdue University, is published by University Microfilms. While it is a comprehensive bibliography, unfortunately it gives no abstracts. Thesis titles are arranged under 45 subject fields, excluding mathematics and life sciences. Volume XV, for July 1971, listed 7,437 theses from 209 universities.

One concluding remark about dissertations and theses: a number of universities still publish their own abstracts and/or bibliographies of their students' work. In addition, many professional societies publish annual lists of dissertations in their official organ, covering one subject discipline. These sources of information should not be overlooked when making a literature search for dissertations and theses.

CONCLUSION

In conclusion, five types of special materials were considered. Although diverse in subject and format, they have certain characteristics in common. First, they all pose acquisition problems. Second, they often require special indexing and classification. Third, they necessitate housing separately from the regular collection. Fourth, they usually involve the use of special bibliographic tools different from the ones normally found in small or medium-sized libraries. Fifth, they are often difficult for the reader to locate or use without help from a reference librarian. An attempt has been made to present each of the five types of special materials with these factors in mind, and to point to possible solutions to the problems involved.

Bibliography

PATRICIA ROGERS
FRANCES E. KAISER

1. Special Materials—General Information and Management

1. Allerton Park Institute, 10th, 1963/ *The school library materials center: its resources and their utilization.* Papers presented at an institute conducted by the Univ. Illinois Grad. Sch. Libr. Sci., Nov 3-6, 1963. Alice Lohrer, ed. Champaign, Ill., Illini Union Bookstore, 1964.
2. American Council of Learned Societies. Committee on Research Libraries / *On research libraries: statement and recommendations of the committee . . . .* Cambridge, Mass., MIT Press, 1967.
3. Annan, Gertrude L. and Jacqueline W. Felter, eds. / *Handbook of medical library practice.* 3d ed. Chicago, Med. Libr. Ass., 1970. (Med. Libr. Ass. Publ. no. 4)
4. Ashworth, Wilfred / *Handbook of special librarianship and information work.* 3d ed. London, Aslib, 1967.
5. Astall, Roland / Stock. In *Special libraries and information bureaux.* London, C. Bingley, 1966. p. 58-65. (Examination Guide Series)
6. Bakewell, K.G.B. / *Industrial libraries throughout the world.* Elmsford, N.Y., Pergamon, 1969.
7. Burkett, Jack / *Special libraries and documentation centres in the Netherlands.* Elmsford, N.Y., Pergamon, 1968.
8. Burkett, Jack, ed. / *Special library and information services in the United Kingdom.* 2d rev. ed. London, Libr. Ass., 1965.
9. Burkett, J., ed. / *Special materials in the library.* A series of fourteen lectures held at the Library Association and Aslib Headquarters, Jan 17 to Apr 11, 1962, organized by the Dept. of Librarianship, Northwestern Polytechnic, London. London, Libr. Ass., 1963.
10. Collison, Robert L. / *The treatment of special materials in libraries.* Aslib Manuals v. 2. London, Aslib, 1955.
11. Davies, Ruth Ann / *The school library, a force for educational excellence.* New York, Bowker, 1969.
12. Egan, Margaret E., ed. / *The communication of specialized information.* Chicago, Distributed by the Amer. Libr. Ass. for the Univ. Chicago Grad. Libr. Sch., 1954. (Papers presented before the 17th Annual conference of the Graduate Library School of the University of Chicago, 1952)
13. Fisher, Eva Lou / *A checklist for the organization, operation, and evaluation of a company library.* 2d ed. New York, Spec. Libr. Ass., 1966.
14. Foskett, D.J. / *Information service in libraries.* 2d ed. Hamden, Conn., Archon, 1967.
15. Gould, Geraldine N. and C. Wolfe Ithmer / *How to organize and*

Patricia Rogers is information specialist, Center for Disease Control, Training Methods Reference Collection, Atlanta, Ga.

Frances E. Kaiser is head of the Department of Library Instruction, Price Gilbert Memorial Library, Georgia Institute of Technology, Atlanta, Ga.

maintain the library picture/pamphlet file. Dobbs Ferry, N.Y., Oceana Publ., 1968.

16. Hamlin, Talbot / *Some European architectural libraries: their methods, equipment and administration.* New York, AMS Press, 1967.

17. Hicks, Warren B. and Elma Tillin / *Developing multimedia libraries.* New York, Bowker, 1970.

18. Hilligan, Margaret P., ed. / *Libraries for research and industry.* New York, Spec. Libr. Ass., 1955. (SLA Monograph no. 1) (out-of-print)

19. Knight, Douglas M., comp. / *Libraries at large: tradition, innovation, and the national interest . . . .* New York, Bowker, 1969.

20. Kruzas, Anthony T. / *Business and industrial libraries in the United States, 1820–1940.* New York, Spec. Libr. Ass., 1965.

21. Kujoth, J.S., ed. / *Readings in nonbook librarianship.* Metuchen, N.J., Scarecrow, 1968.

22. Mason, Donald / *A primer of nonbook materials in libraries.* With an appendix on sound recordings by Jean C. Cowan. London, Ass. Asst. Librn., 1958.

23. Monypenny, Phillip / *The library functions of the states, commentary on the survey of library functions of the states.* Chicago, Amer. Libr. Ass., 1966.

24. Rabinowicz, Harry M. / *Treasures of Judaica.* South Brunswick, T. Yoseloff, 1971.

25. Rogers, Rutherford D. and David C. Weber, Special types of materials. In *University library administration.* Bronx, N.Y., H.W. Wilson, 1971. p. 247–273.

26. Rufsvold, Margaret Irene / *Audiovisual school library service, a handbook for librarians.* Chicago, Amer. Libr. Ass., 1949.

27. Saunders, Helen E. / *The modern school library, its administration as a materials center.* Metuchen, N.J., Scarecrow, 1968.

28. Silva, Manil / *Special libraries.* London, Andre Deutsch, 1970.

29. Special Libraries Association. Illinois Chapter / *Special libraries: a guide*

for management. New York, Spec. Libr. Ass., 1966.

30. Special Libraries Association. Social Science Group / *Public administration libraries.* Chicago, Public Admin. Serv., 1941. (Publ. no. 75).

31. Strauss, Lucille J., et al. / *Scientific and technical libraries: their organization and administration.* 2d ed. New York, N.Y., Becker and Hayes, 1972.

32. United Nations Educational Scientific and Cultural Organization / *The libraries of the United Nations, a descriptive guide.* New York, U.N., 1966.

33. Wright, Gordon H., ed. / *The library in colleges of commerce and technology.* A guide to the use of a library as an instrument of education. New York, London House and Maxwell, 1966.

34. Wright, J.E. / *Manual of special library technique.* With particular reference to the technical special libraries of commercial and government establishments. 2d ed., rev. London, Aslib (Ass. of Spec. Libr. and Inform. Bureaux), 1946. (Aslib manuals, v. 1).

2. Special Materials—Selection & Acquisition

1. California, Univ., Univ. Extension/ *Continuing Education in Librarianship.* Acquisition of special materials. Isabel H. Jackson, ed. San Francisco, San Francisco Bay Region Chapter, Spec. Libr. Ass., 1966.

2. Carter, Mary Duncan and Wallace John Bonk / Selection of non-book materials. In *Building library collections.* Metuchen, N.J., Scarecrow, 1964. p. 119–130.

3. Delaney, Jack J. / Selecting materials . . . non-book materials. In *The new school librarian.* Hamden, Conn., Shoe String, 1968.

4. De Vore, Helen L. / Acquisition policy. *Spec. Libr.* 61: 381–384 (Sep 1970).

5. Enoch Pratt Free Library / Principles

of selection in specific areas . . . according to form and nature of materials (as distinct from subject) . . . materials other than books. In *Book selection policies*, rev. ed. Baltimore, Md., Enoch Pratt Free Libr., 1961. p. 25–33.

6. Gaver, Mary Virginia / Developing special collections and collections of special materials. In *Background readings in building library collections*. vol. II. Metuchen, N.J., Scarecrow, 1969. p. 1026–1046.

7. Gaver, Mary Virginia / Theory of building library collections . . . (standards). In *Readings in building library collections*. Metuchen, N.J., Scarecrow, 1969. p. 113–145.

8. Goldhor, Herbert, ed. / *Selection and acquisition procedures in medium sized and large libraries.* Papers presented at an institute conducted by the Univ. of Illinois Grad. Sch. Libr. Sci., Nov. 11–14, 1962. Champaign, Ill., Illini Union Bookstore, 1963.

9. Horn, Andrew H., ed. / Special materials and services. *Libr. Trends* 4: 117–212 (Oct 1955).

10. Kent, Allen / Acquisition of materials. In *Specialized Information Centers*. Washington, D.C., Spartan, 1965. p. 37–65.

11. McDaniel, Roderick D. / Audiovisual reviews—the state of the art. *Audiovisual Instr.* 15: 63–65 (Dec 1970).

12. Rippon, J.S. and S. Francis / Selection and acquisition of library materials. In *Handbook of Special Librarianship and Information Work*. 3d ed. Wilfred Ashworth, ed. London, Aslib, 1967. p. 35–78.

13. Rufsvold, M.I. and C. Guss / Software: bibliographic control and the NICEM (Nat. Inform. Center for Educ. Media) indexes. *Sch. Libr.* 20: 11–20 (Winter 1971).

14. Sgro, L. and R. Munger / Audiovisual materials: purchase or produce. *Wis. Libr. Bull.* 66: 88–90 (Mar 1970).

15. Special Libraries Ass. Illinois Chapter / Estimating costs and planning budgets—Reports, Documents and Pamphlets. In *Special Libraries: a guide for management.* Edward C. Strable, ed. New York, Spec. Libr. Ass., 1966. p. 56.

16. Strauss, Lucille J., et al. / Books and other publications. In *Scientific and technical libraries: their organization and administration.* 2d ed. New York, N.Y., Becker and Hayes, 1972. p. 120–137.

17. U.S. Office of Education. Bureau of Elementary and Secondary Education / *Aids for media selection for students and teachers.* Yvonne Carter, et al., Comps. Washington, D.C., U.S. Govt. Print. Off., 1971. (Cat. no. HE5.234:34045)

18. Wulfenkoetter, Gertrude / *Acquisition work: processes in building library collections.* Seattle, Univ. of Washington, 1961.

3. Special Materials— Organization

1. Akers, Susan Grey / Audio-visual materials. In *Simple library cataloging.* 5th ed. Metuchen, N.J., Scarecrow, 1969. p. 199–222.

2. American Library Association. Editorial Committee's Subcommittee on the ALA rules for filing catalog cards / Sec. 37. Non-book material arrangement. In *ALA rules for filing catalog cards.* 2d ed. Chicago, Amer. Libr. Ass., 1969. p. 218–232.

3. *Anglo-American Cataloging Rules.* Prepared by the American Library Ass., the Library of Congress, the Library Ass., the Canadian Library Ass. / North American text, with supplement of additions and changes. Chicago, Amer. Libr. Ass., 1970. (Supersedes the ALA Cataloging rules for author and title entries, and includes a revision of the rules of descriptive cataloging in the Library of Congress.) Part III. Non-Book Materials, p. 258ff.

4. Association for Educational Communications and Technology. Information Science Committee / *Standards for cataloging nonprint materials.* 3d ed. Washington, D.C., Ass. for Educ.

Commun. and Tech., 1972.

5. Anthony, L.J. / Filing and storing material. In *Handbook of special librarianship and information work.* 3d ed. Wilfred Ashworth, ed. London, Aslib, 1967. p. 233–273.

6. *Bibliographic control of nonprint media.* Pearce S. Grove, ed. Chicago, Amer. Libr. Ass., 1972.

7. Bidlock, Russell E. and Constance Rinehart / [Examples of special library materials] In *Typewritten catalog cards: a manual of procedure and form with 300 sample cards.* 2d ed. Ann Arbor, Mich., Mich. Campus Publ., 1970. p. 83–106.

8. Cataloging nonbooks. *Liaison,* p. 39. Jun 1971. (Libr. Ass. Newsletter)

9. *Cataloging standards for non-book materials.* Portland, Ore., Northwest Libr. Serv., 1968.

10. Clark, Virginia / *The organization of nonbook materials in the Laboratory School Library, North Texas State University: An outline.* Rev. ed. Denton, North Texas State University, 1969. EDRS: ED 043 349; MF $0.50. For sale by Northeast Campus Bookstore, 828 Harwood Rd., Hurst, Texas 76053. $2.25.

11. Collison, Robert L. / *The cataloging, arrangement and filing of special materials in special libraries.* London, Aslib, 1950. (Aslib manuals, v. 2)

12. Colvin, Laura C. / Sec. IX. Works of special type and special collections, and Sec. X. Nonbook materials. In *Cataloging sampler, a comparative and interpretive guide.* Hamden, Conn., Archon, Shoe String, 1963. p. 231–246, 247–287.

13. Cox, Carl T. / The cataloging of nonbook materials: basic guidelines. *Libr. Res. & Tech. Serv.* 15: 472–478 (Fall 1971).

14. Croghan, Antony / *A thesaurus-classification for the physical forms of non-book media.* London, Antony Croghan, 1970. (Address: 17 Coburgh Mansions, Handel St., London, W.C. 1, England)

15. Daily, Jay E. / *Organizing nonprint materials: a guide for librarians.* New York, M. Dekker, 1972.

16. Dewey, Harry / *Fundamentals of cataloging and classification.* vol. 2. Specialized cataloging and classification, theory and technique. 3d ed. (Prelim.) Madison, Wis., College Typing, 1956.

17. Eaton, Thelma / The organization of special materials. In *Cataloging and classification, an introductory manual.* 4th ed. Ann Arbor, Mich., Edwards Bros. (dist.), 1967. p. 166–183.

18. Field, F. Bernice / The rules for description and for nonbook materials. In *New rules for an old game.* (Proceedings of a workshop on the 1967 Anglo-American cataloging code held by the Sch. Librn., Univ. of British Columbia, Apr 13 and 14, 1967). Thelma E. Allen and Doryl Ann Dickman, eds. Vancouver, Publ. Centre, Univ. British Columbia, 1967. p. 81–95.

19. Foskett, D.J. / Classification—special materials. In *Handbook of special librarianship and information work.* 3d ed. Wilfred Ashworth, ed. London, Aslib, 1967. p. 109–114, 138, 139.

20. Genesee Valley School Development Ass. / *Design for cataloging non-book materials: adaptable for computer use.* Rochester, N.Y., Genesee Valley School Development Ass., 1969. EDRS: ED 045 153; HC $1.65, MF $0.25.

21. Hopkinson, Shirley L. / Card forms for special types of library materials. In *The descriptive cataloging of library materials.* 3d ed. San Jose, Calif., Claremont House, 1968. p. 32–57.

22. Johnson, Jean, et al. / *AV cataloging and processing simplified.* Raleigh, N.C., Audiovisual Catalogers, 1971.

23. National Education Ass. Audio-Visual Instruction Dept. / *Standards for cataloging, coding, and scheduling educational media.* Washington, D.C., NEA, 1968.

24. The new rules in action: a symposium. *Libr. Res. and Tech. Serv.* 13: 5–41 (Winter 1969).

25. Piercy, Esther J. / Non-book and near-book materials. In *Common-*

sense cataloging. A manual for the organization of book and other materials in school and small public libraries. New York, H.W. Wilson Co., 1965. p. 94–110.

26. Riddle, Jean, Shirley Lewis, and Janet MacDonald / Bibliographical chaos and control in the multi-media centre. *Can. Libr. J.* 27: 444–449 (Nov–Dec 1970).

27. Schutze, Gertrude / *Documentation sourcebook.* Metuchen, N.J. Scarecrow, 1965.

28. *Seminar on the Anglo-American cataloging rules (1967):* Proceedings of the Seminar organized by the Cataloging and Indexing Group of the Library Association, at the University of Nottingham, 22nd–25th March 1968. J.C. Downing and N.F. Sharp, eds. London, Library Ass., 1969.

29. Sharp, J.R. / Information retrieval— cataloging and indexing nonbibliographical material. In *Handbook of special librarianship and information work.* 3d ed. Wilfred Ashworth, ed. London, Aslib, 1967. p. 164– 171, 226–227.

30. Silva, Manil / Indexing and filing of non-book material. In *Special libraries.* London, Andre Deutsch, 1970, p. 44–52.

31. Slocum, Robert B. and Lois Hacker / *Sample cataloging forms; illustrations of solutions to problems in descriptive cataloging.* 2d rev. ed. Metuchen, N.J., Scarecrow, 1968.

32. Southern Baptist Convention. Church Library Dept. / *Church library classification and cataloging guide: books, filmstrips, recordings, tape recording, slides.* rev. and enl. ed. Nashville, Tenn., Broadman, 1969.

33. Strauss, Lucille J., et al. / Indexing and filing of non-book materials. In *Scientific and technical libraries: their organization and administration.* 2d ed. New York, N.Y., Becker and Hayes, 1972. p. 184–214.

34. Strauss, Lucille J., et al. / Technical processes cataloging, classification, and subject headings. In *Scientific and technical libraries: their organization and administration.* 2d ed.

New York, N.Y., Becker and Hayes, 1972. p. 157–183.

35. Table I checklist of items for physical description of non-book materials. *Wis. Libr. Bull.* 66: 72–73 (Mar 1970).

36. U.S. Library of Congress. Descriptive Cataloging Div. / *Rules of descriptive cataloging in the Library of Congress* (adopted by the Amer. Libr. Ass.). Washington, D.C., 1949.

37. Volkersz, Evert / Neither book nor manuscript; some special collections. *Libr. Res. and Tech. Serv.* 13: 493– 501 (Fall 1969).

38. Weihs, Jean Riddle, et al. / *Nonbook materials; the organization of integrated collections.* 1st ed. Ottawa, Can. Libr. Ass., 1973.

39. Westhuis, Judith Loveys, and Julia M. DeYoung / *Cataloging manual for nonbook materials in learning centers and school libraries.* Rev. ed. Mich. Ass. Sch. Librns., Bureau of School Services, Univ. Mich. Ann Arbor, Univ. Mich. Press, 1967.

40. Witmore, Rosamond B. / Non-book materials. In *A guide to the organization of library materials in schools and small public libraries.* rev. Muncie, Ind., Ball State Univ., 1967. p. 102–130.

41. Wynar, Bohdan / Cataloging of non-book materials. In *Introduction to cataloging and classification.* 3d ed. Rochester, N.Y., Libraries Unlimited, 1967. p. 149–164.

4. Special Materials— Standards, Storage, Use

1. American Library Ass. Committee on Library Terminology / *ALA glossary of library terms.* Prepared by Elizabeth H. Thompson under direction of the committee. Chicago, Amer. Libr. Ass., 1943.

2. American Library Ass. Library Technology Program / *Library technology reports.* A service to provice information on library systems, equipment and supplies to the

library profession. Chicago, 1965– (loose-leaf). Kept up to date by supplementary material issued bimonthly.

3. American Library Ass. Public Lib. Ass. Audiovisual Committee / *Guidelines for audiovisual materials and services for public libraries.* Chicago, Amer. Libr. Ass., 1970.

4. American Library Ass. Statistics Coordinating Project / Statistics of special libraries. In *Library statistics: a handbook of concepts, definitions and terminology.* Joel Williams, ed. Chicago, Amer. Libr. Ass., 1966. p. 95–116.

5. American National Standards Institute, Committee Z39 / *Standardization in the field of library work, documentation, and related publishing practices.* ANSI Standard Z39–. New York, ANSI, 1943–.

6. American National Standards Institute / *Vocabulary for information processing.* New York, ANSI, 1970. (ANSI Standard X-3.12-1970. Approved Feb 18, 1970.)

7. Appraisals of "Objectives and Standards for Special Libraries." *Spec. Libr.* 56: 197–201 (Mar 1965).

8. Association of College and Research Libraries / *Guidelines for audiovisual services in academic libraries.* Chicago, Ass. of Coll. and Res. Libr., 1968.

9. Association of Hospital and Institution Libraries. Hospital Library Standards Committee / *Standards for library services in health care institutions.* Chicago, Amer. Libr. Ass., 1970.

10. *Audiovisual equipment directory.* 17th ed. 1971. Fairfax, Va., National Audiovisual Ass., Annual.

11. Conference on the Use of Printed and Audio-Visual Materials for Instructional Purposes: First Report, prepared by M.F. Tauber and I.R. Stephens. New York, Columbia Univ. Sch. of Libr. Serv., 1966.

12. Davies, Ruth Ann / Appendix C. Terminology. In *The School library, a force for educational excellence.* New York, Bowker, 1969. p. 265–272.

13. Elstein, Herman, and Frederic R. Hartz / *Standards, selection and the media center: where are we now? Audiovisual Instr.* 15: 35–39 (Dec 1970).

14. Ellsworth, Ralph E., and Hobart D. Wagener / *The school library, facilities for independent study in the secondary school.* New York, Educ. Facilities Lab., 1963.

15. Hines, Theodore C., and Jessica L. Harris / *Terminology of library and information science: a selective glossary.* Preliminary ed. New York, Columbia Univ. Sch. of Libr. Serv., Mar. 1971. 41 p.

16. Mount, Ellis, ed. / *Planning the special library.* New York, Spec. Libr. Ass., 1972. (Spec. Libr. Ass. monograph no. 4)

17. Objectives and Standards for Special Libraries. *Spec. Libr.* 55: 672–680 (Dec 1964).

18. Orne, Jerrold / The place of standards in the new technology of information science. *Spec. Libr.* 58: 703–706 (Dec 1967).

19. Palmer, David C. / *Planning for a nationwide system of library statistics.* U.S. Dep. of Health, Educ. and Welfare, Off. of Educ. Washington, D.C., Supt. of Docs., U.S. Govt. Print. Off., 1970.

20. Pula, Fred J. / *Application and operation of audiovisual equipment in education.* New York, Wiley, 1968.

21. Randall, G.E. / Special library standards, statistics, and performance evaluation. *Spec. Libr.* 56: 379–386 (Jul–Aug 1965).

22. Strauss, Lucille J., et al. / Reference procedures and literature searches. In *Scientific and technical libraries: their organization and administration.* 2d ed. New York, N.Y., Becker and Hayes, 1972. p. 261–305.

23. United Nations Educational Scientific and Cultural Organization / *Vocabularium bibliothecarii.* (English, French, German, Spanish, Russian) New York, UNESCO, 1962.

24. Weber, Olga S., ed. / *Audiovisual market place,* 1971. New York, Bowker, 1971.

5. Special Materials—Records Management

1. Collison, Robert L. / *Commercial and Industrial Records Storage.* Tuckahoe, N.Y., John De Graff, 1969.
2. Collison, R.L. / *Modern Business Filing and Archives.* New York, John De Graff, 1963.
3. Donahoe, Alice M. / Putting automation into hospital record-keeping. *Spec. Libr.* 61: 223–228 (May–Jun 1970).
4. Holmstrom, J.E. / *Facts, files and action in business and public affairs. vol II. Filing, indexing, and circulation.* London, Chapman & Hall, 1953.
5. Jones, H.G. / *The records of a nation: their management, preservation, and use.* New York, Atheneum, 1969. 309 p.
6. Leahy, Emmett J. and Christopher A. Cameron / *Modern records management—a basic guide to records control, filing and information retrieval.* New York, McGraw-Hill, 1965.
7. U.S. Office of the Federal Register / *Guide to records retention requirements.* Washington, D.C., U.S. Govt. Print. Off., 1970.
8. Wright, Gordon H., ed. / A Syllabus for management and business studies. In *The library in colleges of commerce and technology.* A guide to the use of a library as an instrument of education. New York, London House & Maxwell, 1966. p. 150–161.

6. Special Materials—Archives

1. Alldredge, E.O. / Combining archival and records management terminology. *Amer. Arch.* 33: 61–65 (Jan 1970).
2. Allen, John C. / Commercial clearinghouse for the business community; a suggestion. *Spec. Libr.* 62: 185–188, (Apr 1971).
3. Atkinson, Gloria L. / Archives of the USAF Historical Division. *Spec. Libr.* 59: 444–446 (Jul–Aug 1968).
4. Brichford, M. J. / *Scientific and tech-nological documentation.* Archival evaluation and processing of university records relating to science and technology. Urbana-Champaign, Univ. of Ill., 1969.
5. Brichford, M.J. / University archives: relationships with faculty. *Amer. Arch.* 34: 173–181 (Apr 1971).
6. Burke, F.G. / Automation and historical research. *Libri.* 19 (no. 2): 81–91 (1969).
7. Business archives and records. In Burnette, O.L. / *Beneath the footnote.* Madison, State Hist. Soc. of Wis., 1969. p. 104–129.
8. Cavanagh, G.S.T. / Rare Books, archives, and the history of medicine. In Annan, G.L. and J.W. Felter, eds. *Handbook of medical library practice.* 3d ed. Chicago, Med. Libr. Ass., 1970. p. 254–283, bibliog.
9. Cushman, H.M.B. / Modern business archivist. *Amer. Arch.* 33: 19–24 (Jan 1970).
10. Evans, F.B., comp. / *Administration of modern archives.* A select bibliographic guide. Washington, D.C., Off. National Arch., 1970 [i.e., 1971].
11. Evans, F.B. / Modern concepts of archives administration and records management. *Unesco Bull. Libr.* 24: 242–247 (Spring 1970).
12. Fishbein, M.H. / Viewpoint on appraisal of national records. *Amer. Arch.* 33: 175–187 (Apr 1970).
13. Formation of a consortium for the microfilming of manuscript and documentary collections in the Austrian state archives. *Libr. Cong. Inform. Bull.* 29: 344 (Jul 1970).
14. Guidelines for Unesco's policy on archives development. *Bibliogr. Doc. Terminol.* 10: 178–179 (Sep 1970).
15. Harlow, Neal / Managing manuscript collections. *Libr. Trends* 4: 203–212 (Oct 1955).
16. Hasznos, L. / Modern methods for the protection of archival and library material. Care and restoration of badly damaged documents. *Unesco Bull. Libr.* 24: 302–304 (Nov 1970).
17. Heysworth, P. / Manuscripts and non-book materials in libraries. *Arch.* 9: 90–97 (Oct 1969).

18. Houze, R.A. / Texas consortium for microfilming the Mexican archives. *Texas Libr. J.*45: 120-2+ (Fall 1969).

19. Leisinger, A.H. / *Microphotography for archives.* Washington, D.C., Intern. Council on Archives, 1968.

20. Lewis, J.C. / Research on conservation of library materials. *Arch.* 9: 101 (Oct 1969).

21. Lightwood, Martha / Corporation documents—sources of business history. *Spec. Libr.* 57: 336-337 (May–Jun 1966).

22. McAllister, D.T. / Collecting archives for the history of science. *Amer. Arch.* 32: 327-332 (Oct 1969).

23. *Micropublishing for learned societies.* Hatfield, Herts., College of Technology, 1968.

24. Mitchell, T.W. / New viewpoints on establishing permanent values of state archives. *Amer. Arch.* 33: 163–174 (Apr 1970).

25. Muller, Samuel / *Manual for the arrangement and description of archives . . .* translation of the 2d ed. New York, H.W. Wilson, 1968.

26. National Fire Protection Ass. / Standard for the protection of records. In *National fire codes.* v. 9. Occupancy standards and process hazards. Boston, NFPA, 1972-73. p. 232-1-232-93.

27. National Fire Protection Ass. / Manual for fire protection for archives and record centers. In *National Fire Codes.* v. 9. Occupancy standards and process hazards. Boston, NFPA, 1972-73. p. 232AM-1-232AM-26.

28. Nelson, C.W., ed. / Technical notes: new products and data; technical mailbag. See issues of *Amer. Arch.*

29. New programme for archives preservation continues the work of Unesco's Mobile microfilm units. *Bibliogr. Doc. Terminol.* 10: 48–49 (Mar 1970).

30. Oswald, Genevieve / Creating tangible records for an intangible art. *Spec. Libr.* 59: 146-151 (Mar 1968).

31. Pinkett, H.T. / Glossary of records terminology: scope and definitions. *Amer. Arch.* 33: 53-56 (Jan 1970).

32. Posner, Ernst / *American state archives.* Chicago, Univ. of Chicago Press, 1964.

33. Pye, J.M. / Archives of twentieth century scientists and technologists: arranging and listing three collections. *Aslib. Proc.* 23: 122-126 (Mar 1971).

34. Recorded sound archives facing legal risks? *Libr. J.* 34: 4480 (Dec 15, 1969).

35. *Restaurator.* An international journal for the preservation of library and archival material. v. 1, no. 1-1969- . Copenhagen, Restaurator Press.

36. Rundell, W. / Personal data from university archives. *Amer. Arch.* 34: 183-188 (Apr 1971).

37. Santen, V.B. / Appraisal of financial records. *Amer. Arch.* 32: 357-361, (Oct 1969).

38. Schellenberg, Theodore R. / *The management or archives.* New York, Columbia Univ. Press, 1965.

39. Schellenberg, T.R. / *Modern archives: principles and techniques.* Chicago, Univ. Chicago Press, 1956.

40. Simmons, Joseph M. / Business records in the company archives. *Spec. Libr.* 59: 20-23 (Jan 1968).

41. Simmons, Joseph M. / The special librarian as a company archivist. *Spec. Libr.* 56: 647-650 (Nov 1965).

42. Stevens, Rolland E. / *University archives.* Papers presented at an Institute conducted by the University of Illinois Graduate School of Library Science, Nov. 1-4, 1964. Champaign, Ill., Illini Union Bookstore, 1965.

43. Stone, R.C.J. / Business archives and the librarian. *New Zealand Libr.* 33: 208-213 (Dec 1970).

44. Wessel, C.J. / Environmental factors affecting the permanence of library materials. In Chicago, Univ. Grad. Libr. Sch. / *Deterioration and preservation of library materials.* Chicago, Univ. Chicago Press, 1970. p. 39-84. Same, *Libr. Quart.* 40: 39-84 (Jan 1970).

45. West, H.G. / Business financial records. *New Zealand Libr.* 33: 214-222 (Dec 1970).

46. Wickman, John E. / The Dwight D. Eisenhower Library. *Spec. Libr.* 60: 590-595 (Nov 1969).

47. Woadden, A.R.N. / Cultural factors

and records terminology. *Amer. Arch.* 33: 57–59 (Jan 1970).

7. Special Materials—Government Publications—General

1. Childs, J.B. / Current bibliographical control of international intergovernmental documents. *Libr. Res. & Tech. Serv.* 10: 319–331 (Summer 1966).
2. Citro, Constance F. / The Census Bureau as an information system: developments in increasing access to census data. *Spec. Libr.* 60: 10–16 (Jan 1960).
3. Fry, B.M., et al. / *Research design for a comprehensive study of the use, bibliographic control, and distribution of government publications.* Washington, D.C., U.S. Off. of Educ. Bur. of Res., 1970.
4. Hartford, P.J. and J. Osborn / Government publications course: a survey. *J. Educ. Librarianship* 11: 251–260 (Winter 1971).
5. Intergovernmental Task Force on Information Systems / *The dynamics of information flow: recommendations to improve the flow of information within and among Federal, state and local governments.* n.p., 1968.
6. Kerbec, M.J., comp. and ed. / *Legally available U.S. government information as a result of the Public Information Act.* Output Systems Corp., 1911 Jefferson Davis Highway, Arlington, Va. 22202. 1970. 2v.
7. Kerbec, M.J. / Public Information Act: a potent tool for librarians and citizens seeking information from the government. *Libr. J.* 95: 4229–4231 (Dec 15, 1970).
8. Kling, R.E. / *Government Printing Office.* New York, Praeger, 1970.
9. Rawson, Nancy / For the businessman engaged in foreign trade. *Spec. Libr.* 59: 447–451 (Jul–Aug 1968).
10. Schmeckebier, Laurence F. / *Government publications and their use.* 2d rev. ed. Washington, D.C., Brookings Institution, 1969.

11. Strauss, Lucille J., et al. / Government documents. In *Scientific and technical libraries: their organization and administration.* 2d ed. New York, N.Y., Becker and Hayes, 1972. p. 121–127.

8. Special Materials—Government Publications—Management

1. Beckman, Margaret / *Documentation system for the organization of government publications within a university library.* Rep. RR-2; UG-LIB-GLPH-RR-69-2. Guelph, Ont., Canada, Libr. Admin., Univ. of Guelph Library, 1969. 81p. EDRS: ED-044 159; MF $.50
2. Carter, C. / Cataloging and classification of state documents. *Penn. Libr. Ass. Bull.* 25: 86–97 (Mar 1970).
3. Casey, Genevieve M. and Edith Phillips. *The management and use of state documents in Indiana.* Indianapolis, Indiana State Library, 1970. ED-046 473.
4. Dale, Doris Cruger / The development of classification systems for government publications. *Libr. Res. and Tech. Serv.* 13: 471–483 (Fall 1969).
5. Govt. docs. in microfilm from GPO? *Amer. Libr.* 2: 667 (Jul 1971).
6. Grossman, Julian A. / Putting government documents to work. *RQ* 11: 42–45 (Fall 1971).
7. Henrick, F.K. / Fallacy of corporate authorship; how its continuance prevents effective cataloging of govt. docs. In *Proceedings ASIS Conference, 1970.* Philadelphia, 1970. v. 7: Information conscious society. Washington, D.C., ASIS, 1970. p. 233–5.
8. Herold, Althea Conley / Government publications . . . microcards. In *Processing Manual.* A pictorial workbook of catalog cards. Teaneck, N.J., Fairleigh Dickinson Univ. Press, 1963. p. 69–83.
9. Hoduski, B.E. / CIP: a basic social responsibility. *Choice* 7: 1345–1346 (Dec 1970).
10. Jackson, Ellen P. / *A manual for the*

administration of the federal documents collection in libraries. Prep. for the Amer. Libr. Ass. Committee on Public Docs. Chicago, Amer. Libr. Ass., 1955.

11. King, J.A. / Explanation of the Sup. of Docs. classification system. In S.G. Mechanic, comp. / *Annotated list of selected U.S. govt. publ. available to depository libraries.* New York, H.W. Wilson, 1971. 281-293.

12. Levy, Grace / "Cuttering" the corporate entry. *Spec. Libr.* 60: 657-658 (Dec 1969).

13. Markley, Anne E. / Library records for government publications. Berkeley, Univ. of Calif. Press, 1951.

14. Miele, A.W. / Technical services dept. of the Illinois State Library. *Ill. Libr.* 53: 298-309 (Apr-May 1971).

15. Shannon, Michael O. / For the control of municipal documents. *Spec. Libr.* 61: 127-130 (Mar 1970).

16. Simmons, Robert M. / Handling changes in Superintendent of Documents classification. *Libr. Res. and Tech. Serv.* 15: 241-244 (Spring 1971).

17. Spalding, C.S. / LC practice with regard to U.S. documents. *Libr. Res. and Tech. Serv.* 14: 609-610 (Fall 1970).

9. Special Materials—Government Publications—Acquisition

1. Brewster, J.W. / To catch a government document: Doc. ex. *Wilson Libr. Bull.* 45: 941-946 (May 1970).

2. Chona, Harbans S. / Professional developments reviewed: Doc. ex. revisited: does it answer the needs? *Wilson Libr. Bull.* 45: 513-515 (Jan 1971).

3. Cook, Frederick G. / State manual procurement guide. *Spec. Libr.* 62: 88-93 (Feb 1971).

4. Darling, R.E. / Government bookstore. *Spec. Libr.* 62: 8 (Jan 1971).

5. Free, Opal M. / Commercial reprints of federal documents: their significance and acquisition. *Spec. Libr.*

60: 126-131 (Mar 1969).

6. Kiraldi, L. / Cooperation between map and documents librarians; common problems and concerns. SLA Geogr. and Map Div. *Bull.* no. 80: 32-34 (Jun 1970).

7. Locker, B. / Expediting acquisition of government documents. *Spec. Libr.* 62: 9 (Jan 1971).

10. Special Materials—Government Publications—Bibliography

1. Andriot, John L. / *Guide to popular U.S. Government publications.* Arlington, Va., Documents Index, 1960.

2. Andriot, John L. / *Guide to U.S. Government serials and periodicals.* McLean, Va. Documents Index., 1959- .

3. Bernier, Bernard A., Jr., Comp. / *Popular names of U.S. government reports; a catalog.* 2d ed. U.S. Library of Congress, Reference Dept. Washington, D.C., Sup. of Docs., U.S. Govt. Print. Off., 1970.

4. Body, Alexander C. / *Annotated bibliography of bibliographies on selected government publications, and supplementary guides to the Superintendents of Documents classification system.* Kalamazoo, Western Mich. Univ., 1967.

5. Body, Alexander C. / *Annotated bibliography . . .* 1st suppl. Kalamazoo, Western Mich. Univ., 1968- .

6. Boyd, Anne M. / *U.S. Government publications as sources of information for libraries.* 3d ed. New York, H.W. Wilson, 1949.

7. Brown, Everett S. / *Manual of government publications, U.S. and foreign.* New York, Appleton-Century-Crofts, 1950.

8. Congressional Information Service / *CIS index to publications of the United States Congress.* v. 1-. 1970-.

9. Congressional Information Service / *CIS annual.* 1970-. pt. 1: Abstracts of congressional publications and legislative histories. Pt. 2: Index to congressional publications and

public laws. Washington, D.C.

10. *Government reference books*. 1st ed. 1968/69-. Littleton, Colo., Libraries Unlimited. (A biennial guide to U.S. Government publications)

11. Hirshberg, Herbert S. / *Subject guide to U.S. government publications*. Chicago, *Amer. Libr. Ass.*, 1947.

12. Inventory of lists, indexes and catalogues of publications and documents of inter-governmental organizations other than the United Nations. *Unesco Bull. Libr.* 21: 263-270 (Sep 1967).

13. Jackson, Ellen P. / *Subject Guide to major U.S. Government publications*. Chicago, Amer. Libr. Ass., 1968.

14. Leidy, William P. / *A popular guide to government publications*. 3d ed. New York, Columbia Univ. Press, 1968.

15. Mechanic, S.G., comp. / *Annotated list of selected United States Government publications available to depository libraries*. New York, H.W. Wilson, 1971.

16. O'Hara, F.J. / *Over 2000 free publications, yours for the asking*. New York, New American Library, 1968.

17. O'Hara, F.J. / Selected government publications. See issues of *Wilson Libr. Bull.*

18. Poore, Benjamin P. / *A descriptive catalogue of the government publications of the United States, Sep 5, 1774–Mar 4, 1881*. Washington, D.C., U.S. Gov't Print. Off., 1885.

19. Press, Charles / *State manuals, blue books, and election results*. Berkeley, Inst. Govt. Studies, Univ. of Calif., 1962.

20. Schmeckebier, L.F. and R.B. Eastin / *Government publications and their use*. 2d rev. ed. Washington, D.C., Brookings Institution, 1969.

21. United Nations. Dag Hammerskjold Library / *United Nations documents index*. v. 1 Jan, 1950- . Monthly with annual cumulative indexes.

22. U.S. Library of Congress. Processing Dept. / *Monthly checklist of state publications*. v. 1- 1910- . Washington, D.C., U.S. Govt. Print. Off.

23. U.S. Superintendent of Documents / *Catalogue of the public docs. of the fifty-third–seventy-sixth Congress and of all depts. of the government of the United States for the period from Mar 4, 1893, to Dec 31, 1940* (being the "Comprehensive index" provided for by the act approved Jan 12, 1895) Washington, D.C., U.S. Govt. Print. Off., 1896-1944. 25 v. in 40.

24. U.S. Superintendent of Documents / *Monthly catalog of United States Government publications*. no. 1- Jan 1895- . Washington, D.C., U.S. Govt. Print. Off.

25. Vashishth, C.P. / Organization of the documents of the UN and its specialized agencies. *Libr. Her.* 11: 182-193 (Oct 1969).

26. Wilcox, Jerome K., ed. / *Manual on the use of state publications*. Chicago, Amer. Libr. Ass., 1940.

27. Wood, Jennings, ed. / *United States Government publications: a partial list of non-GPO imprints*. Chicago, Amer. Libr. Ass., 1965.

28. *Guide to U.S. Government statistics* 1956- . Arlington, Va., Documents Index.

11. Special Materials—Technical Reports—General Information and Management

1. Boylan, Nancy / Technical reports. *RQ* 10: 18-21 (Fall 1970).

2. Carter, Launor F., et al. / *National document-handling systems for science and technology*. New York, Wiley, 1967.

3. *Dictionary of report series codes*. 2d ed. Lois E. Godfrey and Helen F. Redman, eds. New York, Spec. Libr. Ass., 1973.

4. Fry, Bernard M. / *Library organization and management of technical reports literature*. Washington, D.C., Catholic Univ. of America Press, 1953.

5. Gibson, Eleanor B. / KWIC-software for automating a small metals re-

search report collection. *Spec. Libr.*
56: 175–178 (Mar 1965).

6. Grosch, Audrey N. / Application of
uniterm coordinate indexing to a
marketing research report collection.
Spec. Libr. 56: 303–311 (May/Jun
1965).

7. Grosch, Audrey N. / Thesaurus construction: a small collection of non-
scientific reports. *Spec. Libr.* 60:
87–92 (Feb 1969).

8. Hall, J. / Technical report literature.
In *Handbook of special librarianship
and information work.* 3d ed. Wilfred Ashworth, ed. London, Aslib,
1967. p. 287–308.

9. Hogenauer, A.K. / Aviation firm catalogs its special collection. *Spec. Libr.*
62: 234–237 (May 1971).

10. Hope, Nelson W. / A check list for
classified documents. *Spec. Libr.* 57:
120–121 (Feb 1966).

11. Houghton, Bernard / *Technical information sources: a guide to patent
specifications, standards, and technical reports literature.* 2d ed. [Ham-
den, Conn., London, Eng.] Linnet
Books & Clive Bingley, 1972.

12. *Information Hang-Ups.* Problems en-
countered by users of the technical
information services offered by DDC
and CFSTI, with recommendations
for the future. Comm. of DDC Users
in the Greater Washington, D.C.
Area, 1969. ED-044 156.

13. Linder, L.H. / Comparative costs of
document indexing and book cataloging. *Spec. Libr.* 56: 724–726 (Dec
1965).

14. McKenna, F.E. / An abstract bulletin
for corporate R&E reports. *Spec.
Libr.* 56: 318–322 (May/Jun 1965).

15. Microcard Corporation / *Planning
guide for a miniaturized document
distribution system.* Charles P.
Yerkes, ed. New York, 1962. 1v.

16. North, Jeanne B. / A look at the new
COSATI standard. *Spec. Libr.* 58:
582–584 (Oct 1967).

17. Regional Workshop on the Report
Literature, Albuquerque, N.M. 1965
/ *Proceedings.* Lois E. Godfrey and
Helen S. Keller, eds. North Holly-
wood, Calif., Western Periodicals,
1966.

18. Report literature and sources of information (Special issue, Workshop
proceedings. Workshop on Report
Literature and Sources of Information, sponsored by New Jersey Chapter, Special Libraries Association,
April 5, 1967, Edison, N.J.). *Spec.
Libr.* 59: 84–106 (Feb 1968).

19. Smith, Ruth S. / Information hang-
ups; some suggestions for DDC and
the Clearinghouse. *Spec. Libr.* 60:
672–676 (Dec 1969).

20. Strain, Paula M. / Information hang-
ups; reactions to DDC and CFSTI information services. *Spec. Libr.* 60:
619 (Nov 1969).

21. Strain, Paula M. / KWIC and easy? A
librarian's view of a computer-based
technical reports announcement system. *Spec. Libr.* 55: 614–618 (Nov
1964).

22. Strickland, Helen D. / Regional workshop on report literature. *Spec. Libr.*
57: 52–53 (Jan 1966).

23. U.S. Federal Council for Science and
Technology. Committee on Scientific
and Technical Information / *Standards for descriptive cataloging of government scientific and technical reports.* Washington, D.C., Off. of Sci.
and Tech., Executive Office of the
President . . . , 1963.

24. Voos, H. / Information explosion or,
Redundancy reduces the charge! *Coll.
and Res. Libr.* 32: 7–14 (Jan 1971).

25. Weil, Ben H. / *The technical report.*
New York, Reinhold, 1958.

26. Joshi, R.C., et al. / An experiment in
mechanical storage and retrieval of information in internal technical reports. *Ann. of Libr. Sci. and Doc.*
16: 119–125 (Sep–Dec 1969).

12. Special Materials—Technical Reports—Bibliography

1. CCM Information Corporation /
*ERIC educational documents index,
1966-1969.* New York, 1970. v. 1:
Major descriptors; v. 2: Minor descriptors. Author index.

2. *Complete guide and index to ERIC
reports through Dec 1969.* Prentice-
Hall Editorial Staff, comp. Engle-

wood Cliffs, N.J., Prentice-Hall, 1970.

3. Davis, Richard A. / *Bibliography of use studies.* Prepared under Nat. Sci. Found. Grant GN-170 for the Off. of Sci. Inform. Serv. (Philadelphia, 1964).

4. Flury, W.R. and D.D. Henderson / User oriented KWIC index: KWOC-ed., tagged and enriched. In *Proceedings of the American Society for Information Science Conference,* 1970. Philadelphia. v. 7. Info. conscious society. Washington, D.C., ASIS, 1970. p. 101-105.

5. Gillies, T.D. / Document serials, technical reports, and the national bibliography. In Ill. Univ., Urbana. Grad. Sch. of Libr. Sci. *Serial publications in large libraries.* Champaign, Ill., Illini Union Bookstore, 1970.

6. *Government reports announcements.* v. 1-41, Jan 11, 1946-Dec 25, 1966; v. 67, Jan 10, 1967- . Title varies. Frequency varies. Published by National Technical Information Service (NTIS), Springfield, Va. 22151.

7. *Nuclear science abstracts.* v. 1- Jul 15, 1948- . Oak Ridge, Tenn., Technical Information Service Extension, etc. Semimonthly. Published by Atomic Energy Commission. For sale by Sup. of Docs., U.S. Govt. Print. Off.

8. *PANDEX Current Index to Scientific and Technical Literature.* New York, N.Y., CCM Information Corporation. Bi-weekly, with quarterly and annual cumulations on microfiche or microfilm, 1967- .

9. Rand Corporation / *Index of Selected publications.* v. 1; 1946-62; Santa Monica, Calif. (Supersedes the corporation's *Index of publications.* Continued in the corporation's *Selected Rand abstracts*)

10. Rand Corporation / *Selected Rand abstracts* v. 1- . 1963- . Santa Monica, Calif. Quarterly.

11. *Research in Education.* (Educational Resources Information Center, ERIC) v. 1- . Nov/Dec 1966- . (Available from Sup. Docs., U.S. Govt. Print. Off., Washington, D.C.)

12. *Scientific and technical aerospace re-ports.* v. 1- . Jan 8, 1963- . Washington, D.C. Semimonthly. Published by the National Aeronautics and Space Administration. For sale by Sup. of Docs., U.S. Govt. Print. Off.

13. Special Materials—Dissertations, Academic

1. *American doctoral dissertations.* Ann Arbor, Mich., Univ. Microfilms, 1963- .

2. Aslib / *Index to theses accepted for higher degrees in the universities of Great Britain and Ireland.* v. 1- . 1950/51- . London.

3. Black, Dorothy M., comp. / *Guide to lists of master's theses.* Chicago, Amer. Libr. Ass., 1965.

4. Blum, F. / Two machine indexing projects at the Catholic University of America. *J. Amer. Soc. Inform. Sci.* 22: 105-106 (Mar 1971).

5. *Dissertation abstracts international; abstracts of dissertations available on microfilm or as Xerographic reproductions.* v. 1- . 1938. Ann Arbor, Mich., Univ. Microfilms.

6. Dissertation Abstracts Int., retrospective index. Comment with title: $1,000 misunderstanding: UM's index to its Diss. Abs. Int. by R.L. Scott; rejoinder with title: One-million-entry starting place for finding dissertations, by R.F. Asleson. *Wilson Libr. Bull.* 46: 73-77 (Sep 1971).

7. *Doctoral dissertations accepted by American universities.* no. 1-22; 1933/34-1954/55. New York, H.W. Wilson, 1934-55. 17v.

8. *French doctoral theses.* no. 1- . Dec 1955- . New York, French Cultural Services.

9. *Masters abstracts.* v. 1- . 1962- . Ann Arbor, Mich., Univ. Microfilms.

10. Ottervik, Gosta and Paul Hallberg / Microfilming and bibliographic control of European dissertations. *Libri* 19: 138-141 (1969).

11. U.S. Library of Congress. Catalog Division / *List of American doctoral dissertations printed in 1912-38.* Washington, D.C., U.S. Govt. Print. Off., 1913-40 (27v in 7).

12. Urquhart, D.J. / Doctoral theses. *NLL Rev.* 1: 8-9 (Jan 1971).

14. Special Materials—Standards and Specifications

 1. American National Standards Institute / *Catalog, 1973.* Annual. (Order from ANSI, 1430 Broadway, New York, N.Y. 10018. Also includes partial listing of ISO, IEC, COPANT, and CEE standards.)
 2. *ANSI Reporter / Standards Action.* v. 1- . 1967- . New York, Amer. Nat. Stand. Inst.
 3. British Standards Institution / *British Standards Yearbook, 1971.* (Order from BSI, 2 Park St., London WIA 2BS, Eng.)
 4. *BSI news.* v. 1- . 1956- . London, Brit. Stand. Inst. Monthly
 5. Hartman, Joan E. / *Directory of United States standardization activities.* Washington, D.C., U.S. Dept. of Commerce, National Bureau of Standards; for sale by Sup. of Docs., U.S. Govt. Print. Off., 1967. (National Bureau of Standards. Misc. Publ. 288).
 6. Houghton, Bernard. / *Technical information sources: a guide to patent specifications, standards, and technical reports literature.* 2d ed. [Hamden Conn.] , London, Eng., Linnet Books & C. Bingley, [1972] .
 7. International Organization for Standardization / *ISO catalog, 1970.* Annual. $6.00. (Order from ANSI, 1430 Broadway, New York, N.Y. 10018, or ISO, 1 rue de Varembe, Geneva, Switz.)
 8. *Journal of materials.* v. 1- . Mar 1966- . Philadelphia, Pa. American Society for Testing and Materials. Quarterly.
 9. *Magazine of standards.* Jun 1930- Jul 1970. Superseded by *ANSI Reporter/Standards Action.* New York, Amer. Nat. Stand. Inst.
10. *Materials Research and Standards.* v. 1- . Jan 1961- . Philadelphia, Pa. Amer. Soc. for Testing and Mater.
11. Slattery, William J. / *An index of U.S. voluntary engineering standards.*

Covering those standards, specifications, test methods, and recommended practices issued by national standardization organizations in the United States. Washington, D.C., U.S. Nat. Bureau of Stand., for sale by Sup. of Docs., U.S. Govt. Print. Off., 1971. (U.S. Nat. Bureau of Stand. Spec. Publ. 329).
12. Struglia, Erasmus J. / *Standards and specifications information sources.* A guide to literature and to public and private agencies concerned with technological uniformities. Detroit, Gale Research, 1965. (Management Information Guide, 6)
13. Tayal, A.S. / Acquisition and updating of standards and specifications in technical libraries. *Unesco Bull. Libr.* 25: 198-204 (Jul-Aug 1971).
14. U.S. Dept. of Defense / *Index of specifications and standards.* With supplements. (Defense Supply Agency, Defense Dept.) Bimonthly. Pt. 1: Alphabetical listing. Pt. 2: Numerical listing (Jul 1971).
15. U.S. Federal Supply Service. General Services Administration / *Index of Federal specifications and standards.* Jan 1, 1971. (FPMR 101-29.1, 41 CFR 101-29.1) Cumulative supplements. Irregular.
16. U.S. Small Business Administration / *U.S. Government specifications directory.* A guide to reference sources of U.S. govt. specifications and standards, and appropriate indexes. Prepared by the Office of Procurement and Technical Assistants. Washington, D.C., Off. of Inform., 1954.
17. VSMF (Visual Search Microfilm Files) Englewood, Colo., Information Handling Serv. Military Specifications File, MS Drawings, Documentation File.

15. Special Materials—Patents— General Information and Management

For additional titles covering this subject area, see Bibliography at end of paper entitled: "Patent and Trademark Literature," by Safford Harris.

1. Andrew, Lucy Brett / *Practical patent procedure.* 7th ed. Palm Beach, Fla., 1970.
2. Asher, Gordon / International patent co-operation. *J. Chem. Doc.* 11: 14–18 (Feb 1971).
3. Axhausen, Walter E.A. / Tools for retrieving technological information from classified files of the world's patent offices. In *Users of Documentation: FID International Congress on Documentation, Buenos Aires, 21–24 Sept. 1970,* The Hague, FID, 1970 (Paper III a.5).
4. Brenner, Everett H. and D.H. Helander / Petroleum literature and patent retrieval: centralized information processing. *Spec. Libr.* 60: 146–152 (Mar 1969).
5. C/I/L Patent Abstracts (Computer/information/library). Leonard Cohan, ed. v. 1–3 Jul/Aug 1969–1971, New York, Science Associates/International. (Suspended)
6. Council of Europe. Committee of Experts on Patents. Working Party on Classification. / *International Classification of patents for inventions, under the European Convention of 19th December 1954.* London, Eng. Morgan-Grampian Books, 1968. 3v. (Loose-leaf)
7. Danese, Denny M. / Acquisition of U.S. patents pending. *Spec. Libr.* 62: 490–491 (Nov 1971).
8. Fay, R.J. / Full-text information retrieval. *Law Libr. J.* 64: 167–175 (May 1971).
9. Fenner, Terrence W. / *Inventor's handbook.* New York, Chemical Publ., 1969.
10. Houghton, Bernard / *Technical information sources: a guide to patent specifications, standards, and technical reports literature.* 2d ed. [Hamden, Conn., London, Eng.] Linnet Books & C. Bingley, 1972. British.
11. Hurd, Ethan A. / Patent literature: current problems and future trends. *J. Chem. Doc.* 10: 167–173 (Aug 1970).
12. Hyams, M. / Chemical patents information. *Chem. in Brit.* 6: 416–420 (Oct 1970). (Describes Derwent Publications Ltd. services)
13. Jones, Stacy V. / *The inventor's patent handbook.* rev. ed. New York, Dial, 1969.
14. Kessler, Kenneth O. / *The successful inventor's guide; how to develop, protect and sell your invention profitably.* Englewood Cliffs, N.J., Prentice-Hall, 1965.
15. Lamb, J.P. / Patents and trade marks. In *Commercial and Technical Libraries.* London, Eng., George Allen & Unwin, and The Libr. Ass., 1955. p. 173–191.
16. Lang, William / Foreign patent laws, with comparative analysis. Worth Wade, ed. Ardmore, Pa., Advance House, 1968. (Loose-leaf)
17. Pfeffer, Harold / Information retrieval among examining patent offices. *Spec. Libr.* 59: 330–336 (May/Jun 1968).
18. Strauss, Lucille J. et al. / Reference procedures and literature searches—The patent literature. In *Scientific and Technical Libraries: Their Organization and Administration.* 2d ed. New York, N.Y., Becker and Hayes, 1972. p. 291–301.
19. TTA Information Services Company / *Survey of patent and product development organizations.* San Mateo, Calif., 1971. (An affiliate of Technology Transfer Associates, Inc.)
20. U.S. Patent Office / *Index to classification.* Washington, D.C., U.S. Govt. Print. Off., 1972. (Loose-leaf)
21. U.S. Patent Office / *Manual of Classification.* 1969– . Washington, D.C., U.S. Govt. Print. Off., 1969– . (Loose-leaf. Updated quarterly)
22. U.S. Patent Office / *Official gazette.* V. 1–882, Jan 3, 1872–Jan 26, 1971. Washington, D.C., U.S. Govt. Print. Off., 1872–1971. (Superseded by its *Official gazette: Patents,* and its *Official gazette: Trademarks.)*
23. U.S. Patent Office / *Official gazette: Patents.* v. 883– . Feb 2, 1971– . Washington, D.C., U.S. Govt. Print. Off., 1971– .
24. U.S. Patent Office / *Patents & inventions; an information aid for inventors.* rev. ed. Washington, D.C., U.S. Govt. Print. Off., 1964.
25. Wade, Worth / *The corporate patent*

department: its organization, administration, functions. Ardmore, Pa., Advance House, 1963. (Includes minimum list of books, periodicals, & services for a patent dept. library, p. 151-156.
26. Wade, Worth / How to exploit patents and know-how in Europe, a guide for industry, inventors, and attorneys. Overseas ed. Ardmore, Pa., Advance House, 1962.

16. Special Materials—Patents— Bibliography

1. Finlay, Ian F. / Guide to foreign-language printed patents and applications. London, Eng., Aslib, 1969.
2. The International index of patents: Chemical and allied arts, 1790/1960. New York, Interdex Corp., 1964. 6v.
3. The International index of patents: Electrical and allied arts, 1790/1960. New York, Interdex Corp., 1965. 5v.
4. The National catalog of patents: Chemical. 1961-1962. New York, N.Y., Rowman and Littlefield, 1963. 2v./year. (Patent nos. included as given in the Official gazette, 1961-1962)
5. The National catalog of patents. Chemical, allied patents. 1961/62. New York, N.Y., Rowman and Littlefield, 1963. 1v. (Patent nos. included as given in the Official gazette, 1961-1962)
6. The National catalog of patents. Electrical, allied patents. 1961/62. New York, N.Y., Rowman and Littlefield, 1963. 1v. (Patent nos. included as given in the Official gazette, 1961-1962)
7. The National catalog of patents. Electrical, including communications and radiant energy. 1961-1962. New York, N.Y., Rowman and Littlefield, 1963. 2v./year. (Patent nos. included as given in the Official gazette, 1961-1962).
8. U.S. Patent Office / Index of patents issued from the U.S. Patent Office. 1920- . Washington, D.C., U.S. Govt. Print. Off., 1921- . (Preceded by its Annual report of the Commissioner of Patents)

9. United States Patent previews: 1965-1970. Assignments of pending patents recorded in the U.S. Patent Office, Jan 1963-Jul 1965. Washington, D.C., Bowker, 1966.

17. Special Materials—Trade Literature

1. ANSI standard approval (advertising of books). Spec. Libr. 62: 378-379 (Sep 1971).
2. Goodwin, Jack / The trade literature collection of the Smithsonian Library. Spec. Libr. 57: 581-583 (Oct 1966).
3. Kelbrick, N. / Trade literature as a library material. Libr. Ass. Rec. 73: 65-67 (Apr 1971).
4. Meixell, Granville / The trade catalog collection, a manual with source lists. New York, Spec. Libr. Ass., 1934.
5. Micro-Publishing Systems / MPS library file. 1970- . Stamford, Conn. (On microfiche)
6. Perry, M. / College catalog collection; a survey. RQ 10: 240-242 (Spring 1971).
7. Strauss, Lucille J., et al. / Trade literature—equipment catalogs. In Scientific and technical libraries: their organization and administration. 2d ed. New York, N.Y., Becker and Hayes, 1972. p. 133.
8. Sweet's Catalog Service / Catalog file. A classified collection of manufacturers' catalogs. New York, Sweet's Div., McGraw-Hill Inform. Systems. Annual.
9. Thomas Micro-Catalogs. New York, Thomas Microcatalogs Div., Thomas Publishing, 1968-1969. (On microfiche. Ceased publication with 1969).
10. Thomas' register of American manufacturers. 63d ed. New York, Thomas Publishing, 1973. v. 9-11: Catalogs of companies. Annual.
11. UMF catalog publishing—a case history. Microgr. News and Views 1: 5-6 (Sep 25, 1970).

18. Special Materials—
Trademarks

For additional titles covering this subject area, see bibliography at end of paper entitled: "Patent and Trademark Literature," by Safford Harris.

1. *Trademark register of the United States.* 196- . Washington, D.C., Patent Searching Service, 196- . (Cumulated annually. Covers 1881/June 1 of preceding year. Arranged by Class with Trademark names in alphabetical order. May need to examine: *The Trademark renewal register*)
2. *The Trademark renewal register.* 1965, v. 1. Washington, D.C., The Trademark Register, 1964 [i.e. 1965] (Covers every renewed trademark: Oct 25, 1870–1963.)
3. *The Trademark renewal register.* 1966, v. 2. Washington, D.C., The Trademark Register, 1964 [i.e. 1966] (Covers current trademarks up to Dec 31, 1965, and renewed trademarks of 1964 and 1965.)
4. U.S. Patent Office / *General information concerning trademarks.* [Washington, D.C., U.S. Govt. Print. Off., 1966].
5. U.S. Patent Office / *Index of trademarks.* 1927- . Washington, D.C., U.S. Govt. Print. Off., 1928- .
6. U.S. Patent Office / *Official gazette: Trademarks.* 906, 972- . Feb. 2, 1971- . Washington, D.C., U.S. Govt. Print. Off., 1971- .

19. Special Materials—
Translations

1. Bush, Dorcas / Problems in translation. *Spec. Libr.* 58: 173–178, Mar 1967.
2. Chillag, J.P. / Translations and their guides. *NLL Rev.* 1: 46–53 (Apr 1971).
3. Cunningham, D.S. / Multilevel translation: a solution to foreign-language information needs. In *Proceedings of the American Society for Information Science Conference, 1970.*

Philadelphia, v. 7: Information conscious society. Washington, D.C., ASIS, 1970. p. 245–247.
4. European Translations Centre / *Translations journals.* List of periodicals translated cover-to-cover, abstracted publications, and periodicals containing selected articles. Delft, The Netherlands, European Translations Centre, 1970.
5. Gingold, Kurt / A translator's guide to better translations. *Spec. Libr.* 57: 643–644 (Nov 1966).
6. Himmelsbach, Carl J. and Grace E. Brociner, eds. / *A guide to scientific and technical journals in translation.* 2d ed. New York, Spec. Libr. Ass., 1972.
7. *Index Translationum.* v. 1- . 1948- . Paris, Unesco. Annual.
8. *International directory of translators and interpreters.* London, Pond, 1967.
9. Kaiser, Frances E., ed. / *Translators and translations: services and sources in science and technology.* 2d ed. New York, Spec. Libr. Ass., 1965.
10. Kip, Charles E. / The National Translations Center. *Spec. Libr.* 60: 104 (Feb 1969).
11. Linder, L.H. / Translations in a changing world. *Spec. Libr.* 61: 551–553 (Dec 1970).
12. Lufkin, James M. / What everybody should know about translation. *Spec. Libr.* 60: 74–81 (Feb 1969).
13. Millard, Patricia / *Directory of technical and scientific translators and services.* London, Crosby Lockwood & Son, 1968.
14. National Translations Center / *Consolidated index of translations into English.* New York, Spec. Libr. Ass., 1969. (Avail. from National Translations Center.)
15. *Technical translations.* v. 1–18. Jan 2, 1959–Dec 1967. Washington, D.C., U.S. Dept. of Commerce, Off. Tech. Serv.
16. *Translation monthly.* v. 1–4. Jan/Oct 1955–Dec 1958 [Chicago] Published for the Spec. Libr. Ass. by John Crerar Library.
17. Translation services at Aslib. *Aslib*

Proc. 22: 424 (Sep 1970).

18. *Translations register-index.* v. 1- . Jun 15, 1967- . Chicago, Nat. Transl. Center.

19. *World index of scientific translations and list of translations notified to ETC.* v. 6- . Jan 1972- . Delft, European Translations Centre.

20. Special Materials—Special Libraries

1. Ash, Lee, Comp. *Subject collections. A guide to special book collections and subject emphases as reported by university, college, public and special libraries in the United States and Canada.* 3d ed., rev. and enl. New York, Bowker, 1967.

2. Benton, Mildred and Signe Ottersen / *A critique on standards for evaluating library collections.* Supplement I to final report: *A study of resources and major subject holdings available in U.S. Federal libraries maintaining extensive or unique collections of research materials.* George Washington Univ., Washington, D.C., Biol. Sci. Commun. Proj. Apr 1970. 62p. ED-043 351.

3. Benton, Mildred and Signe Ottersen, comps./ *Roster of Federal libraries.* George Washington University, Washington, D.C., Biol. Sci. Commun. Proj., Oct. 1970. ED-044 158.

4. Benton, Mildred, et al. / *A study of resources and major subject holdings available in U.S. Federal libraries maintaining extensive or unique collections of research materials.* Final report. George Washington Univ., Washington, D.C., Biol. Sci. Commun. Proj., Sep 1970. ED-043 350.

5. Federal Council for Science and Technology, Task Group on Library programs / *Federal information resources: identification, availability and use.* Proceedings of a conference, Washington, D.C., Mar 26–27, 1970. Washington, D.C., Task Group on Libr. Prog., Fed. Council for Sci. and Tech., Mar 1970. 129 p. ED-043 792. EDRS: MF $0.75, HC $6.55.

6. Kruzas, Anthony T., comp. / *Directory of special libraries and information centers.* 2d ed. Detroit, Gale Research, 1968. 2v.

7. Kruzas, Anthony T., ed. / *Encyclopedia of information systems and services.* 1st ed. Ann Arbor, Mich., Edwards Brothers, 1971.

21. Special Materials—Reference Materials—Bibliography

1. American Library Ass. Basic Reference Books Committee / *Reference books for small- and medium-sized public libraries.* Chicago, Amer. Libr. Ass. 1969.

2. *American reference books annual.* 1970- . Littleton, Colo., Libraries Unlimited.

3. Barton, M.N. and M.V. Bell, comps. / *Reference books; a brief guide.* 7th ed. Baltimore, Md., Enoch Pratt, 1970.

4. Blake, J.B. and C. Roos, eds. / *Medical reference works, 1679–1966.* A selected bibliography. Chicago, Med. Libr. Ass., 1967. Mary Virginia Clark / *Suppl. I Med. Libr. Ass.* 1970.

5. Cheney, Frances Neel / *Fundamental reference sources.* Chicago, Amer. Libr. Ass., 1971.

6. Coman, Edwin T. / *Sources of business information.* rev. ed. Berkeley, Univ. of California Press, 1964.

7. *Conference on the present status and future prospects of reference/information service.* Proceedings of the conference held at the Sch. Libr. Serv., Columbia Univ., Mar 30–Apr 1, 1966, W.B. Linderman, ed. Chicago, Amer. Libr. Ass., 1967.

8. Galin, Saul / *Reference books: how to select and use them.* New York, Random House, 1969.

9. *Government reference books.* 1st ed., 1968/69- . S. Wynkoop, comp. Littleton, Colo., Libraries Unlimited. (A biennial guide to U.S. Govt. publ.)

10. *Guide to American directories.* Englewood Cliffs, N.J., Prentice-Hall. Biennial.

11. Herner, Saul / *A brief guide to sources of scientific and technical information.* Washington, D.C., Information Resources Press, 1969.
12. Heggins, J.H. and A.A. Stellwag / Mini reference library: 21 paperbacks. *Libr. J.* 96: 245-247 (Jan 15); *Sch. Libr. J.* 18: 29-31 (Jan 1971).
13. Jenkins, F.B. / *Science reference sources.* 5th ed. Cambridge, MIT Press, 1969.
14. Katzel, R. / *Guide to libraries and reference books.* An introduction to the organization of libraries and an annotated guide to 463 reference books with questions designed to reveal their content. Norkan, 212 West Adams, Pittsburg, Kan. 66762. 1970.
15. Malinowsky, Harold R. / *Science and engineering reference sources.* A guide for students and librarians. Littleton, Colo., Libraries Unlimited, 1967.
16. Manheim. T., G. Dardarion, D. Satterthwaite / *Sources in Educational Research.* A selected & annotated bibliography, Part VIII: Instructional technology. Detroit, Wayne State Univ. Press, 1969.
17. *New reference tools for librarians.* 1962/63- . Oxford, N.Y., R. Maxwell. Annual.
18. Purcell, G.R. / Reference books of 1970. *Libr. J.* 96: 1325-1329. (Apr 15, 1971).
19. *The Reader's advisor and bookman's manual.* 1st ed., 1921- . New York, Bowker.
20. Reference sources: little-known to basic. *RQ* 10: 22-32 (Fall 1970).
21. Sheehy, E.P. / Selected reference books of 1969-1970. *Coll. and Res. Libr.* 32: 36-45 (Jan 1971).
22. Sheehy, E.P. / Selected reference books of 1970-71. *Coll. and Res. Libr.* 32: 304-314 (Jul 1971).
23. *Subscription books bulletin reviews.* 1956-60- . Chicago, Amer. Libr. Ass.
24. Walford, Albert J., ed. / *Guide to reference material.* 2d ed. London, Libr. Ass., 1966. 3v.
25. Walsh, S.P., comp. / *Home reference books in print; a comparative analysis.* New York, Bowker, 1969.
26. Winchell, C.M. / *Guide to reference books.* 8th ed. Chicago, Amer. Libr. Ass. 1967. Suppl. 1st-, 1965-66, Chicago, Amer. Libr. Ass.
27. Wynar, Bohdan S. / *Introduction to bibliography and reference work; a guide to materials and sources.* 4th rev. ed. Rochester, N.Y., Libraries Unlimited, 1967.
28. Wynar, Bohdan S. / *Reference books in paperback; an annotated guide.* Littleton, Colo., Libraries Unlimited, 1972.
29. Wynkoop, S. / *Subject guide to government reference books.* Littleton, Colo., Libraries Unlimited, 1972.
30. Ziskin, Sylvia / *Reference readiness; a manual for librarians and students.* Hamden, Conn., Linnet Books, 1971.

21s. Special Materials—Reference Materials—Bibliography—Supplement

1. Adams, Scott, ed. / *Guide to Russian medical literature.* Washington, D.C., U.S. Dept. of Health, Education, and Welfare, Public Health Service, 1958. (U.S. Pub. Health Serv. Publ. 602).
2. American Bankers Ass. Automation and Technology Research Dept. / *A guide to information systems literature.* P. I and II. Washington, D.C., Amer. Bankers Ass., n.d. Part I: 51p. Part II: 43p.
3. American Historical Ass. / *Guide to historical literature.* New York, Macmillan, 1961.
4. Aslib. Textile Group, comp. / *A guide to sources of information in the textile industry.* London and Manchester, Aslib and the Textile Institute, 1970.
5. Babb, Janice B. / *Real estate information sources.* Detroit, Gale Research, 1963.
6. Bakewell, K.G.B. / *How to find out: management and productivity.* A guide to sources of information arranged according to the Universal Decimal Classification. Elmsford,

N.Y., Pergamon, 1970.

7. Bate, John / *How to find out about Shakespeare.* Elmsford, N.Y., Pergamon, 1968.

8. Battelle Memorial Institute, Columbus, Ohio / *A guide to the scientific and technical literature of Eastern Europe.* Prepared for the Nat. Sci. Found. Washington, D.C., Nat. Sci. Found., 1962.

9. Bentley, Howard B. / *Building construction information sources.* Detroit, Gale Research, 1964.

10. Blanchard, J. Richard and Harold Ostwold / *Literature of agricultural research.* Berkeley, Univ. of Calif. Press.

11. Borchardt, Dietrich H. / *How to find out in psychology.* Elmsford, N.Y., Pergamon, 1968.

12. Bottle, R.T., ed. / *The use of chemical literature.* 2d ed. London, Butterworths (Archon); Hamden, Conn., Shoe String, 1969.

13. Brimmer, Brenda, et al. / *A guide to the use of United Nations documents, including reference to the specialized agencies and special U.N. bodies.* Dobbs Ferry, N.Y., Oceana Publ., 1962.

14. Brown, Russell and G.A. Campbell / *How to find out about the chemical industry.* Elmsford, N.Y., Pergamon, 1963.

15. Burgess, Norman / *How to find out about exporting.* Elmsford, N.Y., Pergamon, 1971.

16. Burkett, Jack and Philip Plumb / *How to find out in electrical engineering.* A guide to sources of information arranged according to the universal decimal classification. 1st ed. Elmsford, N.Y., Pergamon, 1967.

17. Burman, C.R. / *How to find out in chemistry.* Elmsford, N.Y., Pergamon, 1965.

18. Butterworth, Joanne / *A guide for the use of the textile information system.* Atlanta, Ga., Ga. Inst. of Tech., 1964.

19. California. Univ. at Los Angeles. Libr. / *A guide to research materials for graduate students.* Ardis Lodge, comp. Los Angeles, 1964.

20. Carrick, Neville / *How to find out about the arts; a guide to sources of information.* Elmsford, N.Y., Pergamon, 1965.

21. Chandler, George / *How to find out: a guide to sources of information for all.* Arranged by the Dewey Decimal Classification. 2d ed. Elmsford, N.Y., Pergamon, 1966.

22. Chandler, G. / *How to find out about literature.* Elmsford, N.Y., Pergamon, 1968.

23. Christian, Portia / *Ethics in business conduct: selected references from the record—problems, attempted solutions, ethics in business education.* Detroit, Gale Research, 1970.

24. Coman, Edwin T., Jr. / *Sources of business information.* rev. ed., Berkeley, Univ. of Calif. Press, 1964.

25. Cosgrove, Carol Ann / *A reader's guide to Britain and the European communities.* London, Chatham House: PEP, 1970.

26. Crane, Evan Jan, et al. / *A guide to the literature of chemistry.* 2d ed. New York, Wiley, 1957.

27. Davenport, Donald Hills / *An index to business indices.* Ann Arbor, Mich., Gryphon, 1971.

28. Damarest, Rosemary R. / *Accounting: information sources.* Detroit, Gale Research, 1971.

29. Elliott, C.K. / *A guide to the documentation of psychology.* London, Clive Bingley, Linnet, 1971.

30. *Encyclopedia of business information sources.* Paul Wasserman, ed. Detroit, Gale Research, 1970. 2v.

31. Fleener, Charles J. and R.L. Seckinger / *Guide to Latin American paperback literature.* Gainesville, Fla., Center for Latin Amer. Studies, Univ. of Fla., 1966.

32. Fletcher, John / *The use of economics literature.* Hamden, Conn. Archon, 1971.

33. Flood, Kenneth U. / *Research in transportation, legal/legislative and economic sources and procedure.* Detroit, Gale Research, 1971.

34. Fry, Bernard M. and Foster E. Mohrhardt, eds. / *A guide to information sources in space science and technology.* New York, Wiley, 1963.

35. Fundaburk, Emma Lila / *Reference*

materials and periodicals in economics, an international list in five volumes. Metuchen, N.J., Scarecrow, 1971.

36. Gibson, Eleanor B. and Elizabeth W. Tapia, eds. / Guide to metallurgical information. 2d ed. New York, Spec. Libr. Ass., 1965.

37. Goldman, Sylvia / Guide to the literature of engineering, mathematics, and the physical sciences. Silver Spring, Md., Johns Hopkins Univ., Appl. Phys. Lab., 1959.

38. Grogan, Denis Joseph / Science and technology; an introduction to the literature. London, Clive Bingley, 1970.

39. A guide to historical literature. William Henry Allison, et al., eds. New York, Macmillan, 1931.

40. Henderson, G.P., comp., ed. / European companies, a guide to sources of information. 2d ed. Beckenham, Kent, C.B.D. Research, 1966.

41. Hepworth, Philip / How to find out in history, a guide to sources of information for all. Elmsford, N.Y., Pergamon, 1966.

42. Jackson, Lucille, comp. / Guide to mineral industries literature. State College, Pa., Pennsylvania State Univ., 1940. (Penn. State Univ. Libr. Studies, no. 2.)

43. Jenkins, Frances Briggs / Science reference sources. 5th ed. Cambridge, Mass., MIT Press (1969).

44. Johnson, Donald C. / A guide to reference materials on Southeast Asia (based on the collections in the Yale and Cornell University Libraries) New Haven, Conn., Yale Univ. Press, 1970.

45. Jones, Gwendolyn / Packaging information sources. An annotated guide to the literature, associations, and educational institutions concerned with containers and packaging. Detroit, Gale Research, 1967.

46. Kaplan, Stuart R., ed. / A guide to information sources in mining, minerals, and geosciences. New York, Wiley, 1965.

47. Knox, Vera H. / Public finance: information sources. Detroit, Gale Research, 1964. (Management Inform. Guide 3)

48. Kopycinski, Joseph V. / Textile industry information sources, an annotated guide to the literature of textile fibers, dyes and dyeing, design and decoration, weaving, machinery, and other subjects. Detroit, Gale Research, 1964.

49. Lemon, Hugo / How to find out about the wool textile industry. Elmsford, N.Y., Pergamon, 1968.

50. Lovett, Robert Woodberry / American economic and business history information sources. An annotated bibliography of recent works pertaining to economic, business, agricultural, and labor history and the history of science and technology for the U.S. and Canada. Detroit, Mich., Gale Research, 1971. (Management Inform. Guide 23.)

51. McDermott, Beatrice S. / Government regulation of business including antitrust information sources. A comprehensive annotated bibliography of work pertaining to the Antitrust Div., Dep. of Justice, and to the major regulatory agencies of the Fed. Govt. Detroit, Mich., Gale Research, 1967. (Management Inform. Guide 11)

52. Madden, Lionel / How to find out about the Victorian period: a guide to sources of information. Elmsford, N.Y., Pergamon, 1970.

53. Maichel, Karol / Guide to Russian reference books. Stanford, Calif., Hoover Institution, Stanford Univ., 1962- .

54. Malinowsky, Harold R. / Science and engineering reference sources, a guide for students and librarians. Littleton, Colo., Libraries Unlimited, 1967.

55. Marke, Julius J. / Commercial law information sources. Detroit, Gale Research, 1971. (Management Inform. Guide 17.)

56. Mason, John Brown / Research resources, annotated guide to the social sciences. vol. 1. International relations and recent history: indexes, abstracts, and periodicals. Santa Barbara, Calif. Amer. Bibliog. Center—Clio Press, 1968.

57. Mayhew, Lewis B. / *The literature of higher education.* San Francisco, Jossey-Bass Publ., 1971.

58. Melnyk, Peter / *Economics: bibliographic guide to reference books and information resources.* Littleton, Colo., Libraries Unlimited, 1971.

59. Metcalf, Kenneth N. / *Transportation information sources.* An annotated guide to publications, agencies, and other data sources concerning air, rail, water, road, and pipeline transportation. Detroit, Gale Research, 1965. (Management Inform. Guide 8.)

60. Milek, John T. / *Guide to foreign sources of metallurgical literature.* Pittsburgh, R. Rimbach, 1951.

61. Mints, Charles S. / *How to find out in geography.* A guide to current books in English. Elmsford, N.Y., Pergamon, 1966.

62. Morrill, Chester, Jr. / *Computers and data processing information sources.* Detroit, Gale Research, 1969. (Management Inform. Guide 15.)

63. Morrill, Chester / *Systems and procedures including office management: information sources.* A guide to literature and bodies concerned with the systems and procedures aspects of organization and management including office management, whether in business, industry or government. Detroit, Gale Research, 1967. (Management Inform. Guide 12.)

64. Neiswender, Rosemary / *Guide to Russian reference and language aids.* New York, Spec. Libr. Ass. 1962.

65. Newby, Frank / *How to find out about patents.* Elmsford, N.Y., Pergamon, 1967.

66. Nihon No Sanko Tosho Henshu Iinkai / *Guide to Japanese reference books.* Chicago, Amer. Libr. Ass., 1966.

67. Norton, Alice / *Public relations . . . information sources.* Detroit, Gale Research, 1970. (Management Inform. Guide 22.)

68. Parke, Nathan Grier / *Guide to the literature of mathematics and physics including related works in engineering science.* 2d rev. ed. New York,

Dover Publ., 1958.

69. Passwater, Richard A. / *Guide to fluorescence literature.* New York, Plenum, Data Div., 1967.

70. Pearl, Richard M. / *Guide to geologic literature.* New York, McGraw-Hill, 1951.

71. Pemberton, John E. / *How to find out in mathematics.* A guide to sources of information. 2d rev. ed. Elmsford, N.Y., Pergamon, 1969.

72. Pendleton, Oswald W. / *How to find out about insurance; a guide to sources of information.* Elmsford, N.Y., Pergamon, 1967.

73. Penn, Colin T. / *A guide to official publications on buildings.* London, published for the Royal Inst. Brit. Architects by the Architectural Press. 1946.

74. Pennington, Allan L. and Robert A. Peterson / *Reference guide to marketing literature.* Braintree, Mass., D.H. Mark Publ., 1970.

75. Phillips, Margaret / *Guide to architectural information.* Lansdale, Pa., Design Data Center, 1971.

76. Pritchard, Alan / *A guide to computer literature.* An introductory survey of the sources of information. London, Archon and Clive Bingley, 1969.

77. Randle, Gretchen R. / *Electronic industries information sources.* A comprehensive guide to the literature and other data sources. Detroit, Gale Research, 1968.

78. ReQua, Eloise and Jane Statham, eds. / *The developing nations.* A guide to information sources concerning their economic, political, technical, and social problems. Detroit, Gale Research, 1965. (Management Inform. Guide 5.)

79. Schalit, Michael / *Guide to the literature of the sugar industry.* Amsterdam, The Netherlands, Elsevier Publ., 1970.

80. Signeur, Austin V. / *Guide to gas chromatography literature.* New York, Plenum, 1964–67.

81. Smith, Denison L. / *How to find out in architecture and building.* A guide to sources of information. Elmsford, N.Y., Pergamon, 1967.

82. Smith, Julian F. and W.G. Brombacher / *Guide to instrumentation literature.* Washington, D.C. For sale by the Supt. of Docs., U.S. Govt. Print. Off., 1965. (Nat. Bureau of Stand. Misc. Publ. 271.)

83. Smith, Roger C. and Reginald H. Painter / *Guide to the literature of the zoological sciences.* 7th ed. Minneapolis, Minn., Burgess Publ., 1966.

84. Snape, Wilfred H. / *How to find out about local government.* Elmsford, N.Y., Pergamon, 1969.

85. Taylor, Marion R. / *Guide to Latin American reference materials.* A union list for use in the Atlanta-Athens area. Atlanta, Ga. Chapter, Spec. Libr. Ass., 1958.

86. Thomas, Roy Edwin / *Insurance.* A guide to information sources. Detroit, Gale Research, 1971. (Management Inform. Guide 24.)

87. Vara, Albert C. / *Food and beverage industries: a bibliography and guidebook.* Detroit, Gale Research, 1970. (Management Inform. Guide 16.)

88. Wolford, Albert J. / *A guide to foreign language grammars and dictionaries.* 2d ed., rev. and enl. London, Libr. Ass., 1967.

89. Walsh, Dorothy / *A guide for software documentation.* New York, Advanced Computer Techniques Corp., 1969.

90. Wheeler, Lora Jeanne / *International business and foreign trade; information sources.* Detroit, Gale Research, 1968. (Management Inform. Guide 14.)

91. White, Carl M., et al. / *Sources of information in the social sciences.* A guide to the literature. Totowa, N.J., Bedminster, 1964.

92. White, D. / *How to find out in iron and steel.* Elmsford, N.Y., Pergamon, 1970.

93. Woy, James B. / *Business trends and forecasting information sources.* Detroit, Gale Research, 1965. (Management Inform. Guide 9.)

94. Woy, James B. / *Investment information; a detailed guide to selected sources.* Detroit, Gale Research, 1971. (Management Inform. Guide 19.)

95. Wynar, Lubomyr R. / *Guide to reference materials in political science; a selective bibliography.* Denver, Colorado Bibliog. Inst., 1966–68. 2v.

96. Yates, Bryan / *How to find out about the United Kingdom cotton industry.* Elmsford, N.Y., Pergamon, 1967.

22. Special Materials—Abstracts

1. Collison, Robert / *Abstracts and abstracting services.* Santa Barbara, Calif. ABC-Clio Press, Riviera Campus, 1971.

2. International Federation for Documentation / *Abstracting Services.* v. 1: Science and technology. v. 2: Social sciences and humanities. The Hague, Netherlands, FID, 1969.

3. U.S. Library of Congress. Science and Technology Div. / *A guide to U.S. indexing and abstracting services in science and technology.* Prepared for the National Federation of Science Abstracting and Indexing Services. Washington, D.C., 1960. (Nat. Fed. of Sci. Abstr. and Indexing Serv. Rep. 101.)

4. U.S. Library of Congress. Science and Technology Div. / *A guide to the world's abstracting and indexing services in science and technology.* Prepared for the National Federation of Science Abstracting and Indexing Services. Washington, D.C., 1963. (Nat. Fed. of Sci. Abstr. and Indexing Serv. Rep. 102.)

5. Wilson, Thomas D. and James Stephenson / Abstracts and abstracting. In *Dissemination of Information.* New York, Philosophical Libr., 1965. p. 44–47.

23. Special Materials—Indexes

1. American National Standards Institute / *USA standard basic criteria for indexes.* New York, ANSI, 1968. (ANSI Z39.4–1968. Revision of Z39.4–1959).

2. Burkett, Jack / Published indexing and abstracting services. In *Trends in*

special librarianship. Hamden,
Conn., Archon, [1968] p. 37–72.
3. Collison, Robert / *Indexes and indexing.* 3d ed. Tuckahoe, N.Y.,
John De Graff, 1969.
4. Klempner, Irving M. / *Diffusion of
abstracting and indexing services for
government-sponsored research.*
Metuchen, N.J., Scarecrow, 1968.
5. Rothman, John / Communicating
with indexes. *Spec. Libr.* 57: 569–
570 (Oct 1966).

24. Special Materials—Conference Literature

1. Baum, Harry / Scientific and technical meeting papers: transient value or
lasting contribution. *Spec. Libr.* 56:
651–653 (Nov 1965).
2. *Current index to conference papers:
science and technology* v. 2– . Jan
1971– . New York, CCM Information
Corporation. Monthly. (Supersedes
and continues vol. numbering of *Current index* to conference papers in
chemistry, in engineering, and in life
sciences) (3 series)
3. *Directory of published proceedings.*
Series SEMT (Science, Engineering,
Medicine, Technology) v. 1– . Sept
1965– . White Plains, N.Y., InterDok
Corp. Monthly, annual cumulation.
4. *Directory of published proceedings.*
Series SSH (Social Sciences and Humanities) v. 1– . 1968– . White Plains,
N.Y., InterDok Corp. Quarterly,
annual cumulation.
5. Pflueger, Margaret L. / Bibliographic
control of conference literature. *Spec.
Libr.* 55: 230–232 (Apr 1964).
6. *Proceedings in print.* Oct 1964– .
(Aerospace Section, Science-Technology Div., Spec. Libr. Ass.) (Current publisher: Proceedings in Print,
Inc., Mattapan, Mass.)
7. *Scientific Meetings.* New York, Spec.
Libr. Ass. Quarterly. Spring 1957– .
8. *World Meetings outside U.S.A. and
Canada.* Jan 1968– . New York, CCM
Information Corp. Quarterly.
9. *World Meetings: social & behavioral
sciences, education & management.*
Jan 1971– . New York, CCM Informa-

tion Corp. Quarterly.
10. *World meetings, United States and
Canada.* Sept 1963– . New York, CCM
Information Corp. Quarterly

25. Special Materials—Vertical Files (General, Pamphlets, Clippings)

1. ANPA Survey of newspaper libraries—
how they operate and look to the future. *Spec. Libr.* 57: 654–657 (Nov
1966).
2. Barnes, M. / National Geographic Society Library vertical files. Spec. Libr.
Ass., *Geog. and Map Div. Bull.* no.
80: 35–36 (Jun 1970).
3. Condit, Lester / *A pamphlet about
pamphlets.* Chicago, Univ. Chicago,
1939.
4. Gould, Geraldine N. / *How to organize and maintain the library picture/
pamphlet file.* Dobbs Ferry, N.Y.,
Oceana Publ., 1968.
5. Ireland, Norma Olin / *The pamphlet
file in school, college, and public
libraries.* rev. ed. Westwood, Mass.,
F.W. Faxon, 1954.
6. Johnpoll, Bernard K. / The Canada
news index: a report on computerized indexing of news in selected
Canadian dailies. *Spec. Libr.* 58:
103–105 (Feb 1967).
7. Lieberman, Sharon / Vertical file job-
bers do exist. *RQ* 11: 48–49 (Fall
1971).
8. Miller, Shirley / *The vertical file and its
satellites.* A handbook of acquisition,
processing, and organization. Littleton, Colo., Libraries Unlimited, 1971.
9. Rhydwen, David A. / The application
of microphotography to newspaper
clippings. *Spec. Libr.* 55: 28–29 (Jan
1964).
10. Strong, Marilyn / Vertical file footnote *RQ* 11: 49 (Fall 1971).
11. Toronto Public Library / *Subject
headings for vertical files.* Toronto,
Ont., Canada 1964.
12. *Vertical file index.* Subject and title
index to selected pamphlet materials.
Bronx, N.Y., Wilson. Monthly, with
annual cumulation 1935– .
13. Webber, Olga / Trimming the clip-

ping files by the 7 R's. *Spec. Libr.*
60: 82–86 (Feb 1969).

14. Wells, Dorothy / Vertical file sources. *RQ* 10: 150–155 (Winter 1970).

15. Wyllie, John Cook / Pamphlets, broadsides, clippings and posters. *Libr. Trends* 4: 195–202 (Oct 1955).

26. Nonprint Materials—General Information and Management

1. Audiovisual materials and the library. *Wis. Libr. Bull.* 66: 65–98 (Mar 1970).

2. Brong, G.R. Library networks and non-print resources. *Libr. News Bull.* 37: 165–169 (Jul 1970).

3. Brown, James W. / *AV instruction: media and methods.* 3d ed. New York, McGraw-Hill [1969].

4. Church, John G. / *Administration of instructional materials organizations.* Analysis and evaluation criteria for materials centers. Belmont, Calif., Fearon Publ. Lear Siegler, Educ. Div., 1970.

5. Crawford, Susan / Audiovisual Materials. In *Handbook of Medical Library Practice.* 3d ed. Gertrude L. Annan, Jacqueline W. Felter, eds. Chicago Medical Libr. Ass., 1970. p. 222–240.

6. Enright, B.J. / Non-book/media materials and the library: a note. *Libr. Ass. Rec.* 72: 368–369 (Dec 1970).

7. Erickson, Carlton W.H. / *Administering audio-visual services.* New York, Macmillan [1959].

8. Fleischer, E. / Systems for individual study: decks, cassettes, dials or buffers? *Libr. J.* 96: 695–698 (Feb 15, 1971); *Sch. Libr. J.* 18: 27–30 (Feb 1971).

9. Fothergill, Richard / Metabooks: a comment on the educational implications. *Libr. Ass. Rec.* 73: 72 (Apr 1971).

10. Geller, E. / This matter of media. *Libr. J.* 96: 2048–2053 (Jun 15, 1971).

11. Hart, T.L., ed. / Media for the '70's. *Focus* (Mar 1971).

12. Holly, James F. and David J. Camahan / Creating a multi-media library: a case study. *Libr. Trends* 19: 419–436 (Apr 1971).

13. Joint Committe of the American Ass. of School Librarians and the Dept. of Audiovisual Instruction, NEA / *Standards for school media programs* (prepared by the AASL and the Dept. of Audiovisual Instruction of the NEA, in cooperation with representatives of the American Ass. of School Administrators and others) Chicago, Amer. Libr. Ass., 1969.

14. Kenney, Brigitte and Diane Gies, issue eds. / Issues and problems in the management of nonprint media. *Drexel Libr. Quart.* 7: 89–159 (Apr 1971).

15. Lawler, L.J. / Non-book material in the university. (Some thoughts about problems in the university associated with the introduction of education technology) In Aslib Audio-Visual Group / *Audio-Visual Workshop, May 7–8, 1970.* London, Aslib, 1971. p. 24–28.

16. Melinat, Carl H., ed. / *Educational media in the libraries.* Syracuse, N.Y., Syracuse Univ. Press, 1963.

17. Moses, R.B. / Reaching out with the new media. *Conn. Libr.* 13: 17–21 (Summer 1971).

18. Muller, R.E. / Multimedia shelving. *Libr. J.* 95: 750 (Feb 15, 1970); comment (letters) *Libr. J.* 95: 1878 (May 15, 1970).

19. Nelsen, E.N. / Media industry: its growth, structure, and role in education. *Libr. J.* 95: 1159–61 (Mar 15, 1970).

20. Norsworthy, J.A. / Audiovisual services and the media technician. In *Library technical assistant.* Dept. of Libr. Sci., Spalding College, Louisville, Kent, England, 1970. p. 32–34.

21. Peer, C.A. / Reference sources in nonprint media. *Penn. Libr. Ass. Bull.* 25: 168–172 (May 1970).

22. Prostono, Emanual T. / *School media programs: case studies in management.* Metuchen, N.J., Scarecrow, 1970.

23. Rowell, John and M. Ann Heidbreder / *Educational media selection centers: identification and analysis of current practices.* (ALA Studies in Librarianship No. 1) Chicago, Amer. Libr. Ass., 1971.

24. Stone, C.W. / Planning for media

within university library buildings. *Libr. Trends* 18: 233–245 (Oct 1969).

25. Westphal, E.N. / *Patterns of administration and development of audiovisual programs in public junior colleges in Illinois.* Thesis, Univ. of Chicago, 1969.

26. Wittich, Walter A. / *Audiovisual materials; their nature and use.* 4th ed. New York, Harper and Row, 1967.

27. Nonprint Materials—Announcements and Reviews

1. American Musicological Society. *Journal.* (Record Reviews) v. 1– . 1948– . Richmond, Va., William Byrd.

2. *Audio.* (Record Reviews) v. 1– . 1947– . Philadelphia, North. Amer. Publ. Co.

3. *Booklist and Subscription Books Bulletin.* (Reference works; Films, including 16mm, 8mm; Film Loops and Filmstrips; Phonograph Records.) v. 1–. 1905– . Chicago, Amer. Libr. Ass.

4. *Current Geographical Publications.* (Maps) v. 1– . 1938– . New York, Amer. Geogr. Soc.

5. *Geographical Journal.* (Maps) v. 1– . 1893– . London, Royal Geogr. Soc.

6. *Geographical Review.* (Maps) v. 1– . 1916– . New York, Amer. Geogr. Soc.

7. *Library Journal.* (Films, including 16mm and 8mm; Filmstrips; Transparencies; Slides; Disks; Tapes; Prints; Maps; Charts; Academic Games; Multimedia Kits) v. 1– . 1876– . New York, Bowker.

8. *Military Engineer.* (Maps) v. 12– . no. 61– . Jan/Feb 1920– . Washington, D.C., Soc. Amer. Milit. Eng.

9. *Music Index.* (Record Reviews) v. 1– . 1949– . Detroit, Mich., Inform. Coordinators.

10. Music Library Association. *Notes.* (Record Reviews) v. 1– . 1943– . Ann Arbor, Mich. Mus. Libr. Ass.

11. *Musical Quarterly.* (Record Reviews) v. 1–. 1915–. New York, G. Schirmer.

12. *Opera News.* (Record Reviews) v. 1– . 1936– . New York, Metrop. Opera Guild.

13. *School Library Journal.* (Films, 16mm and 8mm; Filmstrips; Transparencies; Slides; Disks; Tapes; Prints; Maps; Charts; Academic Games; Multimedia Kits) v. 1– . 1954– . New York, Bowker.

14. Spec. Libraries Ass. Geography and Map Division / *Bulletin.* (Maps) v. 1– . 1947– .

15. *Stereo Review* (Record Reviews) v. 1– . 1958– . Ziff-Davis Publ.

16. *Subscription Books Bulletin.* (Reference Works) 1956–1960. Chicago, Amer. Libr. Ass. (Continued in *Booklist and Subscription Books Bulletin*)

17. *Surveying and Mapping* (Maps) v. 1– . 1941– . Washington, D.C., Amer. Cong. on Surveying and Mapping.

18. U.S. Copyright Off. / *Catalog of Copyright Entries.* (Maps) 3d Series. Pt. 6: Maps and Atlases. v. 1– . Jan/Jun 1947– . Washington, D.C., U.S. Govt. Print. Off.

19. U.S. Geological Survey / *New Publications.* (Maps) no. 1– . Sep 1907– . Washington, D.C., U.S. Govt. Print. Off.

20. U.S. Library of Congress. Processing Dept. / *Monthly Checklist of State Publications.* (Maps) v. 1– . 1910– . Washington, D.C., U.S. Govt. Print. Off.

21. U.S. Superintendent of Documents / *Monthly Catalog of U.S. Government Publications.* (Maps) no. 1– . Jan 1895– . Washington, D.C., U.S. Govt. Print. Off.

28. Microforms—General Information & Management

1. Asleson, R.F. / Microforms: where do they fit? *Libr. Res. and Tech. Serv.* 15: 57–62 (Winter 1971).

2. Avedon, D.M. / *Computer output microfilm.* Nat. Microfilm Ass., Suite 1101, 8728 Colesville Rd., Silver Spring, Md. 20910, 1969.

3. Ballou, Hubbard W. and John Rather / Microfilm and microfacsimile publications. *Libr. Trends* 4 (2): 182–194 (Oct 1955).

4. Chambers, H.T. / *Copying, duplication and microfilm: systems and*

equipment for use in business and administration. Chicago, Bus. Books, 1970.

5. Conference on microforms. *Calif. Sch. Libr.* 42: 29 (Spring 1971).

6. Damage in proposed govt. micropublishing? *Wilson Libr. Bull.* 45: 717 (Apr 1971).

7. Equipment for photographic files. In Hayes, R.M. and J. Becker / *Handbook of data processing for libraries.* New York, Wiley, 1970. p. 379–397.

8. Hawken, William R. / *Enlarged prints from library microforms; a study of processes, equipment, and materials.* Chicago, Libr. Tech. Proj., Amer. Libr. Ass., 1963. (LTP publications, no. 6)

9. Henderson, Madeline M., comp. / *Proceedings of the conference on image storage and transmission systems for libraries.* Sponsored by the Fed. Libr. Committee's Task Force on Automation, the Lister Hill National Center for Biomedical Communication, COSATI Panel on Information Storage Technology, and the National Bureau of Standards, Dec 1–2, 1969. Gaithersburg, Md., Nat. Bur. of Stands., Sep 1970, var. pages. (PB-193 692).

10. Holmes, Donald C. / *Determination of the environmental conditions required in a library for the effective utilization of microforms.* Interim report, Ass. Res. Libr., Washington, D.C., Nov 1970.

11. Howard, J. / Microfilm system considerations. *MICRODOC* 8: 55–64 (Mar 1969).

12. Iben, Icko / The place of the newspaper. *Libr. Trends* 4: 140–155 (Oct 1955).

13. Janda, Kenneth and David Gordon / A microfilm information retrieval system for newspaper libraries. *Spec. Libr.* 61: 33–47 (Jan 1970).

14. Kiersky, Loretta J. / Developments in photoreproduction. *Spec. Libr.* 59: 261–264 (Apr 1968).

15. Kiersky, Loretta J. / New developments in photoreproduction. *Spec. Libr.* 60: 434–436 (Sep 1969).

16. King, E.M. / Macrocosm in microcopy at Texas A&M. *Texas Libr.* 32: 126–131 (Fall 1970).

17. Lawani, S.M. / Storage and preservation of microfilm under tropical conditions. *Libri* 18: 182–190 (1968).

18. Lee, Thomas Graham / *Microform systems, a handbook for educators.* Ann Arbor, Mich., Audio-Visual Ass., 1970.

19. Lewis, Chester M. / *Microrecording; industrial and library applications.* New York, Interscience Publ., 1956.

20. Massey, D.W. / Aching eye: the use of microforms and viewers by scholars and researchers. *Va. Librn.* 17: 24 (Winter 1970).

21. Microform readers: Readex model 5 (suppl.) *Libr. Tech. Rep.* (Jan 1971).

22. Morgan Information Systems / Microform readers for libraries. *Libr. Tech. Rep.* (May 1971).

23. National Microfilm Ass. / *Glossary of terms for microphotography and reproductions made from microimages.* D.M. Avedon, ed. Annapolis, Md., 1962.

24. National Reprographic Centre for Documentation / University microfilm 1212 reader. *Libr. Tech. Rep.* (Mar 1971).

25. National Reprographic Centre for Documentation / Univ. microfilms 1414 reader. *Libr. Tech. Rep.* (Jan 1971).

26. Nelson, Carl E. / *Microfilm technology; engineering and related fields.* New York, McGraw-Hill, 1965.

27. Nitecki, Joseph Z. / Simplified classification and cataloging of microforms. *Libr. Res. and Tech. Serv.* 13: 79–85 (Winter 1969).

28. Poole, Frazer G. / Preservation costs and standards. *Spec. Libr.* 59: 614–619 (Oct 1968).

29. Reichmann, Felix and Josephine M. Tharpe / *Determination of an effective system of bibliographic control of microform publications.* Interim report. Ass. Res. Libr. Washington, D.C., Nov. 1970.

30. Riker, Elaine M. / Microfilming newspaper clippings. *Spec. Libr.* 56: 655–656 (Nov 1965).

31. Stevens, Rolland E. / The microfilm revolution. *Libr. Trends* 19: 379–395 (Jan 1971).

32. Stevens, Stanley D. / Color microfilming of Sanborn maps for a local
history collection. *Western Ass. Map
Libr. Inform. Bull.* 1: 2–8 (Jun
1970).

33. Sullivan, R.C. / Conference on
microform utilization: the academic
environment. Univ. of Denver, Dec.
7–9, 1970. *Libr. Cong. Inform. Bull.*
30: 27–28 (Jan 14, 1971).

34. Teplitz, Arthur / Microfilm and re-
prography. In *Annual Review of Information Science and Technology.*
vol. 5, 1970, Carlos A. Cuadra, ed.
Chicago, Encycl. Britannica, 1970.
p. 87–111.

35. Thomson, June / Cataloguing of
large works on microform in Canadian university libraries. *Can. Libr.*
26: 446–452 (1969).

36. U.S. Dept. of the Army / *Microfilming of records.* [Washington, D.C.,
U.S. Govt. Print. Off.] 1955. (Technical manual, TM12-257).

37. Veaner, Allen B. / *The evaluation
of micropublications; a handbook
for librarians.* Chicago, Libr. Tech.
Prog., Amer. Libr. Ass., 1971 (LTP
publ. no. 17)

38. Veaner, Allen B. / Micropublica-
tion. In *Advances in librarianship.*
v. 2. Seminar Press, 1971, p. 165–
186.

39. Veenstra, John G. / Microimages and
the library. *Libr. J.* 95: 3443–3447
(Oct 15, 1970).

40. Veit, Fritz / Microforms, microform
equipment and microform use in
the educational environment. *Libr.
Trends* 19: 447–466 (Apr 1971).

41. Weyhrauch, E.E. / Microforms and
their place in academic libraries.
Ky. Libr. Ass. Bull. 35: 15–26 (Jan
1971).

42. Williams, Bernard J.S. / *Evaluation
of microrecording techniques for
information and data storage and
retrieval.* Hatfield (Herts., England),
c/o Hatfield College of Tech.,
1967.

32. Williams, Bernard J.S. / *Miniaturized
communications: a review of microforms.* London, The Libr. Ass. &
Hatfield, The National Reprogr.
Centre for Doc., 1970.

29. Microforms—Bibliography

1. *Guide to microforms in print.* 1961– .
Washington, D.C., Microcard Editions. annual.

2. Hall, L.M. / Bibliographical control
of microforms. *Southeastern Libr.*
20: 258–266 (Winter 1970).

3. Microfilming clearing house bulletin
no. 87. *Libr. Cong. Inform. Bull.* 30:
A 155–157 (Jul 1971).

4. Schneider, L. and D.W. Schneider /
Microfilm masters, a national need.
Southeastern Libr. 20: 106–107
(Summer 1970).

5. *Subject guide to microforms in print.*
1962/63– . Washington, D.C., Microcard Editions. Annual.

6. U.S. General Services Administra-
tion. National Archives and Records
Service / *List of National Archives
Microfilm Publications.* Washington,
D.C., 1966.

30. Microfiche

1. Ardern, L.L. / COM, PCMI and
Books in English. *MICRODOC* 10
(no. 1): 17–21 (1971).

2. Aschenborn, H.J. / International
standardisation of microfiche. *S.
Afr. Libr.* 39: 42–51 (Jul 1971).

3. Campbell, B.W. / A successful microfiche program. *Spec. Libr.* 62: 136–
142 (Mar 1971).

4. Gordon, R.F. / *Microfiche viewing
equipment.* Defense Doc. Center,
Alexandria, Va., 1970.

5. Kennedy, D.T. / Lensman microfiche reader. *MICRODOC* 9 (no. 3):
86–88 (1970).

6. Kristy, N.F. / System design for
microbook publishing. In *Proceedings American Society for Information Science Conference 1970,* Phila.
v. 7: Information conscious society.
Washington, D.C., ASIS 1970, p.
221–223.

7. Microbooks; a new library medium.
Publ. Wkly. 198: 48–50 (Nov 9,
1970).

8. Tressel, G.W., et al. / Automated
retrieval and remote viewing of

COSATI microfiche: problems and prospects. In *Proceedings of the American Society for Information Science Conference, 1970,* Philadelphia. v. 7: Information conscious society. Washington, D.C., ASIS 1970. p. 123–128.

9. UMF libraries: a status report. *Microgr. News and Views* 1: 3–5 (Dec 4, 1970).

10. Wheeler, W.D. / Microfiche—a progress review. *Can. Libr.* 26: 353, 355 (1969).

11. Wicker, Roger, et al. / *Microfiche storage and retrieval system study.* Final rep. TM-WD-(L)-355/000/01. Aug 10, 1970. System Development Corp., Falls Church, Va. NTIS: AD 710 000. ED 046 400.

12. Yerkes, Charles P. / Micro-forum. Indexing ultramicrofiche. *Plan and Print* 42: 14–15 (1969).

31. Aperture Cards

1. Aperture cards for engineering drawing. *Can. Electronics Eng.* 14: 49–50 (Oct 1970).

2. Even, Arthur D. / *Engineering data processing system design.* Princeton, N.J., Van Nostrand, 1960.

32. Instructional Materials— (General)—Bibliography

1. *Abstracts of instructional materials in vocational and technical education* (AIM). Columbus, Ohio, Eric Clearinghouse, Center for Vocat. and Tech. Educ., Ohio State Univ., 1967.

2. *Audiovisual index.* A guide to instructional audiovisual communication & technology. 2d ed. Detroit, Mich., Audio-Visual Res. Inst., 1970.

3. *Audio-visual source directory. Fall-Winter.* Motion Picture Enterprises Publ., Tarrytown, N.Y. (1970–71).

4. Educational Media Council / *Educational media index.* A project of the Educational Media Council. New York, McGraw-Hill, 1964. 14v.

5. *Educator's purchasing master.* Fisher Publ., 1970. 3v.

6. *El-Hi Textbooks in Print.* New York, Bowker. Annual. 1970– .

7. *Guide to simulation games for education and training.* David Zuckerman and Robert Horn, comps. Cambridge, Mass., Inform. Res., 1970.

8. Hendershot, Carl H. / *Programmed learning: a bibliography of programs and presentation devices.* 4th ed. Bay City, Mich., 1967. (loose-leaf)

9. Horkheimer, Foley A. and Louise E. Alley, eds. / *Educators guide to free health, physical education and recreation materials.* 4th ed. Randolph, Wis., Educators Progress Serv., 1971.

10. *Learning Directory, 1970–71.* New York, Westinghouse Learning Corp., 1970. 7 v.

11. Moore, M., comp. / Audiovisual guide: A multimedia subject list: 825 series and individual titles, pre-K through high school, produced between Mar and Aug 1970. *Libr. J.* 95: 1583 (Apr 15, 1970); *Sch. Libr. J.* 17: 65–66 (Apr 1970).

12. Moore, M., comp. / Audiovisual guide. A multimedia subject list: 975 series and individual titles, pre-K through high school produced between Sep 1970 and Feb 1971. *Libr. J.* 95: 3973–3975 (Nov 15, 1970); *Sch. Libr. J.* 17: 37–39 (Nov 1970).

13. *Multi-media reviews index.* Ann Arbor, Mich., Pierian Press. Annual. 1970– . Monthly supplements In *Audiovisual Instruction* (Nat. Educ. Ass., Ass. for Educ. Commun. and Tech.) (Oct. 1945– .)

14. *Programmed instruction guide.* 2d ed. Newburyport, Mass., Entelek, 1969.

15. Rufsvold, Margaret I. and Carolyn Guss / *Guides to educational media.* (films, filmstrips, kinescopes, phonodiscs, phonotapes, programmed instructional materials, slides, transparancies, videotapes) 3d ed. Chicago, Amer. Libr. Ass., 1971.

16. Saterstrom, Mary H., et al., eds. / *Educators guide to free guidance materials, 1970.* 10th ed. Randolph, Wis., Educators Progress Serv., 1971.

17. Saterstrom, Mary H. and John W. Renner, eds. / *Educators guide to free science materials.* 12th ed. Randolph, Wis., Educators Progress Serv., 1971.

18. Suttles, Patricia H. and William H.
Hartley, eds. / *Educators guide to
free social studies materials.* 11th
ed. Randolph, Wis., Educators Progress Serv., 1971.
19. Suttles, Patricia H. and John G.
Fowlkes, eds. / *Elementary teachers
guide to free curriculum materials.*
28th ed. Randolph, Wis., Educators
Progress Serv., 1971.
20. *Yearbook of educational and instructional technology.* Ass. for Programmed Learning and Educ. Tech.
London, Cornmarket, 1969/70- .

33. Pictures

1. American Institute of Architects /
*Filing system for architectural plates
and articles.* 2d ed. Washington,
D.C., 1946 (A.I.A. Doc. no. 261).
2. Dane, William J. / *The picture collection subject headings.* 6th ed.
Hamden, Conn., Shoe String, 1968.
3. Fetros, John G. / Cooperative picture searching & collection development. *Spec. Libr.* 62: 217-226
(May/Jun 1971).
4. Frankenburg, Celestine G. / Compiling a picture-finding reference.
Spec. Libr. 55: 169-170 (Mar 1964).
5. Frankenburg, Celestine G. / The
creative library in an advertising
agency. *Spec. Libr.* 55: 294-299
(May/Jun 1964).
6. Frankenburg, Celestine G., ed. / *Picture Sources.* 2d ed., New York,
Spec. Libr. Ass., 1964.
7. Gould, Geraldine N. / *How to organize and maintain the library pic-
ture/pamphlet file.* Dobbs Ferry,
N.Y., Oceana Publ., 1968.
8. Hill, May D. / Prints, pictures and
photographs. *Libr. Trends* 4: 156-
163 (Oct 1955).
9. Ireland, Norma Olin / *The picture
file in school, college and public
libraries.* rev. ed. Westwood, Mass.,
F.W. Faxon, 1952.
10. Moss, Daphne / Pictures: Radio
Times Hulton Picture Library. In
*Aslib Audio-Visual Group, Audio-
Visual Workshop, May 7-8, 1970.*
London, Aslib, 1971. p. 12-17.

11. Picture and art librarianship / *Spec.
Libr.* 56: 15-48 (Jan 1965).
12. Potter, E.J. and R. Barton / Picture
file of the fine arts department of
the Detroit Public Library. A manual
of procedures and practices. Spec.
Libr. Ass. Pict. Div. / *Picturescope*
18 (no. 3): 135-154 (1970).
13. Rice, Stanley / Picture retrieval by
concept coordination; a self-inter-
preting model file. *Spec. Libr.* 60:
627-634 (Dec 1969).
14. Special Libraries Ass. Picture Div.
Issue. *Spec. Libr.* 45: 269-300 (Sep
1954).
15. U.S. Library of Congress. Descriptive Cataloging Div. / *Rules for descriptive cataloging in the Library of
Congress: pictures, designs, and other
two-dimensional representations.*
Prelim. ed. Washington, D.C., 1959.
16. Vance, Lucile E. / *Illustration index.*
2d ed. New York, Scarecrow, 1966.

34. Photographs

1. Huff, M. / Organizing photographs in
the State library. *Texas Libr.* 32:
154-160 (Fall 1970).
2. McNeil, R.J. / The Shell photographic library. *Aslib Proc.* 18: 128-137
(May 1966).
3. Ostroff, E. / Preservation of photographs. Spec. Libr. Ass. Pict. Div. /
Picturescope 18: 76-84 (1970). (reprinted from *Photographic Journal*
p. 309-314 (Oct 1967).
4. *Spec. Libr.* 47: 439-465 (Dec 1956).
An issue on photographic materials.

35. Special Materials—Art

1. *Art Index.* Bronx, N.Y., H.W. Wilson.
Quarterly. annual cumulation.
1929- .
2. Barton, Margaret / *Guide to color
reproductions.* 2d ed. Metuchen,
N.J., Scarecrow, 1971.
3. Chamberlin, Mary W. / *Guide to art
reference books.* Chicago, Amer.
Libr. Ass., 1959.
4. Gerard, David, ed. / *Libraries and the
arts.* Hamden, Conn., Archon, 1970.

5. Havlice, Patricia P. / *Art in Time* (magazine). Metuchen, N.J., Scarecrow, 1970.

6. Larsen, John C. / The use of art reference sources in museum libraries. *Spec. Libr.* 62: 481–486 (Nov 1971).

7. Martin, Helene / The library at the Willet Stained Glass Studios. *Spec. Libr.* 57: 238–239 (Apr 1966).

8. Monro, Isabel Stevenson and Kate M. Monro / *Index to reproductions of American paintings.* (Also Suppl. 1964.) Bronx, N.Y., H.W. Wilson, 1948, 1964.

9. Monro, Isabel Stevenson and Kate M. Monro / *Index to reproductions of European painting.* Bronx, N.Y., H.W. Wilson, 1956.

36. Special Materials—Maps

1. American Geographical Society of New York / *Cataloging and filing rules for maps and atlases in the Society's collection.* rev. and exp. ed. [by] Roman Drazniowsky. [New York] 1969. (Amer. Geogr. Soc. of New York. Mimeographed and offset publ. no. 4)

2. Baynton-Williams, Roger / *Investing in maps.* New York, C.N. Potter (1969).

3. Boggs, Samuel W. / *The classification and cataloging of maps and atlases.* New York, Spec. Libr. Ass., 1945.

4. Carrington, David K. / *Data preparation manual for the conversion of map cataloging records to machine-readable form.* Washington, D.C., Library of Congress [for sale by the Sup. of Docs., U.S. Govt. Print. Off.] 1971. (Supt. of Docs. no.: LC1.6/4:M32)

5. Christy, Barbara Mae / *Critique of pure labeling for map collections. Western Ass. of Map. Libr. Inform. Bull.* 1:12–22 (Jun 1970).

6. Critchley, W.E. / Old maps: photocopying helps in using them. *MICRODOC* 9: 68–69 (1970).

7. Control of map acquisitions. (Panel II, Spring, 1970, Meeting of Western Ass. of Map Libr.) *Western Ass. of Map Libr. Inform. Bull.* 1: 26–31 (Jun 1970).

8. Current, C.E. / Acquisition of maps for school (and other small) libraries. *Wilson Libr. Bull.* 45: 578–583 (Feb 1971). Correction by W.W. Ristow. *Wilson Libr. Bull.* 45: 737 (Apr 1971).

9. Drazniowsky, Roman / The need for map cataloging. *Spec. Libr.* 61: 236–237 (May/Jun 1970).

10. Easton, William W. / Repair and preservation of map materials. *Spec. Libr.* 61: 199–200 (Apr 1970).

11. Felland, Nordis / On editing current geographical publications. *Spec. Libr.* 61: 538–540 (Dec 1970).

12. Galneder, Mary / Equipment for map libraries. *Spec. Libr.* 61: 271–274, (Jul/Aug 1970).

13. Hagen, Carlos B. / The establishment of a university map library. *Western Ass. of Map Libr. Inform. Bull.* 3: 11 (Oct 1971).

14. Harrison, R.E. / Evaluation of modern maps. *Spec. Libr.* 44: 45–47 (Feb 1953).

15. Hill, J. Douglas / Maps and atlas cases. *Libr. Trends* 13: 481–487 (Apr 1965).

16. Hinckley, Thomas K. / Dewey Decimal Classification for United States Air Force Academy map collection. Spec. Libr. Ass. Geogr. and Map Div. *Bull.* no. 82: 13–20, 25 (Dec 1970).

17. Kiraldi, Louis / Courses in map librarianship. *Spec. Libr.* 61: 496–500 (Nov 1970).

18. Koerner, Alberta G. / Acquisition philosophy and cataloging priorities for university map libraries. *Spec. Libr.* 63: 511–516 (Nov 1972).

19. Landers, John J. / Mending tape for maps. *Spec. Libr.* 61: 466 (Oct 1970).

20. Map preservation (Panel I, Spring, 1970, Meeting of Western Ass. of Map Libr.) *Western Ass. of Map Libr. Inform. Bull.* 1: 22–25 (Jun 1970).

21. Meine, Karl Heinz / Reflections about the organization of a special library on "space cartography." *INSPEL* 5: 85–89 (Jul–Oct 1970).

22. Mittra, D.K. / More about processing

of maps. *Libr. Herald* 10: 268–275 (Jan 1969).

23. Murphy, Mary / Map collection prepares to automate; the U.S. Army Topographic Command Library. *Spec. Libr.* 61: 180–189 (Apr 1970).

24. Nelson, J. / LSU School of Geoscience Map Library. *La. Libr. Ass. Bull.* 33: 87–90, Fall 1970.

25. Parsons, E.J.S. / *Manual of map classification and cataloging prepared for use in the Directorate of Military Survey.* London, War Office, 1946.

26. Ready, William B. / Punched card and/or computer control of a map collection. *Spec. Libr.* 58: 365 (May 1967).

27. Ristow, W.W. and D.K. Carrington / Computerized map cataloging project. *INSPEL* 4: 74–79 (Jul-Oct 1969).—Same, slightly abr., *Intern. Libr. Rev.* 2: 391–397 (Jul 1970).

28. Ristow, Walter W. / The emergence of maps in libraries. *Spec. Libr.* 58: 400–419 (Jul–Aug 1967).

29. Ristow, Walter W. and David K. Carrington / Machine-readable map cataloging in the Library of Congress. *Spec. Libr.* 62: 343–352 (Sep 1971).

30. Ristow, W.W. / Map librarianship. *Libr. J.* 92: 3610–3614 (Oct 15, 1967).

31. Ristow, Walter W. / What about maps? *Libr. Trends* 4: 123–139 (Oct 1955).

32. Sayer, Mimi / Bibliography from: How to start a small map library. (Panel III, Spring, 1970, Meeting of the Western Ass. of Map Libr.) *Western Ass. of Map Libr. Inform. Bull.* 1: 32–38 (Jun 1970).

33. Special Libraries Ass. Geography and Map Div. Directory Revision Committee, comp. / *Map collections in the U.S. and Canada, a directory.* 2d ed. New York, Spec. Libr. Ass., 1970.

34. Special Libraries Association. Washington, D.C., Chapter. Geography and Map Group / *Federal Government map collecting; a brief history.* Richard W. Stephenson, ed. Washington, D.C., 1969.

35. Stephenson, Richard W. / Published sources of information about maps and atlases. *Spec. Libr.* 61: 87–98, 110–112 (Feb 1970).

36. Tessier, Yves / The map library of l'Universite Laval. *Spec. Libr.* 61: 131–132 (Mar 1970).

37. Thiele, Walter / *Official map publications.* An historical sketch, and a bibliographical handbook of current maps and mapping services in the U.S., Canada, Latin America, France, Great Britain, Germany, and certain other countries. Chicago, Amer. Libr. Ass., 1938.

38. Tooley, R.V. / *Maps and mapmakers.* London, B.T. Batsford, 1952.

39. U.S. Copyright Office / *Catalog of copyright entries.* 3d series. Pt. 6: Maps and atlases. v. 1– . Jan/Jun 1947– . Washington, D.C., U.S. Govt. Print. Off.

40. U.S. Library of Congress. Information Systems Office / *Maps, a MARC format: specifications for magnetic tapes containing catalog records for maps.* Prep. by Patricia E. Parker. Washington, D.C., U.S. Govt. Print. Off., 1970.

41. U.S. Library of Congress. Map Div. / *Maps; their care, repair, and preservation in libraries.* by Clara Egli LeGear. rev. ed. Washington, D.C., 1956.

42. U.S. Library of Congress. Subject Cataloging Div. / *Classification.* Class G: Geography, anthropology, folklore, manners and customs, recreation. 3d ed., with supplementary pages. Washington, D.C., U.S. Govt. Print. Off., 1954, reprinted 1966.

43. White, Robert C. / Map librarianship. *Spec. Libr.* 61: 233–235 (May/Jun 1970).

44. Woods, Bill M. / *Map librarianship: a selected bibliography.* Princeton, New Jersey Libr. Ass., 1970.

37. Special Materials—Music

1. Bradley, Carol June, comp. / *Manual of music librarianship.* [Ann Arbor, Mich., Music Libr. Ass., 1966]

2. Brazell, Troy V., Jr. / Comparative

analysis: a minimum music materials budget for the university library. *Coll. Res. Libr.* 32: 110–120 (Mar 1971).

3. Bryant, Eric T. / *Music librarianship: a practical guide.* London, J. Clarke; New York, Hafner Publ., 1959.

4. Bryant, Eric T. / *Music librarianship.* New York, Hafner, 1963.

5. Davies, J.H. / *Musicalia; sources of information in music.* 2d ed. rev. and enl. Elmsford, N.Y. Pergamon, 1969.

6. Duckles, Vincent H., ed. / Music library and librarianship. *Libr. Trends* 8: 493–617 (Apr 1960).

7. Duckles, Vincent H. / *Music reference and research materials; an annotated bibliography.* 2d ed. New York, Free Press, 1967.

8. Duckles, Vincent H. / Musical scores and recordings. *Libr. Trends* 4: 164–173 (Oct 1955).

9. Farish, Margaret K., ed. / *String music in print.* New York, Bowker, 1965.

10. Heyer, Anna Harriet, comp. / *Historical sets, collected editions and monuments of music: a guide to their contents.* 2d ed. Chicago, Amer. Libr. Ass., 1969.

11. Hixon, Donald L. / *Music in early America: a bibliography of music in Evans.* Metuchen, N.J., Scarecrow, 1970.

12. Illing, R. / Dalley-Scarlett collection of music and books about music. *Australian Libr. J.* 19: 459–467 (Dec 1970).

13. Joint Committee on Music Cataloging / *Code for cataloging music and phonorecords.* prep. by a joint comm. of the Music Libr. Ass. and the Amer. Libr. Ass. Div. of Cataloging and Classification, Chicago, Amer. Libr. Ass., 1958.

14. McColvin, Lionel Roy and Harold Reeves / *Music libraries.* Rev. and extended by Jack Dove. London, A. Deutsch, 1965.

15. Music Library Ass. / *Manual of music librarianship.* Carol June Bradley, ed. Ann Arbor, Mich., Music Libr. Ass., 1966.

16. Redfern, Brian L. / *Organizing music in libraries.* London, Clive Bingley, 1966.

17. Tanno, John W. / Automation and music cataloging. *Coll. Mus. Symp. USA* 8: 48–50 (Fall 1968).

18. U.S. Library of Congress / *Library of Congress catalog: a cumulative list of works represented by Library of Congress printed cards. Music and phono-records.* Washington, D.C., U.S. Libr. of Cong., Catalog Maintenance Div., Jan./Mar. 1953– . (semiannual with annual cumulation).

19. U.S. Library of Congress Subject Cataloging Div. / *Classification.* Class M: Music and books on music. 2d

20. U.S. Library of Congress / *Subject Cataloging Div. Classification.* Class M: Music and books on music. 2d ed., with supplementary pages. Washington, D.C. (available from the Card Div., Lib. of Congress, 1917; reissued 1968.)

38. Special Materials—Films General

1. Alexander, William E., et al. / Toward a theory for the scientific management of educational film libraries. *AV Commun. Rev.* 19: 89–101 (Spring 1971).

2. Day, Dorothy L. / Films in the library. *Libr. Trends* 4: 174–181 (Oct 1955).

3. Diffor, John W., et al., eds. / Educators guide to free films, 1971. 31st ed. Randolph, Wis. Educators Progress Serv., 1971.

4. *Educational film index,* 1967– . Ann Arbor, Mich., Audio-visual educ. center, Univ. of Mich. and Instr. Media Center, Mich. State Univ.

5. *Film evaluation guide.* New York, Educational Film Libr. Ass., 1965.

6. *Films for libraries.* (Selected by a committee of the Amer. Libr. Ass. Audio-Visual Committee) Chicago, Amer. Libr. Ass., 1962.

7. Limbacher, James L. / *Feature films on 8mm and 16mm.* A directory of feature films available for rental, sale and lease in the U.S. 3d ed. New York, Bowker, 1971.

8. National Information Center for Educational Media / *Index to 16mm educational films.* 2d ed. New York, Bowker, 1969.

9. Needle-sort system keeps 2000 films in circulation. *Off. Equipment and Methods.* 14: 34–35 (1968).
10. Steele, Robert S. / *The cataloging and classification of cinema literature.* Metuchen, N.J., Scarecrow, 1967.
11. U.S. Federal Advisory Council on Medical Training Aids / *Film reference guide for medicine and allied sciences.* U.S. Dept. HEW, Public Health Serv., Nat'l Institutes of Health,. Nat'l Libr. of Med., Nat'l Med. Audiovisual Center. (Atlanta, Ga.) Washington, D.C., Sup. of Docs. U.S. Govt. Print. Off., 1970. (recurring)
12. U.S. General Services Admin., National Archives and Records Service / *U.S. Government films.* A catalog of motion pictures and filmstrips for sale by the National Audiovisual Center. Washington, D.C., U.S. Govt. Print. Off., 1969.
13. U.S. Library of Congress / *Library of Congress catalog: a cumulative list of works represented by Library of Congress printed cards. Motion pictures and filmstrips.* Washington, D.C., U.S. Libr. of Cong., Catalog Maintenance Div., Jan./Mar. 1953– . (quarterly with an annual cumulation).
14. Wiest, Donald C. / Film, the durable medium. *Spec. Libr.* 62: 475–480 (Nov 1971).

39. Special Materials—8mm Films

1. Educational Film Library Ass. / *8mm film directory.* Grace Ann Kone, comp. and ed. New York, Comprehensive Service Corp., 1969.
2. National Information Center for Educational Media / *Index to 8mm educational motion cartridges.* New York, Bowker, 1969.
3. *Preliminary 8mm film project report and listing of 8mm films.* Reba Benschoter, project director. Omaha, Neb., University of Nebraska, College of Medicine, Sep 1, 1969. (Recurring)

40. Special Materials—Filmstrips

1. Diffor, John W. and Mary F. Horkeimer, eds. / *Educators guide to free filmstrips, 1970.* 23d ed. Randolph, Wis., Educators Progress Serv., 1971.
2. National Information Center for Educational Media / *Index to 35mm educational filmstrips.* 2d ed. New York, Bowker, 1970.
3. U.S. Library of Congress. Descriptive Cataloging Div. / *Rules for descriptive cataloging in the Library of Congress; motion pictures and filmstrips.* Prelim. ed. Washington, D.C., 1952.
4. Wyllie, Diana / Slides and filmstrips: handling and storage. In Aslib Audio-Visual Group *Audio-visual workshop, May 7–8, 1970.* London, Aslib, 1971. p. 20–23.

41. Special Materials—Slides

1. Bird, R.W. / Slides; the cataloging, classification and indexing of a collection of slides. *Catalogue and Index* no. 20: 4 (Oct 1970).
2. Irvine, Betty Jo / Slide classification: a historical survey. *Coll. Res. Libr.* 32: 23–30 (Jan 1971).
3. Simons, W.W. and L.C. Tansey / Automated indexing for a classified 2x2 slide collection. *LARC Rep.* 2: 23–35 (Jun 1969). Same, Spec. Libr. Ass. Picture Div. *Picturescope* 18: 65–75 (1970).
4. Simons, W.W. and L.C. Tansey / *Slide classification systems for the organization and automatic indexing of interdisciplinary collections of slides and pictures.* Santa Cruz, Univ. Calif., 1970.
5. Wyllie, Diana / Slides and filmstrips: handling and storage. In Aslib Audio-Visual Group. *Audio-visual Workshop, May 7–8, 1970.* London, Aslib, 1971. p. 20–23.

42. Special Materials— Transparencies

1. National Information Center for Educational Media / *Index to overhead transparencies.* New York, Bowker, 1969.
2. Wasserman, Morton N. / A computer-prepared book catalog for engineering transparencies. *Spec. Libr.* 57: 111–113 (Feb 1966).

43. Special Materials—Videotape Recordings

1. Burke, J.G. and M.C. Lux / Coming through your front door: pre-recorded video cassettes. *Amer. Libr.* 1: 1069–1073 (Dec 1970).
2. Dessauer, J.P. / Canned video. *Publ. Wkly.* 199: 32–34 (Jan 18, 1971).
3. Jones, R., et al. / VAT (Video-audio tape). *Ga. Librn.* 6: 7–10 (Oct 1969).
4. Kenney, B.L., et al. / Automated index and search system for psychiatric videotapes. In *Proceedings of the American Society for Information Science Conference, 1970.* Philadelphia. v. 7: Information conscious society. Washington, D.C., ASIS, 1970. p. 129–139.
5. Kletter, Richard C. and Heather Hudson / Video cartridges and cassettes. In *Annual review of information science and technology,* v. 7. Washington, D.C., Amer. Soc. Inform. Sci., 1972. p. 197–238.
6. Mount, D.N. / Get yourself a lawyer; it's the only way to understand who owns what in the seething a/v impasse. *Publ. Wkly.* 199: 29–32 (Mar 1, 1971).
7. Video records: everyone's future toy. *Publ. Wkly.* 199: 30–32 (Jan 4, 1971).

44. Special Materials—Computer-Assisted Instruction

1. ENTELEK, Inc. ENTELEK CAI / *CMI Information Exchange.* Newburyport, Mass., ENTELEK, Inc. monthly. 1965– .

2. University of Wisconsin, Milwaukee. Instructional Media Laboratory / *Index to computer assisted instruction.* 2d ed. Helen A. Lekan, ed. Boston, Mass., Sterling Institute, 1970. ED 040 583. (Available from Sterling Institute, Suite 3750, Prudential Tower, Boston, Mass. 02199. $19.50. Not available from EDRS.)

45. Special Materials—Phonograph Recordings

1. Carey, John T. / The visible index method of cataloging phonorecords. *Libr. Res. & Tech. Serv.* 13: 502–510 (Fall 1969).
2. Hagen, C.B. / A proposed information retrieval system for sound recordings. *Spec. Libr.* 56: 223–228 (Apr 1965).
3. International Assn. of Music Libraries, United Kingdom Branch / *Phonograph record libraries: their organization and practice.* Henry F.J. Currall, ed. Hamden, Conn., Archon, 1970. Also publ. as: *Gramophone record libraries.* London, Lockwood, 1970.
4. Langridge, D.W. / *Your jazz collection.* London, C. Bingley, 1970.
5. Lerma, Dominique-René / Philosophy and practice of phonorecord classification at Indiana University. *Libr. Res. & Tech. Serv.* 13: 86–92 (Winter 1969).
6. Pearson, Mary D. / *Recordings in the public library.* Chicago, Amer. Libr. Ass., 1963.
7. Phillips, Dan / An expandable classification scheme for phonograph libraries. *Libr. Res. & Tech. Serv.* 13: 511–515 (Fall 1969).
8. Pickett, A.G. and M.M. Lemcoe / *Preservation and storage of sound recordings.* Washington, D.C., Library of Congress, 1959.
9. Roach, Helen / *Spoken records.* 3d ed. Metuchen, N.J., Scarecrow, 1970.
10. Scholz, D.D. / *A manual for the cataloging of recordings in public libraries.* Baton Rouge, La., State Library, 1964.
11. Sunder, Mary Jane / Organization of

recorded sound. *Libr. Res. and Tech. Serv.* 13: 93–98 (Winter 1969).

12. U.S. Library of Congress. Descriptive Cataloging Division / *Rules for descriptive cataloging in the Library of Congress; phonorecords.* 2d prelim. ed. Washington, D.C., 1964.

13. Van de Voorde, R.A. / *Basic record repertoire for small libraries.* Univ. Arizona, Coll. of Educ., Bur. Educ. Res. and Serv., 1970.

14. Woodward, Robert H. / *Cataloging a home record library.* Bloomington, Ind., Token Publ., 1951.

46. Special Materials—Audiotape Recordings

1. Cassette tape recorders for libraries. In Amer. Libr. Ass. Libr. Tech. Prog. / *Library technology reports.*

Sec. N: Listening equipments. Jan 1965– . (Loose-leaf)

2. National Center for Audio Tapes / *1970-72 Catalog.* Boulder, Colo., Nat. Center for Audio Tapes, Univ. Colorado, 1970.

3. Noble, V. / Chatty chatty bang bang: business information cassettes. *Spec. Libr.* 62: 231–233 (May 1971).

4. Ryan, Noel / Will you have cassette tapes in your library? *Canadian Libr. J.* 28: 106–109 (Mar/Apr 1971).

5. Slocombe, Marie / Tapes and records: BBC Sound Archives. In Aslib Audio-Visual Group / *Audio-Visual Workshop, May 7-8, 1970.* London, Aslib, 1971. p. 18–19.

6. Wittich, Walter A. and Raymond H. Suttles, eds. / *Educators guide to free tapes, scripts, transcriptions, 1970.* Randolph, Wis., Educators Progress Serv., 1971.

INDEX OF MATERIAL TYPES AND MEDIA
(Numbers refer to numbered sections of the bibliography)

Abstracts—1–4, 22
Aperture cards—1–4, 31
Archives—1–4, 6
Art—1–4, 35
Audiotape recordings—1–4, 26, 46

Clippings—1–4, 26
Computer-assisted instruction—44
Conference literature—1–4, 24

Dissertations—1–4, 13

8mm films—1–4, 26, 39

Films—1–4, 26, 27, 38, 39
Filmstrips—1–4, 26, 27, 40

Government publications—1–4, 7–10

Indexes—1–4, 23
Instructional materials—1–4, 26, 27, 32, 33–46

Maps—1–4, 26, 27, 36
Microfiche—1–4, 28–30
Microforms—1–4, 28–31
Music—1–4, 37

Newspapers—1–4, 26
Nonprint materials—1–4, 26, 27

Pamphlets—1–4, 26
Patents—1–4, 15, 16
Phonograph recordings—1–4, 26, 27, 45
Photographs—1–4, 26, 34
Pictures—1–4, 26, 33

Recordings—1–4, 26, 27, 37, 43, 45, 46
Reference materials—1–4, 21
Reports—1–4, 11, 12

Slides—1–4, 26, 27, 41
Special libraries—1–4, 20
Specifications—1–4, 14
Standards—1–4, 14, 26, 28

Technical reports—1–4, 11, 12
Trade & service literature—1–4, 17
Trademarks—1–4, 18
Translations—1–4, 19
Transparencies—1–4, 26, 27, 42

Vertical files—1–4, 25, 26
Videotape recordings—1–4, 26, 27, 43.

SELECTIVE LIST OF PUBLISHERS

1. Advance House Publishers, Box 334, Ardmore, Pa. 19003
2. George Allen & Unwin Ltd., 40 Museum St., London, W.C.1, England
3. American Geographical Society, Broadway at 156 St., New York, N.Y. 10032
4. American Institute of Architects, 107 N. Seventh St., St. Louis, Mo. 63103
5. American Library Association, 50 E. Huron St., Chicago, Ill. 60611
6. American National Standards Institute, 1430 Broadway, New York, N.Y. 10018
7. Appleton-Century-Crofts, Inc., 440 Park Ave., S., New York, N.Y. 10016
8. Archon Books, Shoe String Press, Inc., 995 Sherman Ave., Hamden, Conn. 06514
9. Aslib Publications, London, England (see Chicorel Library Publ. Co.)
10. Association of Assistant Librarians, 49 Halstead Gardens, Winchmore Hill, London, N.21, England
11. Audiovisual Catalogers, Inc., P.O. Box 26002, Raleigh, N.C. 27611
12. Audio-visual Education Center, Univ. of Michigan, Ann Arbor, Mich. 48104
13. Audiovisual Research Institute, 1346 Broadway, Detroit, Mich. 48226
14. Clive Bingley Ltd., 16 Pembridge Rd., London, W.11, England
15. Bowker Associates, Inc., 1677 Wisconsin Ave., Washington, D.C. 20007
16. R.R. Bowker Co., 1180 Ave. of the Americas, New York, N.Y. 10036
17. British Book Centre, Inc., 996 Lexington Ave., New York, N.Y. 10017
18. British Standards Institution, 2 Park St., London WIA 2BS, England
19. Broadman Press, 127 9th Ave. N., Nashville, Tenn. 37203
20. Brookings Institution, 1775 Mass. Ave., N.W. Washington, D.C. 20036
21. Business Books, 49 E. Cedar St., Chicago, Ill. 60611
22. University of California, Institute of Governmental Studies, 348 Library Annex, Berkeley, Calif. 94704
23. University of California at Santa Cruz, Santa Cruz, Calif. 95060
24. University of California Press, 2223 Fulton St., Berkeley, Calif. 94720
25. Canadian Library Association, Room 606, 63 Sparks St., Ottawa 4, Canada
26. Catholic University of America Press, Distributor: Herder & Herder, 232 Madison Ave., New York, N.Y. 10016
27. Chemical Publishing Co., 200 Park Ave. S., New York, N.Y. 10003
28. Chicorel Library Publishing Corp., 275 Central Park West, New York, N.Y. 10024
29. Columbia Univ. Press, 440 W. 110th St., New York, N.Y. 10025
30. Congressional Information Service, 500 Montgomery Bldg., Washington, D.C. 20014
31. Antony Croghan, 17 Coburgh Mansions, Handel St., London W.C.1, England
32. Crosby Lockwood & Son, Ltd., 26 Old Brompton Rd., London, S.W.7, England
33. John De Graff, Inc., 34 Oak Ave., Tuckahoe, N.Y. 10707
34. Andre Deutsch, Ltd., 105 Great Russell St., London W.C.1, England
35. Dial Press, Inc., 750 Third Ave., New York, N.Y. 10017
36. Documents Index, Box 195, McLean, Va. 22101
37. EDRS, ERIC Document Reproduction Service, P.O. Drawer 0, Bethesda, Md. 20014
38. Educators Progress Service, Inc., 212 Center St., Randolph, Wis. 53956
39. Encyclopaedia Brittanica, Inc., 425 N. Michigan Ave., Chicago, Ill. 60611
40. Enoch Pratt Free Library, 400 Cathedral St., Baltimore, Md. 21201
41. European Translations Centre, Doelenstraat 101, Delft, The Netherlands
42. F.W. Faxon Co., Inc., 15 Southwest Park, Westwood, Mass. 02090
43. Fearon Publishers, Lear Siegler Inc., Education Div., 6 Davis Drive, Belmont, Calif. 94002
44. Fisher Publishing Co., Subs. Learning Resources, Inc., 3 W. Princeton, Englewood, Colo. 80110
45. Free Press, Orders to: Macmillan Co., 866 Third Ave., New York, N.Y. 10022
46. French Cultural Services, 972 5th Ave., New York, N.Y. 10021
47. Gale Research Co., Book Tower, Detroit, Mich. 48226
48. Hafner Publishing Co., Inc., 866 Third Ave., New York, N.Y. 10022
49. Harper & Row Publishers, Inc., 49 E. 33rd St., New York, N.Y. 10016
50. Hatfield College of Technology, Hatfield, Herts., England
51. Illini Union Bookstore, 715 S. Wright St., Champaign, Ill. 61822
52. Information Handling Services, Denver Technological Center, P.O. Box 1154, Englewood, Colo. 80110
53. Information Resources Press, 2100 M St. N.W., Washington, D.C. 20037
54. International Council on Archives,

60 rue des Francs-Bourgeois, Paris 3e, France

55. International Organization for Standardization, 1 rue de Varembe, Geneva, Switzerland

56. International Textbook Co., Scranton, Pa. 18515

57. Interscience Publishers, c/o John Wiley & Sons, Inc., 605 Third Ave., New York, N.Y. 10016

58. Libraries Unlimited, Inc., Box 263, Littleton, Colo. 80120

59. Library Association, 7 Ridgmount St., Store St., London, W.C.1, England

60. Linnet Books, c/o Shoe String Press, Inc., 995 Sherman Ave., Hamden, Conn. 66514

61. London House & Maxwell (see British Book Centre)

62. McGraw-Hill Book Co., 330 W. 42 St., New York, N.Y. 10036

63. Macmillan Co., Subs. of Crowell Collier & Macmillan, Inc., 866 Third Ave., New York, N.Y. 10022

64. MIT Press, 28 Carleton St., Cambridge, Mass. 02142

65. Medical Library Association, 919 N. Michigan Ave., Chicago, Ill. 60611

66. Microcard Editions, Washington, D.C., (see NCR/Microcard Editions)

67. Micro-Publishing Systems, Inc., 1860 Utica Ave., Brooklyn, N.Y. 11234

68. Morgan-Grampian Books Ltd. (see International Textbook Co.)

69. NCR/Microcard Editions, 901 26 St., N.W., Washington, D.C. 20037

70. Music Library Association, c/o School of Music, Ann Arbor, Mich. 48105

71. National Audiovisual Association, Inc., 3150 Spring St., Fairfax, Va. 22030

72. National Center for Audio Tapes, University of Colorado, Boulder, Colo.

73. National Education Association, 1201 16 St. N.W., Washington, D.C. 20036

74. National Fire Protection Association, 60 Batterymarch St., Boston, Mass. 02110

75. National Microfilm Association, Suite 1101, 8728 Colesville Rd., Silver Spring, Md. 20910

76. National Technical Information Service (NTIS), Springfield, Va. 22151

77. New American Library, Inc., Subs. of Times Mirror Co., 1301 Ave. of the Americas, New York, N.Y. 10019

78. Norkan, Inc., 212 West Adams, Pittsburg, Kan. 66762

79. Oceana Publications, Inc., Dobbs Ferry, N.Y. 10522

80. Output Systems Corp., 1911 Jefferson Davis Highway, Arlington, Va. 22202

81. Patent Searching Service, Trademark Register, Washington Bldg., Washington, D.C. 20005

82. Pergamon Press, Inc., Maxwell House, Fairview Park, Elmsford, N.Y. 10523

83. Pond Press, 46 St. Augustine's Ave., London, W.5, England

84. C.N. Potter, Inc., Div. of Crown Pubs., Inc., 419 Park Ave. S., New York, N.Y. 10016

85. Praeger, Publishers, Inc., Subs. of Encyclopaedia Britannica, Inc., 111 Fourth Ave., New York, N.Y. 10003

86. Prentice-Hall, Inc., Englewood Cliffs, N.J. 07632

87. Random House, Inc., Subs. of Radio Corp. of America, 201 E. 50 St., New York, N.Y. 10022

88. Robert Maxwell & Co. Ltd., 4 Fitzroy Square, London, W.1, England

89. Rowman and Littlefield, Inc., Div. of Littlefield, Adams & Co., 87 Adams Dr., Totowa, N.J. 07512

90. Scarecrow Press, Inc., 52 Liberty St., Box 656, Metuchen, N.J. 08840

91. Spalding College, Dept. of Library Science, Louisville, Kent, England

92. Spartan Books, Inc., Subs. of Publishers Co., Inc., 432 Park Ave. S., New York, N.Y. 10016

93. Special Libraries Association, 235 Park Ave. S., New York, N.Y. 10003

94. Superintendent of Documents (see U.S. Government Printing Office)

95. Syracuse University Press, Box 8, University Station, Syracuse, N.Y. 13210

96. Thomas Publishing Co., 461 8th Ave., New York, N.Y. 10001

97. Toronto Public Library, Business Office, 40 St. Clair Ave. E., Toronto 7, Ont., Canada

98. Unesco (see Unipub, Inc.)

99. Unipub, Inc., Div. of National Agency for International Publications, Box 433, New York, N.Y. 10016

100. United Nations, Sales Section, Publishing Service, New York, N.Y. 10017

101. U.S. Government Printing Office, Div. of Public Documents, Washington, D.C. 20402

102. U.S. National Archives and Records Service, General Services Administration, National Archives Bldg., Washington, D.C.

103. University Microfilms, 300 N. Zeeb Rd., Ann Arbor, Mich. 48106

104. University of Arizona, College of Education, Bureau of Educational Research and Services, Tucson, Ariz. 85721

105. Van Nostrand, D., Co. (see Van Nostrand Reinhold Co.)

106. Van Nostrand Reinhold Co., Div. of

Litton Educational Publishing Inc., 450 W. 33 St., New York, N.Y. 10001

107. Western Michigan University, Publications Dept., Kalamazoo, Mich. 49001
108. Western Periodicals, 13000 Raymor St., North Hollywood, Calif. 91605
109. Westinghouse Learning Corp., 100 Park Ave., New York, N.Y. 10017

110. John Wiley & Sons, Inc., 605 Third Ave., New York, N.Y. 10016
Becker and Hayes is a subsidiary of John Wiley & Sons. Their present address: 11661 San Vicente Blvd., Los Angeles, Calif. 90049.
111. H.W. Wilson Co., 950 University Ave., Bronx, N.Y. 10452

Index